CWI Tracts

Managing Editors

J.W. de Bakker (CWI, Amsterdam)
M. Hazewinkel (CWI, Amsterdam)
J.K. Lenstra (Eindhoven University of Technology)

Editorial Board

W. Albers (Enschede)
P.C. Baayen (Amsterdam)
R.C. Backhouse (Eindhoven)
E.M. de Jager (Amsterdam)
M.A. Kaashoek (Amsterdam)
M.S. Keane (Delft)
H. Kwakernaak (Enschede)
J. van Leeuwen (Utrecht)
P.W.H. Lemmens (Utrecht)
M. van der Put (Groningen)
M. Rem (Eindhoven)
H.J. Sips (Delft)
M.N. Spijker (Leiden)
H.C. Tijms (Amsterdam)

CWI
P.O. Box 4079, 1009 AB Amsterdam, The Netherlands
Telephone 31 - 20 592 9333, telex 12571 (mactr nl),
telefax 31 - 20 592 4199

CWI is the nationally funded Dutch institute for research in Mathematics and Computer Science.

CWI Tract　　　　84

Computational aspects of Lie group representations and related topics

Proceedings of the
1990 Computational Algebra Seminar
at CWI, Amsterdam

edited by
A.M. Cohen

Centrum voor Wiskunde en Informatica
Centre for Mathematics and Computer Science

1980 Mathematics Subject Classification:
03F65, 05A17, 12E05, 14D25, 15A21,
17B10, 17B45, 20B30, 20G05, 22E46.
ISBN 90 6196 395 8
NUGI-code: 811

Preface

Powerful computer algebra tools have brought new life to the algorithmic study of mathematics. The impact of the algorithmic approach is especially noteworthy in the study of Lie groups. In order to inform the Dutch computer algebraists of developments in this direction, the Spring 1990 sessions of the Computational Algebra Seminar at CWI, Amsterdam, have been mainly devoted to computational aspects of Lie group representations.

At the seminar, on one hand, better ways were brought forward to satisfy the physicists' demands to collect explicit data about representations, tensor product decompositions etc., while, on the other hand, new impulses were given to effective computations of invariants of groups acting on given spaces and even invariants of elements pertaining to these groups. The contributions by Bram Broer, Arjeh Cohen & Bert Ruitenburg, Marc van Leeuwen and Peter Littelmann reflect these activities. Omar Foda and Jan Sanders exploited the use of Lie group notions and techniques in computations for statistical mechanics and differential equations, respectively.

The remaining two contributions are somewhat further away from the theory of Lie groups. Both cover topics of very general interest to computational algebra. Wim Ruitenburg focused on the fundamental theorem of algebra from a constructive point of view: how to find (or, better, construct) roots of polynomials. He stressed that a solution in constructive algebra leads to the existence of an (admittedly, possibly highly impractical) algorithm providing that solution. Van den Essen elaborated on the Jacobian Conjecture. He showed that it is related to various branches of mathematics and how various forms of the conjecture have computational interpretations.

Because many of the talks at the seminar were fine introductions into an active field of research, I have asked the lecturers for a written contribution. These proceedings are the outcome of the enterprise thus started. Several colleagues have given me substantial help in the refereeing. I wish to express my sincere gratitude for their efforts. Most manuscripts were delivered to me electronically. Using TEX, I have forged them into a more or less uniform layout. Marc van Leeuwen's occasional but highly effective assistance is gratefully acknowledged.

In the seminar, the contributors were requested to present elementary introductions, with the aim of reaching a wide audience. We hope that these proceedings still reflect that principle.

Arjeh M. Cohen
CWI, Amsterdam

Contents

Computational Aspects of Lie Group Representations and Related Topics   1
Proceedings of the 1990 Computational Algebra Seminar
pp. 1–18 in CWI Tract 84 (1991)

Hilbert series for ternary forms

Bram Broer

Faculteit Wiskunde en Informatica

Universiteit van Amsterdam

Plantage Muidergracht 24

1018 TV Amsterdam

The Netherlands

0. Introduction

We shall give generating functions for the concomitants of the ternary cubic forms and some types of covariants of the ternary quartics. The method of calculation we used is essentially a combination of nineteenth century techniques; but the calculations were done in the computer algebra package Maple[†].

The method is not restricted to SL_3, but works for any reductive group— as will be explained elsewhere. We tried to be as down to earth as reasonably possible, because the method is elementary and can be of some use for the calculation of other generating functions in the SL_3 (or, equivalently, the SU_3) area. Some other explicit results are given in [Br90].

1. Models for irreducible representations

Let **k** be an algebraically closed field of characteristic zero, for example the field of the complex numbers. One of the basic properties of $G := SL_3(\mathbf{k})$ is the complete reducibility of its (rational) representations, i.e., any representation is a direct sum of representations having no nontrivial subrepresentations. We shall describe a model for any irreducible G-representation, similar to the model used in the last century.

[†] The author thanks the Stichting Computer Algebra Nederland for providing computation facilities with Maple on a Sun workstation.

The restrictions x_{ij} to G of the coordinate functions of $\mathrm{End}(\mathbf{k}^3)$ generate the algebra $\mathbf{k}[G]$ of polynomial functions on G; they are related by $\det(x_{ij}) = 1$. The natural $\tilde{G} := G \times G$-action on G induces an action on $\mathbf{k}[G]$ by algebra automorphisms

$$((g,g')f)(x) := f(g^{-1}xg'),$$

where $(g,g') \in \tilde{G}$, $f \in \mathbf{k}[G]$ and $x \in G$.

Write U for the subgroup of G consisting of upper triangular matrices $u = (u_{ij})$ with $u_{ii} = 1$ for $i = 1,\ldots,n$. The subalgebra of $(1 \times U)$-invariant elements in $\mathbf{k}[G]$ is denoted by $\mathbf{k}[G_U]$ (see [Kr84]); it is generated by

$$u_1 := x_{11}, u_2 := x_{21}, u_3 := x_{31},$$

$$x_1 := x_{21}x_{32} - x_{22}x_{31}, x_2 := x_{31}x_{12} - x_{11}x_{32}, x_3 := x_{11}x_{22} - x_{12}x_{21}.$$

These generators are related by the single relation $\sum_{i=1}^{3} x_i u_i = 0$.

Write B for the subgroup of G consisting of the upper triangular matrices; any character $B \to \mathbf{k}^*$ is of the form $\epsilon_1^n \epsilon_2^m$, where $\epsilon_i(b) = b_{ii}$, $i = 1$ or 2. Now $1 \times B$ acts on $\mathbf{k}[G_U]$ in a completely reducible way determined by its action on the generators

$$b \cdot u_i = \epsilon_1(b)\epsilon_2(b)u_i, \quad b \cdot x_i = \epsilon_1(b)x_i.$$

This action induces an $\mathbf{N}^2$-grading on $\mathbf{k}[G_U]$ by

$$\mathbf{k}[G_U] = \bigoplus_{(n,m)\in\mathbf{N}^2} V_{(n,m)},$$

with

$$V_{(n,m)} := \langle x_1^{n_1} x_2^{n_2} x_3^{n_3} u_1^{m_1} u_2^{m_2} u_3^{m_3}; \sum_{i=1}^{3} n_i = n, \sum_{i=1}^{3} m_i = m \rangle$$

$$= \{f \in \mathbf{k}[G]; f(xb) = \epsilon_1(b)^{n+m}\epsilon_2(b)^n f(x), x \in G, b \in B\},$$

and $V_{(n,m)} \cdot V_{(n',m')} \subset V_{(n+n',m+m')}$. The G ($\simeq G \times 1$)-action on $\mathbf{k}[G_U]$ commutes with the $\mathbf{N}^2$-grading, hence induces a representation on V_μ. These V_μ's are the models of the simple modules.

1.1 Proposition Let $\mu \in \mathbf{N}^2$.

(i)   *The G-module V_μ is simple.*

(ii) *Each simple G-module is isomorphic to some V_μ.*

This can be proved using the following two lemmas. The first lemma generalizes the fact that 1 is the only eigenvalue of any $u \in U$ in any representation. We skip the proof.

1.2 Lemma *Any non-zero representation of U has a non-zero fixed point.*

From this lemma it follows, with the complete reducibility of the representations of G, that a G-representation V is reducible if and only if the dimension of the fixed-points space V^U is at least two. The space of U-invariants $(V_\mu)^U = \langle x_1^{\mu_1} u_3^{\mu_2} \rangle$, $\mu \in \mathbf{N}^2$, is one-dimensional, hence V_μ is irreducible. This proves the first assertion of Proposition 1.1. The second will now be dealt with.

1.3 Lemma *If V is a simple G-module, then it is isomorphic to some V_μ.*

Proof Let v' be a nonzero fixed-point of U in the dual representation V^* to V. Then the action $G \times \mathbf{k}v' \to V^*$, defined by $(g, \lambda v') \mapsto g \cdot (\lambda v')$, induces a non-zero map

$$V \simeq V^{**} \to \mathbf{k}[G] \otimes (\mathbf{k}v')^*,$$

by restricting the coordinate functions on V^* to $G \times \mathbf{k}v'$, commuting with the G-actions. The image of V is isomorphic to V itself, because V is simple, and is contained in the $(1 \times B)$-fixed points of $\mathbf{k}[G_U] \otimes (\mathbf{k}v')^*$, hence is equal to V_μ, $\mu = (n, m) \in \mathbf{N}^2$, if $b.v' = \epsilon_1(b)^{n+m} \epsilon_2(b)^n v'$. $\qquad\square$

The monomials $\prod_{i=i}^{3} x_i^{n_i} u_i^{m_i}$, with $\sum_i n_i = \mu_1$, $\sum_i m_i = \mu_2$ and $n_2 = 0$ or $m_2 = 0$, can be taken as a basis for V^μ, with $\mu = (\mu_1 \lambda, \mu_2)$. Hence by an easy count it follows that the dimension of V_μ is $\frac{1}{2}(n+1)(m+1)(n+m+2)$.

It is also easy to show that, as $\tilde{G}$-modules,

$$\mathbf{k}[G] \simeq \bigoplus_\lambda V_\lambda \otimes V_\lambda^*.$$

2. Concomitants

Let M be any G-module. In the nineteenth century its *concomitants* were studied, i.e., the polynomial (not necessarily linear) maps $c : M \to V_\lambda$. The degree of c in the coefficients of $m \in M$ was called its *degree*, the degree in the x's (i.e., λ_1) its *order* and the degree in the u's (i.e., λ_2) its *class*. If class and order were both zero they were called *invariants*, if only the class was zero *covariants* and if the order was zero *contravariants*. Hilbert's famous basis theorem [H90] says that there are finitely many fundamental concomitants (invariants, covariants, respectively contravariants) such that any concomitant (invariant, covariant, respectively concomitant) can be expressed polynomially in them.

There were various geometric reasons to consider concomitants, in particular for the ternary n-ics, i.e., for $M = V_{(n,0)}$. We give an example of a covariant with geometric importance. The locus of zeros $\mathbf{C}(f)$ of $f \neq 0 \in V_{(n,0)}$ is a curve of degree n in the projective plane. Also, if $n \geq 2$,

$$H(f) := \det \left(\frac{\partial^2 f}{\partial x_i \partial x_j} \right) \in V_{(3n-6,0)}$$

determines a curve $\mathbf{C}(H(f))$, if $H(f)$ is not 0. The intersection points of the two curves are exactly the inflexion points and singularities of either of them. This *Hessian* curve does not depend on a choice of basis. That is, the assignment

$$H : V_{(n,0)} \to V_{(3n-6,0)} : f \mapsto H(f)$$

is a covariant for the ternary n-ics of degree 3 and order $3n - 6$.

We shall give some examples of *complete systems*, i.e., sets of concomitants (covariants, etc.) in which any concomitant (covariant, etc.) can be expressed polynomially.

2.1   The only concomitants for $V_{(1,0)}$ are the powers of f

$$V_{(1,0)} \rightarrow V_{(n,0)} : f \mapsto f^n,$$

of degree n and order n; hence f itself is the basis concomitant.

2.2   The Hessian for the ternary quadrics is an invariant; $H(f) = 0$ if and only if $\mathbf{C}(f)$ degenerates into a union of two lines. Its 'derivative'

$$\partial H : V_{(2,0)} \rightarrow V_{(0,2)} : f = \sum_{i \leq j} a_{ij} x_i x_j \mapsto \sum_{i \leq j} \frac{\partial H(f)}{\partial a_{ij}} u_i u_j$$

is a contravariant of class 2 and degree 2.

Any concomitant $c(f)$ for the ternary quadrics can be expressed polynomially in a unique way by f, $H(f)$ and $(\partial H)(f)$; e.g., any invariant can be expressed as $\sum_{i=0}^{l} b_i H(f)^i$, for some $b_i \in \mathbf{k}$.

2.3   In 1850 Aronhold proved that any invariant for the ternary cubics can be expressed polynomially in a unique way in two invariants, called S and T classically, of degree 4 and 6. We shall give a description of them. Any member of the pencil $\mathbf{C}(\lambda f + \mu H(f))$ of cubic curves has the same set of inflexion points and singularities; and any cubic curve with these inflexion points and singularities is a member of this pencil. In particular we have that $H(H(f)) = A(f)f + B(f)H(f)$, for some invariants A and B. In fact, expressed in S and T:

$$H(H(f)) = 8 \cdot 6^9 S(f)^2 f + 2 \cdot 6^6 T(f) H(f).$$

Using this equation an expression for S and T can be derived. We remark that S has the following curious property that f can be expressed as a sum of three cubes if and only $S(f) = 0$.

Apart from the invariants and the Hessian, there are two more basic covariants.

$$C : f \mapsto \det \begin{pmatrix} \frac{\partial^2 f}{\partial x_1 \partial x_1} & \frac{\partial^2 f}{\partial x_1 \partial x_2} & \frac{\partial^2 f}{\partial x_1 \partial x_3} & \frac{\partial H(f)}{\partial x_1} \\ \frac{\partial^2 f}{\partial x_2 \partial x_1} & \frac{\partial^2 f}{\partial x_2 \partial x_2} & \frac{\partial^2 f}{\partial x_2 \partial x_3} & \frac{\partial H(f)}{\partial x_2} \\ \frac{\partial^2 f}{\partial x_3 \partial x_1} & \frac{\partial^2 f}{\partial x_3 \partial x_2} & \frac{\partial^2 f}{\partial x_3 \partial x_3} & \frac{\partial H(f)}{\partial x_3} \\ \frac{\partial H(f)}{\partial x_1} & \frac{\partial H(f)}{\partial x_2} & \frac{\partial H(f)}{\partial x_3} & 0 \end{pmatrix}$$

has degree 8 and order 6, and

$$K : f \mapsto \det \begin{pmatrix} \frac{\partial f}{\partial x_1} & \frac{\partial H(f)}{\partial x_1} & \frac{\partial C(f)}{\partial x_1} \\ \frac{\partial f}{\partial x_2} & \frac{\partial H(f)}{\partial x_2} & \frac{\partial C(f)}{\partial x_2} \\ \frac{\partial f}{\partial x_3} & \frac{\partial H(f)}{\partial x_3} & \frac{\partial C(f)}{\partial x_3} \end{pmatrix}$$

has degree 12 and order 9.

Any covariant of the ternary cubics can be expressed polynomially by f, $H(f)$, $C(f)$, $K(f)$, $S(f)$ and $T(f)$, but not in a unique way: $K(f)^2$ can be expressed in the other basic covariants.

In 1869 Gordan [G69] found an explicit generating set of *all* the concomitants of the cubic forms; it is considered as one of the crowning pieces of nineteenth century invariant theory. There are 34 generating concomitants needed to express any concomitant polynomially in them, the degrees vary up to 12. We give the triples (class, order, degree) of Gordan's set of generators; there is at most one generator for each given triple.

$$(0,0,0), (3,0,1), (2,2,2), (3,0,3), (0,3,3), (3,3,3), (0,0,4), (4,1,4), (2,2,4),$$

$$(0,6,4), (4,1,5), (0,3,5), (3,3,5), (1,4,5), (0,0,6), (2,2,6), (5,2,6), (2,5,6),$$

$$(4,1,7), (3,3,7), (1,4,7), (1,7,7), (6,0,8), (5,2,8), (1,4,8), (2,5,8), (7,1,9),$$

$$(3,3,9), (1,7,9), (5,2,10), (2,5,10), (7,1,11), (9,0,12), (0,9,12).$$

2.4   For the ternary quartics the situation is much less well understood, not even a generating set of the invariants is known. In 1967, relatively recently, Shioda [Sh67] gave a rational form of the generating function of the linear independent invariants of given degree, and made several conjectures on the algebra of invariants concerning generators and relations. In 1987 Dixmier [D87] proved one of these conjectures by giving a set of algebraically independent invariants, of degrees 3,6,9,12,15,18 and 27, and proving that the full algebra of invariants is finitely generated (and free) considered as a module over the subalgebra generated by these invariants.

2.5   Write $con(\mu; \nu, i)$ for the number of linearly independent concomitants for V_μ of order ν_1, class ν_2 and degree i, and define the generating function for the concomitants of V_μ as

$$Con(\mu; x, y, t) := \sum_{(\nu,i)} con(\mu; \nu, i) x^{\nu_1} y^{\nu_2} t^i.$$

Analogously, $Inv(\mu; t)$, $Cov(\mu; x, t)$ and $Contr(\mu; y, t)$ for the invariants, covariants and contravariants for V_μ are defined. It follows from Hilbert's Basis Theorem that these generating functions can be expressed as (the Taylor expansion at $t = 0$ of) some rational function.

We give generating functions corresponding to the examples above.

$$Con((1,0); x, y, t) = \frac{1}{(1 - xt)}$$

$$Con((2,0); x, y, t) = \frac{1}{(1 - x^2 t)(1 - y^2 t^2)(1 - t^3)}$$

$$Cov((3,0); x, t) = \frac{1 - x^{18} t^{24}}{(1 - x^3 t)(1 - t^4)(1 - t^6)(1 - x^3 t^3)(1 - x^6 t^8)}$$

$$Inv((4,0);t) = \frac{1 + t^9 + t^{12} + t^{15} + \cdots + t^{66} + t^{75}}{(1-t^3)(1-t^6)(1-t^9)(1-t^{12})(1-t^{15})(1-t^{18})(1-t^{27})}$$

In the rest of this paper we give a method for calculating these generating functions, and shall compute, with the aid of a computer, $Con((3,0); x, y, t)$ and some coefficients of $Cov((4,0); x, t)$.

3. Equivariant Hilbert series

The sum of the simple submodules isomorphic to V_λ, $\lambda \in \mathbf{N}^2$, of the G-module M is called the isotypical component M_λ^G with highest weight λ. In particular, if $\lambda = 0$ it is the set of invariants, or the G-fixed points, in M. The multiplicity of V_λ in M is equal to the dimension of the isotypical component of highest weight λ divided by the dimension of V_λ. We have

$$\dim M_\lambda^G / \dim V_\lambda = \dim \operatorname{Hom}_G(V_\lambda, M) = \dim M \otimes_{\mathbf{k}} V_\lambda^*.$$

Any $\lambda \in \mathbf{Z}^2$ determines a character of T, the subgroup of diagonal matrices in G, in the following way:

$$\operatorname{diag}(t_1, t_2, (t_1 t_2)^{-1}) \mapsto t_1^{\lambda_1 + \lambda_2} t_2^{\lambda_2}.$$

For a T-module M write M_λ for the T-eigenspace of M of character (associated with) $\lambda \in \mathbf{Z}^2$. We have that the multiplicity of V_λ in the G-module M equals the dimension of $(M^U)_\lambda$, noting that $T \simeq B/U$ acts on the U-fixed points of M.

Let $M = \bigoplus_{i=0}^\infty M_i$ be a graded G-module with $\dim M_i < \infty$ for any i, then we define the G-Hilbert series $\mathcal{H}_G(M; x, y, t)$ to be the generating function of the multiplicities for all highest weights

$$\mathcal{H}_G(M; x, y, t) := \sum_{i=0}^\infty \sum_{\lambda \in \mathbf{N}^2} \dim \operatorname{Hom}_G(V_\lambda, M_i) e^\lambda t^i,$$

where we use the short-hand $e^\lambda := x^{\lambda_1} y^{\lambda_2}$. Analogously the T-Hilbert series $\mathcal{H}_T$ and the (usual) Hilbert series $\mathcal{H}$ are defined by

$$\mathcal{H}_T(M; x, y, t) := \sum_{i=0}^\infty \sum_{\lambda \in \mathbf{Z}^2} \dim((M_i)_\lambda) e^\lambda t^i;$$

$$\mathcal{H}(M; t) := \sum_{i=0}^\infty \dim M_i t^i.$$

We shall consider the series as elements of the integral domain

$$\mathbf{D} := \mathbf{Q}[x, x^{-1}, y, y^{-1}][\![t]\!].$$

We proceed analogously for multigraded modules. Usually we shall write $\mathcal{H}_G(M)$ for $\mathcal{H}_G(M; x, y, t)$. For generalities on Hilbert series (also known as Poincaré series) we refer to [Sp77], [Sp82].

3.1 We shall use the Hilbert series to derive the character of V_λ, i.e., the T-Hilbert series of the (trivially graded) module obtained by restricting the action of G on V_λ to T.

The double graded ring $\mathbf{k}[G_U]$ has G-Hilbert series

$$\mathcal{H}_G(\mathbf{k}[G_U]; x, y, s, t) = \sum_{\lambda \in \mathbf{N}^2} e^\lambda s^{\lambda_1} t^{\lambda_2} = \frac{1}{(1 - xs)(1 - yt)}.$$

We claim

$$\mathcal{H}_T(\mathbf{k}[G_U]) = \frac{1 - st}{(1 - xs)(1 - x^{-1}ys)(1 - y^{-1}s)(1 - yt)(1 - xy^{-1}t)(1 - x^{-1}t)}.$$

Proof Consider the polynomial ring $A := \mathbf{k}[X_1, X_2, X_3, U_1, U_2, U_3]$, and let T act on X_i and U_i as it does on x_i and u_i. Then there is a surjection $A \to \mathbf{k}[G_U]$ with kernel the principal ideal generated by the irreducible element $\sum_i X_i U_i$ of bidegree $(1, 1)$. Then

$$\mathcal{H}_T(\mathbf{k}[G_U]) = \mathcal{H}_T(A) - \mathcal{H}_T\left(\left(\sum_i X_i U_i\right) A \right) = (1 - st)\mathcal{H}_T(A).$$

Now $A \simeq \bigotimes_{i=1}^3 \mathbf{k}[X_i] \otimes \mathbf{k}[U_i]$, hence

$$\mathcal{H}_T(A) = \prod_{i=1}^3 \mathcal{H}_T(\mathbf{k}[X_i]) \cdot \mathcal{H}_T(\mathbf{k}[U_i]),$$

from which the formula follows. $\qquad\square$

The Weyl group $W = N_G T/T$ is isomorphic to the symmetric group on $\{1, 2, 3\}$ generated by $s_1 = (1, 2)$ and $s_2 = (2, 3)$. It acts on $\mathbf{D}$ by

$$s_1 : x \mapsto y/x, y \mapsto y, t \mapsto t$$
$$s_2 : x \mapsto x, y \mapsto x/y, t \mapsto t.$$

The sign of $\tau \in W$ is denoted by ϵ_τ, and we define the endomorphism $\mathcal{J}$ of $\mathbf{D}$ by $\mathcal{J}(f) := \sum_{\tau \in W} \epsilon_\tau \tau(f)$. Write $\rho = (1, 1)$.

3.2 Proposition (Weyl's Character Formula)

(i) *We have*

$$\mathcal{H}_T(V_\mu) = \mathcal{J}(e^{\mu+\rho})/\mathcal{J}(e^\rho).$$

(ii) *For any (graded) G-module M we have*

$$\mathcal{H}_T(M)\mathcal{J}(e^\rho) = \mathcal{J}(e^\rho \mathcal{H}_G(M)).$$

Proof One can check by hand, or by using a computer algebra package like Maple, that

$$\mathcal{J}\left(\sum_{\lambda \in \mathbf{N}^2} e^{\lambda+\rho} s^{\lambda_1} t^{\lambda_2}\right) / \mathcal{J}(e^\rho) = \mathcal{J}(e^\rho \mathcal{H}_G(\mathbf{k}[G_U])) / \mathcal{J}(e^\rho)$$

$$= \left(\frac{xy}{(1-xs)(1-yt)} - \frac{x^{-1}y^2}{(1-x^{-1}ys)(1-yt)} + \frac{xy^{-2}}{(1-y^{-1}s)(1-xy^{-1}t)} - \frac{x^{-1}y^{-1}}{(1-y^{-1}s)(1-x^{-1}t)} + \frac{x^{-2}y}{(1-x^{-1}ys)(1-x^{-1}t)} - \frac{x^2 y^{-1}}{(1-xs)(1-y^{-1}xt)}\right) /$$

$$/ (xy - x^{-1}y + xy^{-2} - x^{-1}y^{-1} + x^{-2}y - x^2 y^{-1})$$

$$= \frac{1 - st}{(1-xs)(1-x^{-1}ys)(1-y^{-1}s)(1-yt)(1-xy^{-1}t)(1-x^{-1}t)}$$

$$= \mathcal{H}_T(\mathbf{k}[G_U]).$$

By comparing the coefficients of $s^{\mu_1} t^{\mu_2}$ we get the character formula. □

Define the endomorphisms D_1 and D_2 of **D** by

$$D_i(f) := \frac{f \cdot e^\rho - s_i(f \cdot e^\rho)}{e^\rho - s_i(e^\rho)},$$

they are called *Demazure operators*. They have the properties that $D_i^2 = D_i$ and $D_1 D_2 D_1 = D_2 D_1 D_2$. Write $\mathcal{I} = D_1 D_2 D_1$.

3.3 Proposition (Demazure's Character Formula) *We have*

$$\mathcal{I}(f) = \mathcal{J}(e^\rho f) / \mathcal{J}(e^\rho),$$

hence for any (graded) G-module M we have $\mathcal{H}_T(M) = \mathcal{I}(\mathcal{H}_G(M))$.

Proof It is easily proved that $s_i D_i(f) = D_i(f)$, hence $\tau \mathcal{I}(f) = \mathcal{I}(f)$, $\tau \in W$, and $\mathcal{J}(e^\rho D_i(f))/\mathcal{J}(e^\rho) = \mathcal{J}(e^\rho f)/\mathcal{J}(e^\rho)$. Then $\mathcal{I}(f) = \mathcal{J}(e^\rho \mathcal{I}(f))/\mathcal{J}(e^\rho) = \mathcal{J}(e^\rho f)/\mathcal{J}(e^\rho)$. □

3.4 We shall define a kind of reverse of the Demazure operators. We define $\mathcal{D}_1(f)$, $f \in \mathbf{D}$, to be the part of $f - s_1(f)x^{-2}y$ which consists only of nonnegative powers of x, and analogously $\mathcal{D}_2(f)$ the part of $f - s_2(f)xy^{-2}$ which consists of the nonnegative powers of y. For example

$$\mathcal{D}_1(x^i y^j) = \begin{cases} x^i y^j & \text{if } i \geq 0 \\ 0 & \text{if } i = -1 \\ x^{-i-2} y^{i+j+1} & \text{if } i < -1 \end{cases}$$

One can check $\mathcal{D}_i^2 = \mathcal{D}_i$ and $\mathcal{D}_1 \mathcal{D}_2 \mathcal{D}_1 = \mathcal{D}_2 \mathcal{D}_1 \mathcal{D}_2$. We write

$$\mathcal{B}(f) := \mathcal{D}_1(\mathcal{D}_2(\mathcal{D}_1(f))),$$

then $\mathcal{B}(f)$ consists only of nonnegative powers of x and y.

The fundamental property is contained in the next proposition.

3.5 Proposition

(i)　We have $\mathcal{I}(\mathcal{B}(f)) = \mathcal{I}(f)$,

(ii)　$\mathcal{B}(\mathcal{I}(f)) = \mathcal{B}(f)$.

(iii)　For any (graded) G-module M we have $\mathcal{B}(\mathcal{H}_T(M)) = \mathcal{H}_G(M)$.

Proof　We have $\mathcal{D}_i\, D_i = \mathcal{D}_i$ and $D_i\, \mathcal{D}_i = D_i$, hence

$$\mathcal{I}(B(f)) = D_1 D_2 D_1\, \mathcal{D}_1\, \mathcal{D}_2\, \mathcal{D}_1(f) = D_1 D_2 D_1\, \mathcal{D}_2\, \mathcal{D}_1(f)$$

$$= D_2 D_1 D_2\, \mathcal{D}_2\, \mathcal{D}_1(f) = D_2 D_1 D_2\, \mathcal{D}_1(f) = D_1 D_2 D_1(f) = \mathcal{I}(f).$$

And analogously $\mathcal{B}\mathcal{I}(f) = \mathcal{B}(f)$.　　　　　□

4. A relation

We introduce a handy notation first. If V is some T-module, take any basis $\{e_i\}_{i \in I}$ for V consisting of T-eigenvectors e_i with eigencharacter (associated to) $\lambda_i \in \mathbf{Z}^2$. For any function f on $\mathbf{Z}^2$ with values in an abelian group Γ we shall write

$$\sum_{\lambda \vdash V} f(\lambda) := \sum_{i \in I} f(\lambda_i) \in \Gamma.$$

For example $\mathcal{H}_T(V) = \sum_{\lambda \vdash V} e^\lambda$, and

$$\mathcal{H}_T(\mathbf{k}[V]) = \frac{1}{\prod_{\lambda \in V^*}(1 - e^\lambda t)} = \left(\frac{1}{\prod_{\lambda \vdash V}(1 - e^\lambda t)}\right)^*, \qquad (1)$$

where $f \mapsto f^*$ is the involution of $\mathbf{D}$ determined by

$$x \mapsto y, \quad y \mapsto x, \quad t \mapsto t,$$

which commutes with the W-action, and hence with $\mathcal{I}$ and $\mathcal{B}$.

Let M be some G-module, N a T-submodule, and $\mu \in \mathbf{Z}^2$. Write

$$\mathcal{B}(e^\mu \prod_{\lambda \vdash M/N} (1 - e^\lambda t)) =: \sum_{\lambda \in S^{\mu,N}} \alpha_\lambda^{\mu,N} e^\lambda,$$

where $S^{\mu,N}$ is a finite subset of $\mathbf{N}^2$. We shall write α_λ^μ for the polynomials $\alpha_\lambda^{\mu,N}$ in the variable t if no confusion can arise, and S^μ for $S^{\mu,N}$.

The next proposition is fundamental to our approach of calculating G-Hilbert series.

4.1 Proposition *We have*

$$\mathcal{B}\left(\frac{e^{\mu}}{\prod_{\lambda \vdash N}(1 - e^{\lambda}t)}\right)^{*} = \sum_{\lambda \in S^{\mu}} \alpha_{\lambda}^{\mu} \mathcal{H}_{G}(k[M] \otimes V_{\lambda}^{*}).$$

Proof Using Proposition 3.5, equation (1) and the property that $\mathcal{I}(fg) = f\mathcal{I}(g)$, if f is W-invariant, we obtain

$$\mathcal{I}\left(\mathcal{B}\left(\frac{e^{\mu}}{\prod_{\lambda \vdash N}(1 - e^{\lambda}t)}\right)^{*}\right) = \mathcal{I}\left(\frac{e^{\mu}}{\prod_{\lambda \vdash N}(1 - e^{\lambda}t)}\right)^{*} =$$

$$= \left(\frac{1}{\prod_{\lambda \vdash M}(1 - e^{\lambda}t)}\right)^{*} \mathcal{I}\left(e^{\mu} \prod_{\lambda \vdash M/N}(1 - e^{\lambda}t)\right)^{*}$$

$$= \frac{1}{\prod_{\lambda \vdash M^{*}}(1 - e^{\lambda}t)} \mathcal{I}\left(\mathcal{B}(e^{\mu} \prod_{\lambda \vdash M/N}(1 - e^{\lambda}t))\right)^{*}$$

$$= \mathcal{H}_{T}(k[M]) \sum_{\lambda \in S^{\mu}} \alpha_{\lambda}^{\mu} \mathcal{I}(e^{\lambda})^{*}$$

$$= \sum_{\lambda \in S^{\mu}} \alpha_{\lambda}^{\mu} \mathcal{H}_{T}(k[M] \otimes V_{\lambda}^{*}).$$

Now apply $\mathcal{B}$ and use Proposition 3.5 again to finish the proof. $\qquad\square$

5. Ternary quadrics

As a first example we calculate the well-known generating function for the concomitants of the ternary quadrics.

Take $N := \langle x_1^2, x_2, x_1^{-2}x_2^2\rangle$, and $\mu = 0$. Then if

$$f := \prod_{\lambda \vdash M/N}(1 - e^{\lambda}t) = (1 - xy^{-1}t)(1 - x^{-1}t)(1 - y^{-2}t),$$

we have

$$\mathcal{D}_1(f) = 1 - (xy^{-1} + y^{-2}t + (xy^{-3} + y^{-1})t^2 - y^{-3}t^3)$$
$$\mathcal{D}_2 \mathcal{D}_1(f) = 1 - (-x^{-1}t + x^{-1}yt^2 - x^{-2}yt^3)$$
$$\mathcal{B}(f) = \mathcal{D}_1 \mathcal{D}_2 \mathcal{D}_1(f) = 1 - t^3.$$

Next write

$$g := \frac{1}{\prod_{\lambda \vdash N}(1 - e^{\lambda}t)} = \frac{1}{(1 - x^2t)(1 - yt)(1 - x^{-2}y^2t)},$$

then $\mathcal{D}_2(g) = g$, and one checks that

$$g - s_1(g)x^{-2}y = \frac{1 - x^{-2}y}{(1 - x^2t)(1 - yt)(1 - x^{-2}y^2t)}$$

$$= \frac{1}{(1 - x^2t)(1 - y^2t)} + \frac{(y^2t - y)x^{-2}}{(1 - yt)(1 - y^2t^2)(1 - x^{-2}y^2t)}.$$

In the development of the second factor at $t = 0$ only negative powers of x occur; in the first factor only nonnegative. Hence

$$\mathcal{D}_1 \mathcal{D}_2(g) = \frac{1}{(1 - y^2 t^2)(1 - x^2 t)} = \mathcal{D}_2 \mathcal{D}_1 \mathcal{D}_2(g).$$

So it follows from Proposition 4.1 that

$$\mathcal{H}_G(\mathbf{k}[V_{(2,0)}]) = \frac{1}{(1 - y^2 t)(1 - x^2 t^2)(1 - t^3)},$$

and for the concomitants

$$Con((2, 0); x, y, t) = \frac{1}{(1 - x^2 t)(1 - y^2 t^2)(1 - t^3)}.$$

6. Ternary cubics

Taking $N := \langle x_1^3, x_1^2 x_2, x_1 x_2^2, x_2^3, x_3 x_1^2 \rangle$ we have that $GN := \{gn; g \in G, n \in N\}$ is the subvariety of the space of ternary cubics $M := V_{(3,0)}$ defined by the invariant polynomials; this was known to Hilbert [H93]. It consists of the elements $x \in M$ such that 0 is in the closure of the orbit Gx.

6.1 We compute the relation associated to N and $0 \in \mathbf{N}^2$. Write

$$f = \prod_{\lambda \vdash M/N} (1 - e^\lambda t)$$
$$= (1 - t)(1 - x^{-2} y t)(1 - x y^{-2} t)(1 - x^{-1} y^{-1} t)(1 - y^{-3} t).$$

Then

$$\mathcal{D}_1(f) = (1 - t^2)(y^3 - t)(y^{-3} + y^{-6} t^2 - t x y^{-5})$$
$$\mathcal{D}_2 \mathcal{D}_1(f) = (1 - t^2)((1 + t) + y x^{-2}(t - t^2) + y^3(-t^2 x^{-3}) + y^4(t^3 x^{-5}))$$
$$\mathcal{D}_1 \mathcal{D}_2 \mathcal{D}_1(f) = (1 - t^2)((1 + t^2) + t^2 x y - t^3 x^3).$$

Hence $\mathcal{B}(f) = (1 - t^4) + t^2(1 - t^2)xy - t^3(1 - t^2)x^3$. Put $F^\mu := \mathcal{B}\left(\dfrac{e^\mu}{\prod_{\lambda \vdash N}(1 - e^\lambda t)}\right)^*$ and $A := \mathbf{k}[V_{(3,0)}]$, then it follows from Proposition 4.1 that

$$F^{(0,0)} = (1 - t^4)\mathcal{H}_G(A) + t^2(1 - t^2)\mathcal{H}_G(A \otimes V_{(1,1)}) - t^3(1 - t^2)\mathcal{H}_G(A \otimes V_{(0,3)}).$$

The relations associated to $(N$ and$)$ $(1, 1)$, $(3, 0)$ and $(0, 3)$ are

$$F^{(1,1)} = (1 - t)(1 - t^3)\mathcal{H}_G(A \otimes V_{(1,1)}),$$
$$F^{(3,0)} = -t^2(1 - t)(1 - t^2)\mathcal{H}_G(A \otimes V_{(1,1)}) + (1 - t^2)\mathcal{H}_G(A \otimes V_{(0,3)}) -$$
$$\qquad - t^2(1 - t^2)\mathcal{H}_G(A \otimes V_{(3,0)}),$$
$$F^{(0,3)} = -t(1 - t^4)\mathcal{H}_G(A) - t(1 - t^2)\mathcal{H}_G(A \otimes V_{(1,1)}) +$$
$$\qquad + (1 - t^2)\mathcal{H}_G(A \otimes V_{(3,0)}),$$

where we used $V_{(3,0)}^* \simeq V_{(0,3)}$.

These four relations enable us, by elimination of $\mathcal{H}_G(A \otimes V_{(1,1)})$, $\mathcal{H}_G(A \otimes V_{(3,0)})$ and $\mathcal{H}_G(A \otimes V_{(0,3)})$, to express $\mathcal{H}_G(A)$ in terms of F^μ.

6.2 Proposition *We have*

$$\mathcal{H}_G(\mathbf{k}[V_{(3,0)}]) = \frac{F^{(0,0)} - t^2(1-t)F^{(1,1)} + t^3 F^{(3,0)} + t^5 F^{(0,3)}}{(1-t^4)(1-t^6)}.$$

6.3   We give an outline of the calculation of $F^{(0,0)}$. Write $g = 1/(\prod_{\lambda \vdash N}(1 - e^\lambda t))$. Then

$$g - s_1(g)x^{-2}y =$$

$$= \frac{1}{(1-x^3t)(1-xyt)(1-x^{-1}y^2t)(1-x^{-3}y^3t)} \times$$

$$\times \left(\frac{1}{(1-x^2y^{-1}t)} - \frac{x^{-2}y}{(1-x^{-2}yt)} \right)$$

$$= \frac{(1+t)x^4y(x^2-y)}{(1-x^3t)(1-xyt)(y-x^2t) \times (x-y^2t)(x^3-y^3t)(x^2-yt)}.$$

Observe that the degree with respect to x of this rational function is negative, and the two parts of the denominator separated by $\times$ are coprime in $\mathbf{k}(y,t)[x]$. Hence there is a partial fraction decomposition

$$= \frac{A}{(1-x^3t)(1-xyt)(y-x^2t)} + \frac{B}{(x-y^2t)(x^3-y^3t)(x^2-yt)},$$

where both summands have negative degree with respect to x. Using Maple we calculated that A and B could be written with denominator

$$(1 - y^3t^3)(1 - y^3t^5)(1 - y^6t^4),$$

and numerator a for A:

$$\left(-t^{10}y^8 - t^3y^2\right)x^4 + \left(\left(t^9 - t^8 - t^7\right)y^7 + \left(-t^5 - t^6\right)y^4 + yt^2\right)x^3 +$$

$$+ \left(\left(-t^8 - t^5\right)y^6 + \left(t^5 + t^2\right)y^3\right)x^2 +$$

$$+ \left(\left(t^4 + t^5\right)y^5 - t^8y^8 + \left(t^3 + t^2 - t\right)y^2\right)x + y^7t^7 + y.$$

Now one sees that in the development in $t = 0$ of the first summand only non-negative powers of x occur. But in the development of the second

$$\frac{x^{-6}B}{(1-x^{-1}y^2t)(1-x^{-3}y^3t)(1-x^{-2}yt)}$$

only negative powers of x occur, because the degree of B with respect to x is smaller than 6. Hence

$$\mathcal{D}_1(f) = \frac{a}{(y-x^2t) \times (1-x^3t)(1-xyt)(1-y^3t^3)(1-y^3t^5)(1-y^6t^4)}.$$

Again there is a partial fraction decomposition of $D_1(f)$, this time with respect to y, of the form

$$D_1(f) = \frac{C}{(y - x^2 t)} + \frac{D}{(1 - x^3 t)(1 - xyt)(1 - y^3 t^3)(1 - y^3 t^5)(1 - y^6 t^4)},$$

with

$$C = \left((y - x^2 t)\, D_1(f)\right)_{y = x^2 t},$$

and only the second summand gives non-negative powers of y in the development at $t = 0$.

And $s_2(D_1(f)) x y^{-2}$ has a decomposition of the form

$$\frac{F}{(1 - xyt)} + \frac{G}{(1 - x^3 t)(y - x^2 t)(y^3 - x^3 t^3)(y^3 - x^3 t^5)(y^6 - x^6 t^4)},$$

with

$$F = \left((1 - xyt) s_2(D_1(f)) x y^{-2}\right)_{y = x^{-1} t^{-1}} = \left((y - x^2 t)\, D_1(f)\right)_{y = x^2 t} \cdot xt.$$

and only the first summand gives non-negative powers of y in the development at $t = 0$. Combining we get

$$D_2\, D_1(f) = \frac{D}{(1 - x^3 t)(1 - xyt)(1 - y^3 t^3)(1 - y^3 t^5)(1 - y^6 t^4)} - \frac{F}{(1 - xyt)}$$

$$= \left(D_1(f) - \frac{C}{(y - x^2 t)}\right) - \frac{F}{(1 - xyt)}$$

$$= D_1(f) - \frac{(1 - x^3 t^2)}{(y - x^2 t)(1 - xyt)} \times \left((y - x^2 t)\, D_1(f)\right)_{y = x^2 t}.$$

Using Maple we found that the result only involves non-negative powers of both x and y when expanded at $t = 0$, hence $D_1\, D_2\, D_1(f) = D_2\, D_1(f)$.

We also found that $F^{(0,0)} = B(f)^* = D_1\, D_2\, D_1(f)^*$ could be written with denominator

$$(1 - y^3 t)(1 - y^3 t^3)(1 - y^3 t^4)(1 - xyt)(1 - x^3 t^3)(1 - x^3 t^5)(1 - x^6 t^4)$$

and numerator

$$-\left(-x^{11} y^2 t^{13} - x^{10} y^4 t^{14} - x^9 y^6 t^{15} + \left((t^{10} + t^8)\, y^2 - y^8 t^{16}\right) x^8 + \right.$$
$$\left((t^{15} - t^{14} - t^{13})\, y^7 + (t^{10} - t^{12} + t^9)\, y^4 + yt^8\right) x^7 +$$
$$+ \left((-t^{14} - t^{11})\, y^6 + (t^{11} + t^{10} + t^8 + t^7)\, y^3 - t^7\right) x^6 +$$
$$+ x^5 y^2 t^9 + \left((-t^{12} - t^{11})\, y^7 + (t^{10} + t^9 + 2t^8 + t^7)\, y^4 + (-t^5 - t^4)\, y\right) x^4 +$$
$$+ x^3 y^6 t^{11} + \left((t^9 + t^8 + t^6 + t^5)\, y^5 - y^8 t^9 + (-t^6 - t^5 - t^4 - t^2)\, y^2\right) x^2 +$$
$$\left. + \left(y^7 t^8 + (t^6 - t^5 - t^4)\, y^4 + (-t^3 - t^2 + t)\, y\right) x - 1\right).$$

6.4 Remark The expansion of this rational function has an independent interpretation. The ideal of the cone GN is generated by the fundamental, algebraically independent invariants S and T; from this it follows that $\mathcal{H}_G(\mathbf{k}[GN]) = \mathcal{H}_G(A)(1 - t^4)(1 - t^6)$. This cone is not normal, because its singularities form a subvariety of codimension one. Write $\widetilde{GN}$ for the normalization of GN, then the interpretation is $F^{(0,0)} = \mathcal{H}_G(\mathbf{k}[\widetilde{GN}])$.

In an analogous way the other F^μ s can be computed. Together with Proposition 6.2 it gives the following completion of computations by Forsyth [F98].

6.5 Theorem *The SL_3-Hilbert series $\mathcal{H}_G(\mathbf{k}[V_{(3,0)}])$ can be written as a rational function with numerator*

$$
\begin{aligned}
&1 - xyt + x^2y^2t^2 + (-y^3 + xy^4 + x^2y^2)t^4 + (2xy^4 - x^2y^5 + x^4y)t^5 + \\
&+ (x^2y^2 - x^2y^5)t^6 + (xy^4 + x^4y - x^6y^3 + x^7y)t^7 + (y^6 - xy^7 - x^2y^5 + \\
&+ x^4y - x^4y^4 - x^8y^2)t^8 + (-xy^7 + x^2y^8 + x^3y^3 - x^4y^4 - x^5y^2 + x^7y - \\
&- x^7y^4)t^9 + (-2x^4y^4 + x^5y^2 - x^7y^4 - x^8y^2)t^{10} + (-x^3y^6 - x^4y^4 + x^6y^6 - \\
&- 2x^7y^4)t^{11} + (-x^4y^4 + x^4y^7 - x^6y^6 - x^7y^4 + x^8y^5 + x^9 - x^{10}y)t^{12} + \\
&+ (-x^3y^6 - x^7y^4 + x^7y^7 - x^9y^3 - x^{10}y + x^{11}y^2)t^{13} + (x^4y^7 - x^5y^5 + \\
&+ x^7y^7 + x^{10}y^4)t^{14} + (-x^9y^3 + x^9y^6)t^{15} + (x^7y^7 - x^9y^3 + 2x^{10}y^4)t^{16} + \\
&+ (x^9y^6 + x^{10}y^4 - x^{11}y^5)t^{17} + x^9y^6t^{19} - x^{10}y^7t^{20} + x^{11}y^8t^{21};
\end{aligned}
$$

and with denominator

$$
\begin{aligned}
&(1 - y^3t)(1 - y^3t^3)(1 - y^3t^4)(1 - xyt)(1 - x^3t^3)(1 - x^3t^5)(1 - x^6t^4) \times \\
&\times (1 - t^4)(1 - t^6).
\end{aligned}
$$

6.6 Remark The generating function $\mathrm{Con}((3,0); x, y, t)$ of the concomitants of the ternary cubic forms is obtained from the formula above by interchanging x and y. In particular

$$
\mathrm{Cov}((3,0); x, t) = \frac{1 - x^3t^4 + x^6t^8}{(1 - x^3t)(1 - x^3t^3)(1 - x^3t^4)(1 - t^4)(1 - t^6)}.
$$

7. Ternary quartics

In this section we give an outline of the computation of the generating functions associated to some types of covariants of the ternary quartics.

We consider the representation $M = V_{(4,0)}$. Introduce the two functions $\mathrm{ht}_i : \mathbf{Z}^2 \to \mathbf{Z}$, for $i = 1$ or 2, by $\mathrm{ht}_1((n, m)) := n + m$ and $\mathrm{ht}_2(n, m) = n + 2m$. Write N_i for the sum of the T-eigenspaces of M corresponding to $\mu \in \mathbf{Z}^2$ with $\mathrm{ht}_i(\mu) \geq 0$. The union of GN_1 and GN_2 is the cone defined by the invariants.

We used the following procedure to obtain a set of relations. Define $S := S^{(0,0),N_1}$. If $3\mu_1 \geq \mu_2$ put $S^\mu = S^{\mu,N_1}$, else put $S^\mu = S^{\mu,N_2}$. If $\bigcup_{\mu \in S} S^\mu$ is larger than S, replace S by this union and repeat the procedure.

This algorithm stops at the set of weights $\mu \in \mathbf{N}^2$ with $\mathrm{ht}_1(\mu) \leq 7$ together with $\{(8,0),(7,1),(6,2),(5,3),(3,5),(2,4),(6,3)\}$. It consists of 43 elements. Write $A := \mathbf{k}[M]$ and, for $i = 1$ or 2,

$$f_i := \frac{1}{\prod_{\lambda \vdash N_i}(1 - e^{\lambda}t)},$$

then we have 43 relations

$$\mathcal{B}(e^{\mu}f_i)^* = \sum_{\lambda \in S} \alpha_{\lambda}^{\mu,N_i}\mathcal{H}_G(A \otimes V_{\lambda}^*),$$

with $\mu \in S$, and $i = 1$ if $3\mu_1 \geq \mu_2$, else $i = 2$. We observe that $\alpha_{\lambda}^{\mu}(t := 0) = 0$, unless $\lambda = \mu$; in that case it is 1. It follows that the matrix $(\alpha_{\lambda}^{\mu})_{\lambda,\mu \in S}$ is invertible; hence $\mathcal{H}_G(A \otimes V_{\lambda})$, $\lambda \in S$, can be expressed in the $\mathcal{B}(e^{\mu}f_i)^*$ and the coefficients α_{λ}^{μ}.

We were not able to calculate $\mathcal{B}(e^{\mu}f_i)^*$ completely, but at least we can give the coefficient of x^0y^0.

7.1 Lemma

(i) If $\mu \neq 0 \in \mathbf{N}^2$ then the coefficient of x^0y^0 in $\mathcal{B}(e^{\mu}f_i)^*$ is zero, for $i = 0$ or 1.

(ii) The coefficient of x^0y^0 in $\mathcal{B}(f_1)^*$ equals $(1-t^3)^{-2}$.

Proof Any λ such that e^{λ} occurs with a non-zero coefficient in the expansion of $e^{\mu}f_i$ at $t = 0$ has $\mathrm{ht}_i(\lambda) \geq 0$, because any T-eigenvector of N_i has a eigen-character ν with $\mathrm{ht}_i(\nu) \geq 0$, by definition of N_i. If $\mu \neq 0$, then $\mathrm{ht}_i(\mu) > 0$, hence $\mathrm{ht}_i(\lambda) > 0$.

Suppose that $\psi \in \mathbf{Z}^2$ such that $\mathcal{D}_1(e^{\psi}) \neq 0$. If $\mathcal{D}_1(e^{\psi}) \neq e^{\psi}$, then $\psi_1 < -1$ and $\mathcal{D}_1(e^{\psi}) = e^{(-\psi_1-2,\psi_1+\psi_2+1)}$. We have

$$\mathrm{ht}_1((-\psi_1 - 2, \psi_1 + \psi_2 + 1)) = -1 + \psi_2 > \psi_1 + \psi_2 = \mathrm{ht}_1(\psi)$$
$$\mathrm{ht}_2((-\psi_1 - 2, \psi_1 + \psi_2 + 1)) = \psi_1 + 2\psi_2 = \mathrm{ht}_2(\psi).$$

Now suppose that $\mathcal{D}_2(e^{\psi}) \neq 0$. If $\mathcal{D}_2(e^{\psi}) \neq e^{\psi}$, then $\psi_2 < -1$ and $\mathcal{D}_1(e^{\psi}) = e^{(\psi_1+\psi_2+1,-\psi_2-2)}$. We have

$$\mathrm{ht}_1((\psi_1 + \psi_2 + 1, -\psi_2 - 2)) = \psi_1 - 1 > \psi_1 + \psi_2 = \mathrm{ht}_1(\psi)$$
$$\mathrm{ht}_2((\psi_1 + \psi_2 + 1, -\psi_2 - 2)) = \psi_1 - \psi_2 - 3 > \mathrm{ht}_2(\psi).$$

It follows that if $\mu \neq 0$ and e^{λ} occurs with non-zero coefficient in $\mathcal{B}(e^{\mu}f_i)$, then $\mathrm{ht}_1(\lambda)$ and $\mathrm{ht}_2(\lambda)$ both are greater than zero, hence $\lambda \neq (0,0)$. This proves (i).

It also follows that the coefficient of x^0y^0 in $\mathcal{B}(f_1)^*$ equals the coefficient of x^0y^0 in

$$g := \frac{1}{\prod_{\lambda \vdash N_1,\mathrm{ht}_1(\lambda)=0}(1 - e^{\lambda}t)} = \frac{1}{(1 - x^2y^{-2}t)(1 - x^{-1}yt)(1 - x^{-4}y^4t)}$$
$$= \frac{1}{(1 - z^{-2}t)(1 - zt)(1 - z^4t)},$$

if we write $z = x^{-1}y$. Now there is a partial fraction decomposition with respect to z of the form

$$g = \frac{A}{(1 - zt)(1 - z^4t)} + \frac{B}{(z^2 - t)}.$$

Only the first gives non-negative powers of z in the development at $t = 0$. With Maple we computed that

$$A(z := 0) = \frac{1}{(1 - t^3)^2},$$

which is the coefficient of x^0y^0 we searched for.   □

By comparing the coefficient of x^0y^0 on both sides of the equations we get equations involving $\mathcal{H}((A \otimes V_\lambda)^G; s, t)$. By solving the equations we found $\mathcal{H}((A \otimes V_\mu)^G; t)$, $\mu \in S$. This Hilbert series is the generating function of the concomitants of the form $V_{(3,0)} \to V_\mu$. They are of geometrical interest in the case $\mu = (n, 0)$, for some $n \in \mathbf{N}$. We give some of the results in the next proposition.

7.2 Theorem *The Hilbert series* $\mathcal{H}((\mathbf{k}[V_{(4,0)}] \otimes V_\mu)^G; t)$, *for* $\mu \in S$ *as above, can be written as a rational function with denominator*

$$(1 - t^3)(1 - t^6)(1 - t^9)(1 - t^{12})(1 - t^{15})(1 - t^{18})(1 - t^{27}).$$

For $\mu = (m, 0)$ $(m = 0, \ldots, 8)$ *the numerator is*

for $m = 0$:
$$t^{75} + t^{66} + t^{63} + t^{60} + 2t^{57} + 3t^{54} + 2t^{51} + 3t^{48} + 4t^{45} + 3t^{42} + 4t^{39} +$$
$$+ 4t^{36} + 3t^{33} + 4t^{30} + 3t^{27} + 2t^{24} + 3t^{21} + 2t^{18} + t^{15} + t^{12} + t^9 + 1,$$

for $m = 1$:
$$t^{61} + 2t^{58} + 5t^{55} + 8t^{52} + 9t^{49} + 13t^{46} + 16t^{43} + 14t^{40} + 17t^{37} +$$
$$+ 18t^{34} + 13t^{31} + 12t^{28} + 11t^{25} + 5t^{22} + 3t^{19} + 3t^{16},$$

for $m = 2$:
$$t^{71} + 2t^{68} + 3t^{65} + 5t^{62} + 8t^{59} + 10t^{56} + 14t^{53} + 19t^{50} + 20t^{47} +$$
$$24t^{44} + 27t^{41} + 25t^{38} + 27t^{35} + 26t^{32} + 21t^{29} + 19t^{26} + 16t^{23} +$$
$$11t^{20} + 8t^{17} + 7t^{14} + 3t^{11} + 2t^8 + 2t^5,$$

for $m = 3$:
$$t^{66} + 2t^{63} + 6t^{60} + 12t^{57} + 17t^{54} + 28t^{51} + 38t^{48} + 42t^{45} + 51t^{42} +$$
$$+ 55t^{39} + 50t^{36} + 50t^{33} + 46t^{30} + 34t^{27} + 28t^{24} + 21t^{21} + 10t^{18} +$$
$$+ 6t^{15} + 3t^{12},$$

for $m = 4$:

$$t^{73} + t^{70} + 4\,t^{67} + 8\,t^{64} + 11\,t^{61} + 20\,t^{58} + 30\,t^{55} + 36\,t^{52} + 49\,t^{49} + 60\,t^{46} +$$
$$+ 62\,t^{43} + 69\,t^{40} + 73\,t^{37} + 65\,t^{34} + 62\,t^{31} + 57\,t^{28} + 43\,t^{25} + 35\,t^{22} +$$
$$+ 27\,t^{19} + 16\,t^{16} + 10\,t^{13} + 7\,t^{10} + 2\,t^{7} + t^{4} + t,$$

for $m = 5$:

$$3\,t^{65} + 8\,t^{62} + 15\,t^{59} + 30\,t^{56} + 48\,t^{53} + 62\,t^{50} + 82\,t^{47} + 99\,t^{44} + 103\,t^{41} +$$
$$+ 110\,t^{38} + 112\,t^{35} + 97\,t^{32} + 87\,t^{29} + 74\,t^{26} + 50\,t^{23} + 35\,t^{20} + 22\,t^{17} +$$
$$+ 9\,t^{14} + 3\,t^{11} + t^{8},$$

for $m = 6$:

$$t^{72} + 3\,t^{69} + 6\,t^{66} + 15\,t^{63} + 26\,t^{60} + 38\,t^{57} + 59\,t^{54} + 80\,t^{51} + 94\,t^{48} +$$
$$+ 116\,t^{45} + 131\,t^{42} + 130\,t^{39} + 135\,t^{36} + 131\,t^{33} + 111\,t^{30} + 97\,t^{27} +$$
$$+ 81\,t^{24} + 55\,t^{21} + 39\,t^{18} + 27\,t^{15} + 13\,t^{12} + 7\,t^{9} + 4\,t^{6} + t^{3},$$

for $m = 7$:

$$t^{67} + 5\,t^{64} + 17\,t^{61} + 36\,t^{58} + 57\,t^{55} + 90\,t^{52} + 124\,t^{49} + 145\,t^{46} + 173\,t^{43} +$$
$$+ 192\,t^{40} + 185\,t^{37} + 183\,t^{34} + 171\,t^{31} + 136\,t^{28} + 110\,t^{25} + 83\,t^{22} +$$
$$+ 48\,t^{19} + 27\,t^{16} + 14\,t^{13} + 3\,t^{10},$$

for $m = 8$:

$$t^{71} + 4\,t^{68} + 12\,t^{65} + 23\,t^{62} + 45\,t^{59} + 73\,t^{56} + 100\,t^{53} + 138\,t^{50} + 173\,t^{47} +$$
$$+ 192\,t^{44} + 216\,t^{41} + 228\,t^{38} + 214\,t^{35} + 203\,t^{32} + 183\,t^{29} + 143\,t^{26} +$$
$$+ 112\,t^{23} + 84\,t^{20} + 50\,t^{17} + 30\,t^{14} + 17\,t^{11} + 6\,t^{8} + 2\,t^{5} + t^{2}.$$

7.3 Remark We did not calculate $\mathcal{H}((\mathbf{k}[V_{(4,0)}] \otimes V_{(8,0)})^{G})$, i.e., the generating function of all covariants $V_{(4,0)} \to V_{(8,0)}$, but $\mathcal{H}((\mathbf{k}[V_{(4,0)}] \otimes V_{(8,0)}^{*})^{G})$. But they are related to each other by a general result of Stanley, see [St79].

8. Systems of ternary forms

In an analogous way we computed the generating functions of some systems of ternary forms. We give the results.

For a system of a quadric and a cubic form the generating function of the invariants $\mathcal{H}(\mathbf{k}[V_{(2,0)} \oplus V_{(3,0)}]^{G}; t)$ can be written as a rational function with numerator

$$1 + t + t^{7} + t^{8} + t^{9} + 2t^{11} + 3t^{12} + 3t^{13} + 4t^{14} + 6t^{15} + 7t^{16} + 7t^{17} +$$
$$+ 9t^{18} + 9t^{19} + 8t^{20} + 9t^{21} + 9t^{22} + 7t^{23} + 7t^{24} + 6t^{25} + 4t^{26} +$$
$$+ 3t^{27} + 3t^{28} + 2t^{29} + t^{31} + t^{32} + t^{33} + t^{39} + t^{40},$$

and denominator

$$(1+t)(1-t^{3})(1-t^{4})(1-t^{5})(1-t^{6})(1-t^{7})(1-t^{8})(1-t^{9})(1-t^{13}).$$

For a system of two ternary cubic forms the generating function of the invariants $\mathcal{H}(\mathbf{k}[V_{(3,0)} \oplus V_{(3,0)}]^G; t)$ can be written as a rational function with numerator

$$1 - 2t + t^2 - 2t^3 + 5t^4 - 4t^5 + 9t^6 - 16t^7 + 18t^8 - 22t^9 + 29t^{10} - 24t^{11} +$$
$$+ 40t^{12} - 42t^{13} + 38t^{14} - 42t^{15} + 40t^{16} - 24t^{17} + 29t^{18} - 22t^{19} +$$
$$+ 18t^{20} - 16t^{21} + 9t^{22} - 4t^{23} + 5t^{24} - 2t^{25} + t^{26} - 2t^{27} + t^{28},$$

and denominator

$$(1 - t^4)^4 (1 - t^6)^4 (1 - t^3)^2 (1 - t)^2.$$

9. References

[Br90]   A. Broer, *Hilbert series in invariant theory*, Thesis Rijksuniversiteit Utrecht, 1990.

[D87]   J. Dixmier, *On the projective invariants of quartic plane curves*, Adv. in Math., **64**(1987), 305–325.

[F98]   A.R. Forsyth, *An essay towards the generating functions of ternariants*, Proc. of the London Math. Soc., **31**(1898), 487–518.

[G69]   P. Gordan, *Über ternäre Formen dritten Grades*, Math. Ann., **1**(1869), 90–129.

[H90]   D. Hilbert, *Über die Theorie der algebraischen Formen*, Math. Ann., **36**(1890), 473–534.

[H93]   D. Hilbert, *Über die vollen Invariantensysteme*, Math. Ann., **42**(1893), 313–373.

[Kr84]   H. Kraft, *Geometrische Methoden in der Invariantentheorie*, Vieweg Verlag, Braunschweig, 1984.

[Sh67]   T. Shioda, *On the graded ring of invariants of binary octavics*, Amer. J. of Math., **89**(1967), 1022–1046.

[Sp77]   T.A. Springer, *Invariant theory*, L.N.M. 585, Springer Verlag, New York, 1977.

[Sp82]   T.A. Springer, *Séries de Poincaré dans la théorie des invariants*, pp. 37–54 in: Séminaire d'Algèbre, P. Dubreil et M.-P. Malliavin, Proceedings, Paris 1982 (35ème Année) (ed.: M.-P. Malliavin), Springer Verlag, New York, 1982L.N.M. 1029.

[St79]   R.P. Stanley, *Combinatorics and invariant theory*, pp. 345–355 in: Relations between combinatorics and other parts of mathematics, Proc. of Symposia in Pure Math. (ed.: D.K. Ray-Chaudhuri), 1979, A.M.S. Providence, Rhode IslandVol. 34.

Computational Aspects of Lie Group Representations and Related Topics
Proceedings of the 1990 Computational Algebra Seminar
pp. 19–28 in CWI Tract 84 (1991)

19

Generating Functions and Lie Groups

Arjeh M. Cohen

CWI

Kruislaan 413

1098 SJ Amsterdam

The Netherlands

and

G.C.M. Ruitenburg

Universiteit van Amsterdam

Pl. Muidergracht 24

1018 TV Amsterdam

The Netherlands

0. Introduction

In their listings [McK], [Bre] of decompositions of characters of semisimple Lie subgroups obtained by restriction from overgroups or by tensor products of irreducible representations, McKay et al. often use generating functions that turn out to be rational. In this paper, we prove that they are always rational and provide an example of how to derive an explicit expression for this rational function in the case $G_2 \downarrow A_2$.

Let G be a semisimple complex connected Lie group of Lie rank n with maximal torus T. The group of all rational characters of T, called *weights*, is denoted by $\Lambda(T)$. As groups, we have $\Lambda(T) \cong \mathbf{Z}^n$. The set of all *roots* (that is, all nonzero weights occurring in the restriction to T of the adjoint representation of G), is denoted by Φ_G. A set of fundamental roots $\alpha_1, \ldots, \alpha_n$ is chosen with respect to a fixed Borel subgroup B of G containing T. We write $W_G = N_G(T)/T$ and $(\cdot, \cdot)$ for the canonical W_G-invariant inner product on $\Lambda(T)$. We also fix the fundamental weights $\omega_1, \ldots, \omega_n$ as the basis dual to the fundamental roots in the following sense: $2(\omega_i, \alpha_j)/(\alpha_j, \alpha_j) = \delta_{i,j}$, $1 \leq i, j \leq n$. The set $\Lambda^+(G,T)$ of dominant weights is the $\mathbf{N}$-span of these fundamental weights. As semigroups we have $\Lambda^+(G,T) \cong \mathbf{N}^n$. The set of positive roots is $\Phi_G^+ = \{\alpha \in \Phi_G | (\alpha, \omega_i) \geq 0$ for $i = 1, \ldots, n\}$ and $\rho_G = \sum_{i=1}^n \omega_i$ is the half sum of all roots in Φ_G^+. A partial ordering $\leq$ on $\Lambda(T)$ is given by $\lambda \leq \mu$ if and only if $\mu - \lambda$ is a non–negative integral linear combination of positive roots. $\Lambda^+(G,T)$ is used to indicate irreducible representations of G and V_λ is the irreducible G–module with highest weight λ. This module can be obtained as $\{f \in \mathbf{C}[G] \mid f(gb) = \lambda(b)f(g)\}$; here λ is viewed as a character of B by $\lambda(b) = \lambda(t)$ for $b = tu$, with $t \in T$ and $u \in U$, where U is the maximal unipotent subgroup of B. There is a straightforward extension from semisimple to reductive groups. If G is a reductive group we also use elements of $\Lambda^+(G,T)$ to indicate the set of all weights that are dominant with respect to the semisimple part of the torus. Thus for example $\Lambda^+(T,T) = \Lambda(T)$.

1. Rational generating functions

Assume that G is a semisimple Lie group. Let $\mu_1, \ldots, \mu_p \in \Lambda^+ = \Lambda^+(G,T)$ and set $M = \mathbf{N}^p$ with standard basis $e_1, \ldots, e_p$. For the G-module $V \cong V_{\mu_1} \oplus \cdots \oplus V_{\mu_p}$, the algebra $\mathbf{C}[V^*]$ of polynomial functions on the dual V^* of V can be M–graded in such a way that $\mathbf{C}[V^*]_{e_i} = V_{\mu_i}$ for each $i \in \{1, \ldots, p\}$. Given $m = (m_1, \ldots, m_p) \in M$, the homogeneous part $\mathbf{C}[V^*]_m$ is a homomorphic image of $V_{\mu_1}^{m_1} \otimes \cdots \otimes V_{\mu_p}^{m_p}$ in which $V_{m_1\mu_1 + \cdots + m_p\mu_p}$ occurs with multiplicity 1 and has a unique G-stable complement J_m. Clearly $\mathbf{C}[V^*]_m \cdot J_{m'} \subset J_{m+m'}$, so $J = \oplus_{m \in M} J_m$ is an M-graded G-stable ideal in $\mathbf{C}[V^*]$. Since the algebra $\mathbf{C}[V^*]$ is Noetherian, J must be finitely generated. In fact

1.1 Theorem ([Bri, 4.1]) *The ideal J is generated by the $J_{e_i+e_j}$ for all $1 \leq i \leq j \leq n$.*

The quotient algebra $A = \mathbf{C}[V^*]/J$ can be provided with the induced M-grading and is preserved by the induced G-action. By construction, $A_m \cong V_{m_1\mu_1 + \cdots + m_p\mu_p}$. In particular, putting $p = n$, $\mu_i = \omega_i$ for all $i \in \{1, \ldots, n\}$ and $M = \Lambda^+$, the direct sum $A = \bigoplus_{\lambda \in \Lambda^+} V_\lambda$ over all irreducible representations of G is a Λ^+-graded G-algebra, with $A_\lambda \cong V_\lambda$. The Poincaré series of A is the expression

$$P_{dim}(x) = \sum_{\lambda \in \Lambda^+} (\dim V_\lambda)x^\lambda,$$

where x stands for $(x_1, \ldots, x_n)$ and x^λ stands for $x_1^{\lambda_1} \cdots x_n^{\lambda_n}$ if $\lambda = \sum_{i=1}^n \lambda_i\omega_i$. Thus, $x_i = x^{\omega_i}$. As A is finitely generated, $P_{dim}(x)$ is a rational function in $x_1, \ldots, x_n$ (this will later be abbreviated to: rational in x). The rational function can be explicitly given:

1.2 Theorem (Weyl's Dimension Formula, cf. [Hum]) *The dimensions of the highest weight modules of G are given by the formula*

$$P_{dim}(x) = \sum_{\lambda \in \Lambda^+} \prod_{\alpha \in \Phi^+} \frac{(\lambda + \rho_G, \alpha)}{(\rho_G, \alpha)} x^\lambda$$

$$= \prod_{\alpha \in \Phi^+} \frac{\sum_{i=1}^n (\omega_i, \alpha) \dfrac{\partial}{\partial x_i} \cdot x_i}{(\rho_G, \alpha)} \left(\prod_{i=1}^n \frac{1}{1 - x_i} \right).$$

The first identity gives an explicit formula for the dimension of V_λ and is more convenient for actual computation. The second identity expresses $D_{dim}(x)$ as a rational function in x; it can easily be derived from the first by use of $\dfrac{\partial}{\partial x_i} \cdot x_i(x^m) = (m_i + 1)x^m$ and $(\lambda + \rho_G, \alpha) = \sum_{i=1}^n (\lambda_i + 1)(\omega_i, \alpha)$.

1.3 Example Let G be a Lie group of type A_1. Then $\rho_G = \omega_1$ and $\Phi^+ = \{\alpha_1\} = \{2\omega_1\}$, so

$$P_{dim}(x) = \sum_{m \geq 0} \frac{((m+1)\omega_1, 2\omega_1)}{(\omega_1, 2\omega_1)} x^m = \sum_{m \geq 0} (m+1)x^m = \frac{\partial}{\partial x} \cdot x \left(\frac{1}{(1-x)} \right)$$

$$= \frac{1}{(1-x)^2}.$$

We shall extend these observations to Weyl's Character Formula. Let H be a reductive closed Lie subgroup of the semisimple Lie group G. The fact that H is reductive ensures that any finite-dimensional rational representation of H decomposes into a direct sum of irreducibles. *Branching* is the decomposition of a representation of H that is obtained by restriction from a highest weight module of G. Let S be a maximal torus of H and m the Lie rank of H. Then, there is a maximal torus of G containing S, which we may take (up to conjugacy) to be T. Thus for dominant weights $\lambda = (\lambda_1, \ldots, \lambda_n)$ of G and $\mu = (\mu_1, \ldots, \mu_m)$ of H, we are after the multiplicity $(V_\mu, V_\lambda \downarrow_H)$ of the highest weight representation V_μ of H in the highest weight representation V_λ of G restricted to H. In terms of formal power series in the indeterminates $x_1, \ldots, x_n, y_1, \ldots, y_m$, we want to find an explicit description of the *branching series*

$$P_{G \downarrow H}(x; y) = \sum_{\lambda, \mu} (V_\mu, V_\lambda \downarrow_H) x^\mu y^\lambda$$

of H in G.

The coefficients of the branching series have a second interpretation. Given a highest weight module V_μ of the subgroup H there is a unique (possibly infinite dimensional) induced G-module $V_\mu \uparrow^G$. The multiplicity of the highest weight module V_λ in the module $V_\mu \uparrow^G$ is denoted by $(V_\mu \uparrow^G, V_\lambda)$. Frobenius Reciprocity gives that $(V_\mu \uparrow^G, V_\lambda) = (V_\mu, V_\lambda \downarrow_H)$, which is a second interpretation of the power series. However, considered as a power series in x, the coefficients of the series are power series in y that need not be polynomials.

1.4 Lemma $P_{G \downarrow H}(x; y)$ *is a rational function in* x *and* y.

Proof Denote by $B = \bigoplus_{\mu \in \Lambda^+(H,S)} V_\mu^*$ the $\Lambda^+(H, S)$-graded H-algebra of all dual irreducible H–representations, and by $A = \bigoplus_{\lambda \in \Lambda^+(G,T)} V_\lambda$ the $\Lambda^+(G, T)$-graded G-algebra of all irreducible G–representations. Then the tensor product $A \otimes B$ is a $\Lambda^+(G, T) \oplus \Lambda^+(H, S)$–graded algebra with a $G \times H$-action preserving the grading. Considering H as a diagonally embedded subgroup of $G \times H$, we get for $\lambda \in \Lambda^+(G, T)$ and $\mu \in \Lambda^+(H, S)$

$$(A \otimes B)^H_{(\lambda, \mu)} \cong (V_\lambda \downarrow_H \otimes V_\mu^*)^H \cong \operatorname{Hom}_H(V_\lambda \downarrow_H, V_\mu).$$

Since the dimension of the latter complex vector space is the multiplicity $(V_\mu, V_\lambda \downarrow_H)$, the Poincaré series of $(A \otimes B)^H$ is precisely $P_{G \downarrow H}(x; y)$. On the other hand, it is a rational function too, as $(A \otimes B)^H$ is finitely generated, for H is reductive and acts grade preserving on the finitely generated graded ring $A \otimes B$. (cf. [Spri, Proposition 2.4.14]). $\qquad\square$

Weyl's Dimension Formula handles the special case $H = 1$. In the case of the reductive subgroup $H = T$, an explicit rational form is known. For any $\lambda \in \Lambda^+(G, T)$ set $\Theta_\lambda(x) = \sum_{w \in W_G} \det w\, x^{w\lambda}$.

1.5 Theorem (Weyl's Character Formula, cf. [Hum]) *The branching series of the maximal torus* T *in the semisimple Lie group* G *is*

$$P_{G \downarrow T}(x; y) = \sum_{\lambda \in \Lambda^+(G,T)} \frac{\Theta_{\lambda + \rho_G}(x)}{\Theta_{\rho_G}(x)} y^\lambda$$

$$= \frac{1}{x^{\rho_G} \prod_{\alpha \in \Phi^+}(1 - x^{-\alpha})} \sum_{w \in W_G} sgn(w) x^{w\rho_G} \left(\sum_{\lambda \in \Lambda^+(G,T)} x^{w\lambda} y^\lambda \right).$$

This is indeed a rational function since $\sum_{\lambda \in \Lambda^+(T)} x^{w\lambda} y^\lambda$ is rational for each $w \in W_G$. If G is of type E_8, the expression consists of $|W_G| = 696729600$ summands, which is unrealistically high for computations.

1.6 Example Let G be a simply connected Lie group of type A_1. Then

$$P_{G \downarrow T}(x; y) = \frac{1}{x(1 - x^{-2})} \left(\frac{x}{1 - xy} - \frac{x^{-1}}{1 - x^{-1}y} \right)$$

$$= \frac{1}{(1 - xy)(1 - x^{-1}y)}$$

$$= \sum_m (x^m + x^{m-2} + \cdots + x^{2-m} + x^{-m}) y^m,$$

which is a well-known fact.

2. Tensor decomposition and plethysms

Computing the decomposition of the tensor product $V_\lambda \otimes V_\mu$ of two irreducible G-modules can be viewed as branching the irreducible $G \times G$-module

$V_\lambda \otimes V_\mu$ to the diagonal subgroup isomorphic to G. Denote by $(V_\lambda, V_\mu \otimes V_\nu)$ the multiplicity of V_λ in $V_\mu \otimes V_\nu$ and identify $\Lambda^+(G \times G, T \times T)$ with $\Lambda^+(G, T) \times \Lambda^+(G, T)$. Then, as we have seen in the previous section, the power series in $x_1, \ldots, x_n, y_1, \ldots, y_n, z_1, \ldots, z_n$

$$P_\otimes(x; y; z) = \sum_{\lambda, \mu, \nu \in \Lambda^+(G,T)} (V_\lambda, V_\mu \otimes V_\nu) x^\lambda y^\mu z^\nu$$

is rational in x, y, z. Again, let $A = \bigoplus_{\lambda \in \Lambda^+(G,T)} V_\lambda$ and $A^* = \bigoplus_{\lambda \in \Lambda^+(G,T)} V_\lambda^*$. By the proof of the lemma in the previous section, the power series can be considered as the Poincaré series of $(A \otimes A \otimes A^*)^G$, where G must be considered as the diagonal subgroup of $G \times G \times G$. If we use an automorphism of G to identify A^* with A, the entries of the multidegrees in $\Lambda^+(G, T)$ must be permuted in an appropriate way. Therefore the series can be considered as the Poincaré series of $(A \otimes A \otimes A)^G$ and is invariant under permutation of the names x, y, z.

2.1 Example Take G a Lie group of type A_1. Then $A = \bigoplus_{n \geq 0} V_n$ is a polynomial algebra in two variables. $(A \otimes A)_{(1,1)} \cong V_2 \oplus V_0$, and if we take $p \in (A \otimes A)_{(1,1)}$ a generator for V_0, then it follows by Theorem 2.1 that $A \otimes A/(p) \cong \bigoplus_{n,m \geq 0} V_{n+m}$. On the other hand $(A \otimes A)^G \cong \mathbf{C}[p]$, because $(V_n \otimes V_m)^G$ has dimension 1 if $n = m$ and dimension 0 otherwise. Therefore, $A \otimes A$ is a free $(A \otimes A)^G$–module, or equivalently $A \otimes A \cong (A \otimes A/(p)) \otimes (A \otimes A)^G$. This yields the generating function for the tensor product of G:

$$\frac{1}{(1 - xy)(1 - xz)(1 - yz)}.$$

This formula can also be used to compute the power series of the l-fold tensor products. If $P_l(x_1; \ldots; x_l; y) = \sum c_{k,m_1,\ldots,m_l} y^k x_1^{m_1} \cdots x_l^{m_l}$, where the sum is taken over all $k, m_1, \ldots, m_l \geq 0$ and $c_{k,m_1,\ldots,m_l}$ denotes the multiplicity of V_k in $V_{m_1} \otimes \cdots \otimes V_{m_l}$, then $P_0 = 1$ and, for $l > 0$,

$$P_{l+1} = \frac{x_{l+1} P_l(x_1; \ldots; x_l; x_{l+1}) - y P_l(x_1; \ldots; x_l; y)}{(1 - y x_{l+1})(x_{l+1} - y)}.$$

The factor $x_{l+1} - y$ in the denominator always divides the numerator.

As we will see, also symmetric and skew-symmetric powers, and more general plethysms, lead to rational functions. Let $d \in \mathbf{N}$. Identify $\Lambda^+(G^d, T^d)$ with $(\Lambda^+(G, T))^d$, and set $\mu_i = \omega_i^d = (\omega_i, \ldots, \omega_i)$, d times ω_i, for $i = 1, \ldots, n$. Then $B = \bigoplus_{m \in M} V_{m_1 \mu_1 + \cdots + m_n \mu_n}$, where $M = \mathbf{N}^n$, is a M-graded algebra, which is preserved by the G^d action. Restricted to the subgroup G, embedded diagonally in G^d, we get $B = \bigoplus_{m \in M} V_{m_1 \omega_1 + \cdots + m_n \omega_n}^{\otimes d}$. The action of Sym_d on B, given by permuting the factors of the d-fold tensor product in each degree, preserves the degree and commutes with the G action. Suppose τ is any irreducible character of Sym_d. Denote by V_μ^τ the τ-homogeneous part of the Sym_d-module $V_\mu^{\otimes d}$, and by (V_λ, V_μ^τ) the multiplicity of V_λ in V_μ^τ. The *Plethysm of V_μ with respect to* τ is the decomposition of V_μ^τ as a G-module. The symmetric and skew-symmetric d-tensors are special cases corresponding to the trivial character $\tau = d+$ and the sign character $\tau = d-$, respectively.

2.2 Theorem *Let τ be a character of Sym_d. The power series*

$$\sum_{\lambda,\mu \in \Lambda^+(G,T)} (V_\lambda, V_\mu^\tau) x^\lambda y^\mu$$

is a rational function in x and y.

Proof Note that for given τ the power series is the Poincaré series of $(B^\tau \otimes A^*)^G$. The algebra $C = (B^{Sym_d} \otimes A^*)^G$ is finitely generated and has rational Poincaré series. This proves the case where τ is the trivial character. $(B \otimes A^*)^G$ is finitely generated and integral over C, thus is a finitely generated C-module. We have the C-module decomposition $(B \otimes A^*)^G = \bigoplus_\tau (B^\tau \otimes A^*)^G$, where the sum is taken over all irreducible representations τ of Sym_d. Thus $(B^\tau \otimes A^*)^G$ is a finitely generated C-module for each τ, and therefore its Poincaré series is rational. □

2.3 Example Take $G = A_1$, $d = 2$ and set $S = Sym_2 \cong \{\pm 1\}$. We have $B = \bigoplus_{k \geq 0} V_k \otimes V_k$ and $A^* = \bigoplus_{k \geq 0} V_k^*$. Let $C = \mathbf{C}[(V_1 \otimes V_1^*]$ an $\mathbf{N}$-graded polynomial algebra provided with the natural $S \times G$ action. There is the natural surjective homomorphism $C \to B$, which preserves the degree and commutes with the $S \times G$ action. The kernel, I say, is graded and $S \times G$ stable. Let p be a generator of the skew-symmetric part V_0 of $C_1 \cong V_2 \oplus V_0$. We have $C = C^S \oplus C^S p$. By Brion's theorem I is generated by elements of degree 2 and from that it follows $I \cap (C^S p) = (I \cap C^S)p = I^S p$. But then $B \cong C/I \cong C^S/I^S \oplus C^S/I^S p \cong B^S \oplus B^S p$. Thus if P_{2+} is the Poincaré series of $(B^S \otimes A^*)^G$ corresponding to the series for the symmetric 2-tensors, then $P_{2-} = y P_{2+}$ is the series corresponding to the skew-symmetric 2-tensors. The Poincaré series $P_{2\otimes} = P_{2+} + P_{2-}$ of $(B \otimes A^*)^G$ can easily be derived from the tensor product series of G above:

$$P_{2\otimes} = \frac{1}{(1 - x^2 y)(1 - y)}.$$

The series of the symmetric 2-tensors becomes

$$P_{2+} = \frac{1}{(1 - x^2 y)(1 - y^2)}$$

and for the skew-symmetric 2-tensors

$$P_{2-} = \frac{y}{(1 - x^2 y)(1 - y^2)}.$$

Write $P_{3\otimes} = \sum_{k,l \geq 0} c_{k,l} x^k y^l$, where $c_{k,l}$ is the multiplicity of V_k in $V_l^{3\otimes}$, then straightforward computations using the above formulas give

$$P_{3\otimes} = \frac{x^2 y^2 + xy + 1}{(1 - x^3 y)(1 - xy)(1 - y^2)}.$$

3. Branching

We now return to the general situation. G is a reductive group with maximal torus T and H a reductive subgroup with maximal torus S, such that $S \subset T$. The most straightforward way to compute a coefficient $(V_\mu, V_\lambda \downarrow_H)$ of the branching series $P_{G \downarrow H}(x; y)$ is by determining the set of all weights of the G-module V_λ, next computing their restrictions to S and then decomposing this set with the inverse of Freudenthal's formula as an H-module. In this section we give an explicit formula for the coefficients of the branching series. Let $r : \Lambda(G) \to \Lambda(H)$ denote the linear map restricting the weights of T to weights on S. Also, by choosing appropriate Borel subgroups, we may assume that for $\alpha \in \Phi_G^+$ we have $r(\alpha) \notin \Phi_H^-$. Let $\Phi = \{\alpha \in \Phi_G \mid r(\alpha) = 0\}$, $\Phi^+ = \Phi \cap \Phi_G^+$ and W_Φ the subgroup of W_G generated by Φ. Each coset in W_G relative to W_Φ has a unique representative in W_G of minimal length, the set of these representatives is denoted by W. Put $A = r(\Phi_G^+) \backslash \{0\}$ and provide each element $\alpha \in A$ with a finite multiplicity $m_\alpha = |\{\beta \in \Phi_G^+ \mid r(\beta) = \alpha\}|$ if $\alpha \notin \Phi_H^+$ and $m_\alpha = |\{\beta \in \Phi_G^+ \mid r(\beta) = \alpha\}| - 1$ if $\alpha \in \Phi_H^+$. Let L be the lattice of non-negative integral linear combinations of elements in A. Kostant's partition function p_A on L is defined by

$$\frac{1}{\prod_{\alpha \in A}(1 - z^\alpha)^{m_\alpha}} = \sum_{\beta \in L} p_A(\beta) z^\beta$$

and is extended to the real span of L by putting $p_A(\beta) = 0$ if $\beta \notin L$. Finally put

$$D(\lambda) = \prod_{\alpha \in \Phi^+} \frac{(\lambda, \alpha)}{(\rho_\Phi, \alpha)}.$$

3.1 Theorem ([Hec])

$$(V_\mu, V_\lambda \downarrow_H) = \sum_{w \in W} \det(w) D(w(\lambda + \rho_G)) p_A(r(w(\lambda + \rho_G)) - (\mu + r(\rho_G))).$$

The theorem can be proved using Weyl's dimension and character formulas above. Conversely Weyl's formulas are special cases of the theorem. The theorem suggests how the branching series can be written as a sum over W of power series, which represent rational functions. Below we indicate by means of a rank 2 example how the actual rational functions can be obtained. Again, a higher rank case such as E_8 seems intractible. Here is a simpler one.

3.2 Example
Let G be a Lie group of type G_2, with root system Φ_G and fundamental roots β_1, β_2, where β_1 is long and β_2 is short. There is a subgroup H of type A_2, whose root system Φ_H is the root subsystem of long roots of Φ_G, and with fundamental roots β_1 and $\beta_1 + 3\beta_2$. We want to give the power series $P_{G \downarrow H} = \sum_{\lambda, \mu} (V_\mu, V_\lambda \downarrow_H) x^{\lambda_1} y^{\lambda_2} z^{\mu_1} u^{\mu_2}$, where the sum is taken over all $\lambda \in \Lambda^+(G, T)$ and $\mu \in \Lambda^+(H, T)$. The restriction map with respect to the bases of fundamental weights is given by $r((1, 0)) = (1, 1)$ and $r((0, 1)) = (0, 1)$. Thus Φ is empty, so $D \equiv 1$, $W_\Phi = \{1\}$ and $W = W_G$. The multiplicities of the

elements in $A = r(\Phi_G^+)$ are one for the images of the short roots and zero for the long roots. The short positive roots are $\gamma_1 = \beta_1 + \beta_2$, $\gamma_2 = \beta_2$ and $\gamma_1 + \gamma_2$. Kostant's partition function p_A at the lattice points $m\gamma_1 + n\gamma_2$, $m, n \geq 0$, is given by

$$\frac{1}{(1-a)(1-b)(1-ab)} = \sum_{m,n \geq 0} p_A(m\gamma_1 + n\gamma_2)a^m b^n$$

and is zero outside these points. We need the following more general formal power series expansion defining the function q_A on the same lattice, whose values are polynomials in z and u.

$$\frac{1}{(1-a)(1-b)(1-ab)(1-az)(1-abu)} = \sum_{m,n \geq 0} q_A(m\gamma_1 + n\gamma_2)a^m b^n \quad (*)$$

The values of q_A are taken to be zero outside the lattice. Thus,

$$q_A(v) = \sum_{\mu} p_A(v - (\mu_1\gamma_1 + \mu_2(\gamma_1 + \gamma_2)))z^{\mu_1} u^{\mu_2}.$$

Since the fundamental weights of the A_2 subsystem of long roots are γ_1 and $\gamma_1 + \gamma_2$, we have $\mu = \mu_1\gamma_1 + \mu_2(\gamma_1 + \gamma_2)$. Consequently, substitution of the formula of Theorem 3.1 in the formal power expansion $P_{G\downarrow H}$, yields

$$P_{G\downarrow H} = \sum_{w \in W} \sum_{\lambda} q_A(r(w(\lambda + \rho_G)) - r(\rho_G))x^{\lambda_1} y^{\lambda_2}.$$

Now $P_{G\downarrow H}$ is computed by finding rational functions for the power series corresponding to each $w \in W$ separately. Let s_1 and s_2 denote the reflections in W_G corresponding to the fundamental roots β_1 and β_2 of G, respectively. In light of the support of q_A, a non–zero series occurs only when w is one of the four elements $1, s_1, s_2, s_1 s_2$.

We indicate how to compute the rational function corresponding to $w = 1$. As $r(\lambda) = \lambda_1(2\gamma_1 + \gamma_2) + \lambda_2(\gamma_1 + \gamma_2)$, we have to compute the rational function expression of

$$\sum_{\lambda} q_A(\lambda_1(2\gamma_1 + \gamma_2) + \lambda_2(\gamma_1 + \gamma_2))x^{\lambda_1} y^{\lambda_2}. \quad (**)$$

But, writing $x = a^2 b$ and $y = a b$, we obtain the subseries of $(*)$ in which precisely those monomials $a^m b^n$ occur that can be written in the form $(a^2 b)^i (ab)^j$ for certain $i, j \geq 0$. The following general identity is useful in finding the required rational function

$$\sum_{\substack{n_1, n_2, \ldots, n_k \geq 0 \\ m_1, m_2, \ldots, m_l \geq 0 \\ n_1 + n_2 + \cdots + n_k \geq m_1 + m_2 + \cdots + m_l}} a_1^{n_1} a_2^{n_2} \cdots a_k^{n_k} b_1^{m_1} b_2^{m_2} \cdots b_l^{m_l} =$$

$$\sum_{i=1}^{k} \sum_{j=1}^{l} \frac{a_i^{k-1} b_j^{l-1}}{\prod_{p \neq i}(a_i - a_p)\prod_{q \neq j}(b_j - b_q)} \frac{1}{(1 - a_i b_j)(1 - a_i)}. \quad (***)$$

We first compute a rational expression for the subseries of (*) in which only monomials $a^m b^n$ occur that are at the same time monomials in the variables ab and a. To this end we need only consider the fraction

$$\frac{1}{(1-a)(1-b)(1-az)}$$

of (*). Letting $k = 2$ and $l = 1$ and substituting $a_1 = a$, $a_2 = az$ and $b_1 = b$ in (***) we obtain the rational expression for the relevant subseries of the above fraction of (*). Thus, the rational expression for the subseries of (*) itself becomes

$$\left(\frac{a}{(1-ab)(1-a)} - \frac{az}{(1-abz)(1-az)} \right) \frac{1}{a-az} \frac{1}{(1-ab)(1-abu)}$$

$$= \frac{(1-a^2bz)}{(1-a)(1-az)(1-ab)(1-abz)(1-ab)(1-abu)}.$$

A look at the denominator of this function shows that a similar step, with $k = 4$ and $l = 2$, and substitution $a_1 = a_2 = ab$, $a_3 = abz$, $a_4 = abu$, $b_1 = a$, and $b_2 = az$ in (***) yields the required expression for (**) upon substitution of x for $a^2 b$ and y for $a\,b$. The resulting rational function for the $w = 1$ summand of $P_{G\downarrow H}$ is

$$\frac{\begin{aligned}-(-1 &+ z^2 u x^2 - xz + x^2 z^2 + yx + x^2 z - z^2 u x^3 + z^3 y^2 x^3 - z^3 u x^3 - z^3 x^2 y - \\ & x^2 yu + y^2 x^2 z^2 - u x^3 z - y^2 x u - y^2 x z - z^2 y^2 x + 3yxz + 2x^2 zu + 2z^2 yx + \\ & 2xyu + 3yxzu + z^3 u^2 x^3 y + u^2 yx^3 z + z^2 x^3 yu^2 + 2yx^3 zu - 3x^2 z^2 y + z^4 u^2 x^5 y^2 + \\ & 4z^2 x^2 y^2 u + 2z^2 x^2 y^2 u^2 - 2z^3 u x^2 y + z^3 x^3 y^2 u^2 - 2x^2 zy - 6x^2 zyu + z^2 xyu - \\ & 2x^2 zyu^2 - 2u^2 x^4 z^3 y^2 - u^2 x^2 z^2 y + z^4 x^4 y^3 u^2 - x^4 z^3 y^2 u - y^3 x^2 z^2 u^2 + z^3 x^4 y^3 u^2 - \\ & z^4 x^4 y^2 u - 2z^4 u^2 x^4 y^2 + z^3 y^2 x^3 u + 2x^2 y^2 uz + x^2 y^2 u^2 z - 6u x^2 z^2 y + z^2 y^3 ux + \\ & z^4 x^3 yu + 3x^3 z^3 yu + 3x^3 z^2 yu - u^2 y^2 x^4 z^2 - 2y^2 xuz^2 + y^3 xzu - 3y^2 xzu + \\ & y^2 x^2 z^3 u - z^3 y^3 x^3 u - y^3 x^2 z^2 u - z^3 y^3 x^3 u^2)\end{aligned}}{(1-x)^2(1-zux)(1-xz)(1-y)^2(1-z^2 x)(1-yz)(1-xu)(1-yu)}$$

For $w \in \{s_1, s_2, s_1 s_2\}$ one can follow the same procedure. In these cases, an additional summand $r(w(\rho_G) - \rho_G)$ occurs in the argument of q_A. However this requires only a shift in the grading or removing some terms of the series. The corresponding rational functions are, respectively,

$$\frac{y^2 x^3 zu + y^3 x^2 zu - 2x^2 y^2 uz - y^2 x^2 u - y^2 x^2 z + xyu + yxz + 2yx - x - y}{(1-xu)(1-xz)(1-x)^2(1-yu)(1-yz)(1-y)^2}$$

$$\frac{-x^2}{(1-y)(1-x)^2(1-xz)(1-xu)}$$

$$\frac{-x(z^4 x^3 yu - z^3 ux^2 y - z^3 ux^3 - z^3 x^2 y + x^3 z^3 yu + 2z^2 x - z^2 yx + yz^2 - z^2 ux^2}{(1-zux)(1-xz)(1-z^2 x)(1-yz)(1-xu)(1-x)^2(1-y)} \\ \quad - z^2 + z^2 xu - z^2 xyu + xz + yz - z + zux - 1)}{}.$$

Adding these series gives the rational form of the branching series of G_2 to the subgroup A_2:

$$P_{G_2 \downarrow A_2}(x, y; z, u) = \frac{1 - xyzu}{(1 - yu)(1 - xu)(1 - yz)(1 - y)(1 - xz)(1 - zux)}.$$

An immediate consequence of the obtained rational function expression is the following recursive expression for the coefficient $q(\lambda_1, \lambda_2)$ of $x^{\lambda_1} y^{\lambda_2}$ in $P_{G_2 \downarrow A_2}$.

$$q(\lambda_1, \lambda_2) = \begin{cases} \sum_{\ell=0}^{\lambda_2} \sum_{m=0}^{\lambda_2 - \ell} z^\ell u^m & \text{if } \lambda_1 = 0 \\ \sum_{\ell=0}^{\lambda_1} \sum_{m=0}^{\lambda_1 - \ell} z^{\lambda_1 - m} u^{\ell + m} & \text{if } \lambda_1 > 0, \lambda_2 = 0 \\ q(\lambda_1, 0)q(0, \lambda_2) - zuq(\lambda_1 - 1, 0)q(0, \lambda_2 - 1) & \text{if } \lambda_1 > 0, \lambda_2 > 0 \end{cases}$$

We recall that $q(\lambda_1, \lambda_2)$ is a polynomial in z and u expressing the decomposition into irreducibles of the restriction to A_2 of the G_2 representation with highest weight (λ_1, λ_2). The computation of $q(\lambda_1, \lambda_2)$ via this method is much faster than the general method as implemented in, e.g., the software package LiE (cf. [Co]).

4. References

[Bre]   M.R. Bremner, R.V. Moody, J. Patera, *Tables of dominant weight multiplicities for representations of simple Lie algebras*, Marcel Dekker, New York, 1985.

[Bri]   M. Brion, *Représentations Exceptionelles des Groupes Semi-simples*, Ann. Scient. École Norm. Sup., **18**(1985), 345-387.

[Co]   Arjeh M. Cohen et al., *LiE Manual*, Computer Algebra Group, CWI, Amsterdam, 1989.

[Hec]   G. Heckman, *Projections of Orbits and Asymptotic Behavior of Multiplicities for Compact Connected Lie Groups*, Inventiones Math., **67**(1982), 333-356.

[Hum]   J.E. Humphreys, *Introduction to Lie algebras and representation theory*, Springer, New York, 1974.

[McK]   W.G. McKay & J. Patera, *Tables of dimensions, indices, and branching rules for representations of simple Lie algebras*, Marcel Dekker, New York, 1981.

[Spri]   T.A. Springer, *Invariant Theory*, Springer Lecture Notes in Math. 585, Springer, Berlin, 1977.

Computational Aspects of Lie Group Representations and Related Topics   29
Proceedings of the 1990 Computational Algebra Seminar
pp. 29–44 in CWI Tract 84 (1991)

Polynomial maps and

the Jacobian Conjecture

Arno van den Essen

Department of Mathematics

Catholic University Nijmegen

Toernooiveld

6525 ED Nijmegen

The Netherlands

0. Introduction

In this paper we describe some of the surprising results which appeared in the study of invertible polynomial maps during the last few years. Our main motivation is the well-known Jacobian Conjecture, formulated by O. Keller in 1939, which asserts that a polynomial map $F : \mathbf{C}^n \to \mathbf{C}^n$ is invertible, if the determinant of the Jacobian matrix of F is a non-zero constant.

Since the literature concerning the Jacobian Conjecture is extensive, we only describe some of the highlights in the first section. At the end of section one we also give references to other papers concerning the Jacobian Conjecture. In section two we give new criteria for the invertibility of a polynomial map and apply these results to the study of the Jacobian Conjecture. Finally in the last section we make some remarks on the automorphism group of a polynomial ring in several variables over a field.

1. The Jacobian Conjecture

Let $F : \mathbf{C}^n \to \mathbf{C}^n$ be a polynomial map, that is a map

$$(x_1, \ldots, x_n) \mapsto (F_1(x_1, \ldots, x_n), \ldots, F_n(x_1, \ldots, x_n))$$

where each F_i belongs to $\mathbf{C}[X] := \mathbf{C}[X_1, \ldots, X_n]$. The central question in this paper is

1.1 Question How can we decide if a given polynomial map is invertible, i.e., has a polynomial map as inverse?

Let us assume that F is invertible with inverse G. Then $G(F(X)) = X$, where $X = (X_1, \ldots, X_n)$. So if we put

$$JF := \left(\frac{\partial F_i}{\partial X_j} \right)_{1 \leq i, j \leq n}$$

then by the chain rule we get $(JG)(F(X)) . JF = I_n$, so $\det (JG)(F(X)) \cdot \det JF = 1$, whence $\det JF \in \mathbf{C}^*$. Summarizing: if F is invertible, then $\det JF \in \mathbf{C}^*$.

Jacobian Conjecture: If $\det JF \in \mathbf{C}^*$, then F is invertible.

This more than 50 year old conjecture is still open for all $n \geq 2$. Before we give some of the history of the Jacobian Conjecture, let us first give a useful criterion for invertibility of F. To this end, observe that if F is invertible with inverse $G = (G_1, \ldots, G_n)$ then $X = G(F(X))$, i.e., $X_i = G_i(F_1, \ldots, F_n)$. So $X_i \in \mathbf{C}[F] := \mathbf{C}[F_1, \ldots, F_n]$ for all i, implying $\mathbf{C}[X] = \mathbf{C}[F]$. Conversely, if $\mathbf{C}[X] = \mathbf{C}[F]$ then $X_i \in \mathbf{C}[F]$ for all i, i.e., $X_i = G_i(F_1, \ldots, F_n)$ for some G_i. Hence $X = G(F(X))$, where $G = (G_1, \ldots, G_n)$. It is a well-known fact that this relation also implies that $F(G(X)) = X$ (see [11], §4). Hence F is invertible. So we obtain

1.2 Lemma F is invertible if and only if $\mathbf{C}[F] = \mathbf{C}[X]$.

1.3 Some history of the Jacobian Conjecture

For two nice survey papers concerning the Jacobian Conjecture, we refer the reader to [7] and [46].

The Jacobian Conjecture was first formulated by O. Keller ([25], 1939) with $\mathbf{Z}$ instead of $\mathbf{C}$. In fact he was considering the problem of describing all transformations between several $\mathbf{Z}$-transcendency bases of a given ring (with finite $\mathbf{Z}$-transcendency bases). The main result of his paper states that if $F : \mathbf{C}^n \to \mathbf{C}^n$ is a polynomial map with $\det JF \in \mathbf{C}^*$ and which has a rational inverse, i.e., $X_i = a_i(F_1, \ldots, F_n)/b_i(F_1, \ldots, F_n)$ for some $a_i, b_i \in \mathbf{C}[F]$, $b_i \neq 0$, then actually this inverse is a polynomial inverse. So writing the quotient field of $\mathbf{C}[X]$ as $\mathbf{C}(X)$ we have

1.4 Theorem (Keller) *Let $F = (F_1, \ldots, F_n)$ with* $\det JF \in \mathbf{C}^*$. *If* $\mathbf{C}(F) := \mathbf{C}(F_1, \ldots, F_n) = \mathbf{C}(X)$, *then* $\mathbf{C}[F] = \mathbf{C}[X]$.

In a completely different setting the Jacobian problem was studied by Arne Magnus ([29], 1955). He considered volume preserving transformations of complex planes given by analytic functions in two variables, i.e.,

$$(z_1, z_2) \longmapsto (f(z_1, z_2), g(z_1, z_2)) \qquad \text{with } \det J(f, g) = 1.$$

Let now $f, g \in \mathbf{C}[z_1, z_2]$ with $n = \deg f$, $m = \deg g$. Then Magnus showed that (f, g) is invertible if n or m is a prime number. This result was generalized by Nakai and Baba ([41], 1977): if n or m is prime or n or m is 4 or $m > n$, $m = 2p$ and $p > 2$ is prime, then (f, g) is invertible. This result was in turn generalized by Appelgate and Onishi ([6], 1985): if n or m has at most 2 prime factors, then (f, g) is invertible. This result was recently reproved by Nagata ([40], 1988). In this context we also refer to the paper [42] of Nowicki.

Also several wrong "proofs" of the Jacobian Conjecture were published. The first one appeared in 1955, [19]. Engel "proved" the Jacobian Conjecture for $n = 2$. It took 18 years until Vitushkin [55] discovered two errors in Engel's proof. In the meantime Segre had produced three incomplete "proofs" in 1956, '57, '60 [48], [49], [50], all using topological methods. In the third paper he asked for a purely algebraic proof. This was given in 1961 by Gröbner [22]. However Zariski showed that formula 14 was wrong. A more dramatic "proof" was given by S. Oda in 1980, [43]: he cited a lemma from a book of Murre [38] incorrectly.

After all these negative results one more positive result in case $n = 2$. In 1983 Moh [36] showed, using a computer search, that the Jacobian Conjecture is true if both $\deg F_1$ and $\deg F_2 \leq 100$. He reduces the problem to four problem cases namely $(\deg F_1, \deg F_2) \in \{(64, 48), (75, 50), (84, 56), (99, 66)\}$ and then eliminates these cases by a reduction of degree trick. The reduction to the above four cases is also obtained in a recent paper [23] by Heitmann.

Now we return to the study of the Jacobian Conjecture. The first question which comes up is: what is the connection between the Jacobian Conjecture (over $\mathbf{C}$) and Keller's problem (over $\mathbf{Z}$)? Can we replace $\mathbf{C}$ by an arbitrary field, or even better by a "nice" ring such as $\mathbf{Z}$? The example $F(X) = X + X^p \in \overline{\mathbf{F}}_p[X]$ $(n = 1)$ shows that, for characteristic $p > 0$, the Jacobian Conjecture does not hold; for $\frac{dF}{dX} = 1$, but for every $G \in \overline{\mathbf{F}}_p[X]$ we have $\deg G(X + X^p) = p \deg G > 1$ so that $G(X + X^p) \neq X$.

Therefore, let R be a subring of a $\mathbf{Q}$-algebra and $F_1, \ldots, F_n \in R[X] := R[X_1, \ldots, X_n]$. Arguing as above we obtain: if $R[X] = R[F]$ then $\det JF$ is a unit in $R[X]$. Denoting the units of $R[X]$ by $R[X]^*$ we get

1.5 Generalized Jacobian Conjecture $(JC_n(R))$: let R be a subring of a $\mathbf{Q}$-algebra. If $\det JF \in R[X]^*$, then $R[F] = R[X]$.

So in the case $R = \mathbf{C}$ we get the usual Jacobian Conjecture and if $R = \mathbf{Z}$ we get Keller's problem. Now the question arises: how much more general is the generalized Jacobian Conjecture then the usual Jacobian Conjecture? It was shown in [7] that for each $n \in \mathbf{N}$ the conjecture $JC_n(\mathbf{C})$ implies $JC_n(R)$ for every R as above. However at the cost of enlarging the number of variables we obtain

1.6 Theorem *Let R be a subring of a $\mathbf{Q}$-algebra. Then $JC_n(R)$ is true for all $n \geq 1$ if and only if $JC_n(\mathbf{C})$ is true for all $n \geq 1$.*

Proof By the observation above we only need to show that if $JC_n(R)$ is true for all $n \geq 1$, the same holds for all $JC_n(\mathbf{C})$. Observe that R has no $\mathbf{Z}$-torsion since it is a subring of a $\mathbf{Q}$-algebra. Hence R contains $\mathbf{Z}$. Suppose now that there is a number n for which $JC_n(\mathbf{C})$ is not true. Then there exists an n variable counter example. So by [16], Theorem 1.5 there exists an m ($> n$) variable counter example with integer coefficients and hence with coefficients in R, a contradiction. So $JC_n(\mathbf{C})$ is true for all $n \geq 1$, as described. $\square$

So by this theorem we can safely return to the study of the usual Jacobian conjecture (over $\mathbf{C}$). The advantage of working with $\mathbf{C}$ (instead of R as above) is that you can use methods of complex analysis (see for example the paper of Campbell, [13] and the papers [53] and [54] of Stein and Comment 1.14 below).

A question which arises in this context is: can we generalize the Jacobian Conjecture to analytic functions on $\mathbf{C}^n$, i.e., if $F_1, \ldots, F_n$ are analytic on $\mathbf{C}^n$ with $\det JF \in \mathbf{C}^*$ does there exist an inverse $G = (G_1, \ldots, G_n)$ where each G_i is analytic on $\mathbf{C}^n$? Already for $n = 2$ we get a counterexample namely $F_1 = e^X$, $F_2 = Ye^{-X}$, which satisfy $\det JF = 1$, however $F(2\pi i k, 0) = (1, 0)$ for all $k \in \mathbf{N}$. So F is not injective. In this example the map F is not injective. It can even be worse. There exists an $F = (F_1, F_2) : \mathbf{C}^2 \to \mathbf{C}^2$ where each F_i is analytic on $\mathbf{C}^2$, $\det JF = 1$ and F is injective. However $\mathbf{C}^2 \backslash F(\mathbf{C}^2)$ contains a non-empty open set ([10], Chapter III, §1). In the light of this example the next result is a surprising contrast (see also remark 1.13 below).

1.7 Proposition *Let $F : \mathbf{C}^n \to \mathbf{C}^n$ be a polynomial map with $\det JF \in \mathbf{C}^*$. If F is injective, then F is invertible.*

Proof Since $\det JF \in \mathbf{C}^*$ certainly $\det JF \neq 0$ in $\mathbf{C}[X]$. Hence $F_1, \ldots, F_n$ are algebraically independent over $\mathbf{C}$ ([45], Satz 61). So both $\text{trdg}_\mathbf{C}\mathbf{C}(F) = \text{trdg}_\mathbf{C}\mathbf{C}(X) = n$, which implies that $\mathbf{C}(F) \subset \mathbf{C}(X)$ is an algebraic, hence finite extension. Let $e = |\mathbf{C}(X) : \mathbf{C}(F)|$. Then by [26], AI 3.5 for almost all $x \in \mathbf{C}^n$ (i.e., for all x in a Zariski open set of $\mathbf{C}^n$) the fiber $F^{-1}(x)$ contains e points. Since F is injective it follows that $e = 1$. So $\mathbf{C}(X) = \mathbf{C}(F)$ which implies $\mathbf{C}[X] = \mathbf{C}[F]$ by Keller's theorem. Hence F is invertible by Lemma 1.2. $\square$

So the Jacobian Conjecture is equivalent to: if $\det JF \in \mathbf{C}^*$ then F is injective. In other words it is equivalent to: if F is not injective then $F' := \det JF \notin \mathbf{C}^*$ so F' has a zero in $\mathbf{C}^n$. So we obtain

1.8 Corollary ("Rolle" formulation of the Jacobian Conjecture) *The Jacobian Conjecture is equivalent to: (R) If $F(a) = F(b)$ with $a \neq b$ in $\mathbf{C}^n$, then there exists $\xi \in \mathbf{C}^n$ such that $F'(\xi) = 0$.*

Let us give one more application of Proposition 1.7.

1.9 Theorem (S.S. Wang [56], 1980) *Let $\det JF \in \mathbf{C}^*$ and $\deg F_i \leq 2$ for all i. Then F is invertible.*

Proof By proposition 1.7 it suffices to prove that F is injective. So suppose $F(a) = F(b)$ for some $a, b \in \mathbf{C}^n$, $a \neq b$. We first show that we can assume that $b = 0$. To see this, we define $G(X) := F(X + a) - F(a)$. Then $\deg G \leq 2$, $G(0) = 0$ and putting $c := b - a$ we have $c \neq 0$ and $G(c) = 0$. Observe that $(JG)(X) = (JF)(X + a)$, so $\det JG \in \mathbf{C}^*$. Now write $G = G_{(1)} + G_{(2)}$, its decomposition in homogeneous components. Consider $G(tc) = tG_{(1)}(c) + t^2 G_{(2)}(c)$. Differentiation gives

$$G_{(1)}(c) + 2tG_{(2)}(c) = \frac{d}{dt}G(tc) = (JG)(tc) \neq 0, \quad \text{all } t \in \mathbf{C}$$

since $c \neq 0$ and $\det JG \in \mathbf{C}^*$. Substituting $t = \frac{1}{2}$ gives $G(c) \neq 0$, a contradiction with $G(c) = 0$. So F is injective as required. $\square$

One could object that this result is only a very special case of the Jacobian Conjecture. However the next theorem, proved independently by Yagzhev in [57] and Bass-Connell-Wright in [7] (1980) shows that theorem 1.9 is "almost" the general case:

1.10 Theorem (Yagzhev, Bass-Connell-Wright, 1980) *If the Jacobian Conjecture holds for all $n \geq 2$ and all polynomial maps F with $\deg F_i \leq 3$ all i, then the Jacobian Conjecture holds.*

1.11 Remark One may wonder where the three in theorem 1.10 comes from: the idea in the proof given in [7] is to get rid of all monomials of degree d to obtain a reduction of the degree by multiplying F by so-called elementary polynomial maps (see §3). By the method used a monomial M of degree d can be eliminated if it can be written as a product PQ of two monomials which are both of degree $\leq d - 2$. Therefore take P a divisor of M of degree $d - 2$. Then degree $Q = 2$ and $2 \leq d - 2$ as soon as $d \geq 4$. So all monomials of degree ≥ 4 can be eliminated and one remains with polynomials of degree ≤ 3.

The following improvement of theorem 1.10 was obtained by L. Druzkowski ([18], 1983).

1.12 Theorem (Druzkowski) *If the Jacobian Conjecture holds for all $n \geq 2$ and all F of the form*

$$F = \left(X_1 + \left(\sum a_{j1}X_j \right)^3, \ldots, X_n + \left(\sum a_{jn}X_j \right)^3 \right)$$

then the Jacobian Conjecture holds.

1.13 Remark The result in Proposition 1.7 even holds without the assumption det $JF \in \mathbf{C}^*$: every injective polynomial map $F : \mathbf{C}^n \to \mathbf{C}^n$ is invertible ([9]). See also [46], Theorem 6.2 and [47] where $\mathbf{C}^n$ is replaced by an (irreducible) affine algebraic variety over an algebraically closed ground field.

1.14 Comment In two recent papers Y. Stein takes the example $F_1 = e^X$, $F_2 = Ye^{-X}$ as a starting point for a new analytic approach to the Jacobian Conjecture: Let E be the Frechet space of entire functions on $\mathbf{C}^2$. Let $f, g \in E$.

Analytic Jacobian Conjecture: if det $J(f, g) = 1$, then $\frac{d}{df}(E)$ is dense in E (where $\frac{d}{df}$ is the linear operator $\frac{\partial g}{\partial Y} \frac{\partial}{\partial X} - \frac{\partial g}{\partial X} \frac{\partial}{\partial Y}$).

It is proved in [53] that this conjecture for polynomials implies the Jacobian Conjecture. Furthermore the conjecture is proved for $f = e^X$, $g = Ye^{-X}$. In [54] it is shown that $\frac{d}{df}(E)$ is closed in E (with the standard Frechet space topology).

1.15 Comment A topic which we will not discuss in this paper is the global asymptotic stability Jacobian Conjecture (see [34] for a nice survey). This conjecture, which is due to Markus and Yamabe ([30], 1960) asserts that if $f : \mathbf{R}^n \to \mathbf{R}^n$ is a C^1-function with $f(0) = 0$ and such that for each $p \in \mathbf{R}^n$ the origin is a locally asymptotic rest point of the linearized system $\dot{y} = (JF)(p)y$, then the origin is a globally asumptotic rest point of $\dot{x} = f(x)$. For $n = 2$ this conjecture was recently solved in the affirmative by Meisters and Olech ([35], 1988). In this context we also mention the paper [21] of the author.

2. New Criteria for the Invertibility of a Polynomial Map and the Relationship with the Jacobian Conjecture

Now we return to Question 1.1. In 1986 I gave an answer to this question based on methods from computer algebra, namely from the theory of Gröbner bases for ideals in polynomial rings (for a nice survey of this subject we refer the reader to the paper [12] of Buchberger).

Before recalling the main definitions in order to understand the following theorem let us first mention the main point of the Gröbner basis theory. In a polynomial ring in one variable over a field every ideal is generated by one element. If we choose this element to be monic it is unique. Furthermore this unique element can be constructed by using Euclidean division several times (every reduction gives a polynomial of lower degree). In a completely analogous way one can proceed in the case of a polynomial ring $k[X] := k[X_1, \ldots, X_n]$ $(n \geq 1)$ over a field k. Let us give some more details: to have the notion of "degree" one has to order the set T of terms $X_1^{i_1} \ldots X_n^{i_n}$, $i_1, \ldots, i_n \geq 0$. More precisely, a total order $<$ on T is called *admissible* if $1 < t$ for all $t \in T$, $t \neq 1$; and if $s < t$ then $su < tu$ for all $s, t, u \in T$. (An example of an admissible order on T is the lexicographical order with $X_1 < X_2 < \cdots < X_n$).

Now choose a fixed admissible order on T. For each $f \in k[X]$ we write $f \in \sum f_t t$, $f_t \in k$, $t \in T$. If $f \neq 0$ define $Lp(f) = \max\{t \in T \mid f_t \neq 0\}$ and $Lc(f) := $ the coefficient of $Lp(f)$ in f. If $f = 0$ define $Lp(f) = 0$ and $Lc(0) = 0$. Let E be a finite subset of $k[X]$ and $g \in k[X]$, then we say that g is *reducible* mod E if $t = sLp(f)$ for some $t \in T$ with $g_t \neq 0$, $s \in T$ and $f \in E$. The set of all terms $t \in T$ which are reducible mod E is denoted by $\overline{Lp(E)}$. Let I be an ideal in $k[X]$. A finite subset $E \subset I$ is called a *Gröbner basis* of I in $I = (E)$ (= the ideal generated by E) and $Lp(I) = \overline{Lp(E)}$. A Gröbner basis G of I is called a *reduced Gröbner* basis of I if for each $f \in G$ we have: f is not reducible mod $G\backslash\{f\}$ and $Lc(f) = 1$. It can be shown that for each ideal I there exists a unique reduced Gröbner basis (only depending on the admissible order $<$ chosen on T). Furthermore, given an arbitrary finite basis E of I there exist algorithms with input E and output the reduced Gröbner basis of I.

Now we are able to describe the first invertibility criterion for a polynomial map $F : k^n \to k^n$ when k is an arbitrary field. So let $F_1, \ldots, F_n \in k[X_1, \ldots, X_n]$. Introduce n more variables $Y_1, \ldots, Y_n$ and consider the ideal I in $k[X, Y] := k[X_1, \ldots, X_n, Y_1, \ldots, Y_n]$ generated by $Y_1 - F_1(X), \ldots, Y_n - F_n(X)$. On $k[X, Y]$ we choose a fixed admissible order such that any power product in $Y_1, \ldots, Y_n$ any power product in $X_1, \ldots, X_n$ (for example the lexicographical order with $Y_1 < Y_2 < \cdots < Y_n < X_1 < \cdots < X_n$).

2.1 Theorem (van den Essen, [20], 1986) *Let G be the reduced Gröbner basis of I. Then $F = (F_1, \ldots, F_n)$ is invertible if and only if $G = \{X_1 - G_1(Y), \ldots, X_n - G_n(Y)\}$ for some $G_i \in k[Y]$. Furthermore, if F is invertible the inverse is given by $G = (G_1, \ldots, G_n)$.*

Let us compare the possible Jacobian criterion "F is invertible if and only if $\det JF \in k^*$" with Theorem 2.1.

+ our theorem works for all characteristics. The Jacobian criterion only when char $k = 0$.

+ our theorem also computes the inverse. The Jacobian criterion doesn't.

− our algorithm is slow if the number of variables or the degree is large. The Jacobian criterion is comparable faster.

2.2 Remark Some theoretical applications of Theorem 2.1 are mentioned below.

As already observed before, for practical computations the above algorithm is too slow. So the question arises: How can we make the algorithm faster? The idea is to make bigger steps in the reduction process: looking at the Gröbner basis G above we see that the ideal I contains an element of the form $X_1 - G_1(Y)$. So in the case $n = 2$ this means that I contains an element from which X_2 is eliminated. This observation guides us to elimination theory. Its main tool is the resultant, a device which was often used in the early days of algebraic geometry, but which was gradualy eliminated from the theory and replaced by methods from modern algebra. However, together with the birth of computer algebra there was a renewed interest in the study of resultants. Several new papers appeared see for example [14] and [15]. Now let us recall the Resultant (see [45], §43 for more details).

Let A be a commutative ring without zero divisors, K its quotient field and $A[T]$ the polynomial ring in the variable T with coefficients in A. Let $f = f_n T^n + f_{n-1} T^{n-1} + \cdots + f_0 \in A[T]$ with $f_n \neq 0$ and $g = g_m T^m + g_{m-1} T^{m-1} + \cdots + g_0 \in A[T]$ with $g_m \neq 0$.

i) If $n, m \geq 1$ the resultant of f and g, denoted $R_T(f, g)$ is defined as

$$R_T(f, g) := \det \begin{pmatrix} f_n & \cdots & f_0 & & & \\ & \ddots & & \ddots & & \\ & & f_n & \cdots & & f_0 \\ g_m & \cdots & g_0 & & & \\ & \ddots & & & \ddots & \\ & & g_m & \cdots & & g_0 \end{pmatrix} \begin{matrix} \left.\vphantom{\begin{matrix}a\\b\\c\end{matrix}}\right\} m \\ \left.\vphantom{\begin{matrix}a\\b\\c\end{matrix}}\right\} n \end{matrix}$$

ii) If $m = 0$ we put $R_T(f, g) = g_0^n$, if $n = 0$ we put $R_T(f, g) = f_0^m$.

The main property of the resultant is

(2.3) f and g have a common zero (in some finite field extension of K) if and only if $R_T(f, g) = 0$.
Furthermore

(2.4) $R_T(f, g) \in A[T]f + A[T]g.$

Now we are able to formulate the main theorem of [3].

2.5 Theorem (Adjamagbo, van den Essen, 1988) *Let k be an arbitrary field and $F = (F_1, F_2) : k^2 \to k^2$ a polynomial map. There is equivalence between*
  i) *F is invertible.*
  ii) *There exist $\lambda_1, \lambda_2 \in k^*$ and $G_1, G_2 \in k[Y]$ such that $R_{X_2}(F_1 - Y_1, F_2 - Y_2) = \lambda_1(X_1 - G_1)$ and $R_{X_1}(F_1 - Y_1, F_2 - Y_2) = \lambda_2(X_2 - G_2)$. Furthermore, if F is invertible then $G = (G_1, G_2)$ is the inverse of F.*

This algorithm is extremely fast, works in all characteristics and computes the inverse (in case F is invertible). A generalization of this result to rational maps in two variables, can be found in [2].

In the remainder of this section we derive two consequences from Theorem 2.5. Each of these conclusions will be generalized to the case of several variables. At the end of this section we relate these results to the Jacobian Conjecture.

2.6 Border polynomials To derive the first corollary from Theorem 2.5 we substitute $X_1 = 0$ resp. $X_2 = 0$ in the two resultant expressions of Theorem 2.5. We obtain

(2.7) $\begin{cases} R_{X_2}(F_1(0, X_2) - Y_1, F_2(0, X_2) - Y_2) = \lambda_1(-G_1(Y)) \\ \\ R_{X_1}(F_1(X_1, 0) - Y_1, F_2(X_1, 0) - Y_2) = \lambda_2(-G_2(Y)). \end{cases}$

From (2.7) we see that up to some constants λ_1, λ_2 G is completely determined by the so-called border polynomials $F_1(0, X_2), F_2(0, X_2), F_1(X_1, 0), F_2(X_1, 0)$.

In fact also λ_1, λ_2 are determined by these border polynomials which can be seen as follows: the linear part of G and hence of G_1 is determined by the linear part of F and so by its border polynomials. Obviously the left hand side of the first equation in (2.7) is determined by the border polynomials of F. So equating the linear parts in this equation we see that λ_1 is determined by the border polynomials of F. The constant λ_2 is treated similarly. In [31] explicit formulas for λ_1 and λ_2 are given: $\lambda_1 = (-1)^n cJ$, $\lambda_2 = (-1)^{m+1} dJ$, where $J = \det JF$, $n = \deg F_1(0, X_2)$, $m = \deg F_1(X_1, 0)$, $c = R_{X_2}(F_1(0, X_2)/X_2,$ $F_2(0, X_2)/X_2)$, and $d = R_{X_1}(F_1(X_1, 0)/X_1, F_2(X_1, 0)/X_1)$ (here it is assumed that $F(0) = 0$). These formulas show once more that λ_1 and λ_2 are determined by the border polynomials of F.

Summarizing: the inverse G of an invertible polynomial map $F : k^2 \to k^2$ is completely determined by the border polynomials of F. Since F is the inverse of G, F is determined by the border polynomials of G. However G is determined by the border polynomials of F. So we obtain our first conclusion.

2.8 Corollary If $F : k^2 \to k^2$ is invertible, then F is determined by its border polynomials.

This result was first obtained in [31], Corollary 13. See also [3], Corollary 2.2.

2.9 Remark For formal power series a similar result as Corollary 2.8 does not hold as can be seen from the following example:

$$F_1(X_1, X_2) = X_1(1 - \alpha X_1 X_2), \quad F_2(X_1, X_2) = X_2(1 - \alpha X_1 X_2)^{-1}, \quad \alpha \in k.$$

Then $\det JF = 1$ and for each $\alpha \in k$ the border polynomials of F are the same as the border polynomial of the identity map ($\alpha = 0$).

The following generalization of Corollary 2.8 to several variables was given by McKay and Wang in [32], 1988.

2.10 Theorem (McKay, Wang) Let $\phi = (F_1, \ldots, F_n)$ define a k-automorphism of $k[X]$. Then ϕ is determined by its face polynomials

$$F_i(X_1, \ldots, X_{j-1}, 0, X_{j+1}, \ldots, X_n).$$

Proof Let $\hat{\phi} = (\hat{F}_1, \ldots, \hat{F}_n)$ be another k-automorphism of $k[X]$ with the same face polynomials. This can be expressed by saying that $\pi_i \circ \phi = \pi_i \circ \hat{\phi}$ for all $1 \le i \le n$, where $\pi_i : k[X] \to k[X]$ is the k-endomorphism defined by $\pi_i(X_i) = 0$ and $\pi_i(X_j) = X_j$ if $j \ne i$. We show that $\phi^{-1} = \hat{\phi}^{-1}$. So let $R_i = \phi^{-1}(X_i)$ and $\hat{R}_i = \hat{\phi}^{-1}(X_i)$. We show that $R_1 = \hat{R}_1$. Observe that

$$\ker \pi_1 \circ \phi = \{g \in k[X] \mid \phi(g) \in (X_1)\} = (R_1).$$

Similarly $\ker \pi_1 \circ \hat{\phi} = (\hat{R}_1)$. Since $\pi_1 \circ \phi = \pi_1 \circ \hat{\phi}$ we get $(R_1) = (\hat{R}_1)$ and hence $R_1 = \lambda \hat{R}_1$ for some $\lambda \in k[X]^* = k^*$. Applying $\hat{\phi}$ gives $\hat{\phi}(R_1) = \lambda X_1$. Also $\phi(R_1) = X_1$. Now apply π_2. Then

$$X_1 = \pi_2 \circ \phi(R_1) = \pi_2 \circ \hat{\phi}(R_1) = \lambda X_1.$$

So $\lambda = 1$ implying $R = \hat{R}_1$. Similarly we get $R_i = \hat{R}_i$ for all i, which implies $\phi = \hat{\phi}$, as desired. □

2.11 Remark The above proof is given in [17] and also works in the case that k is a reduced ring (since then $k[X]^* = k^*$).

2.12 Remark The generalization to the case that k is a reduced ring was first obtained by Li in [28]; his proof is based on a result from [20].

2.13 Remark If k is not a reduced ring, the result of Theorem 2.10 does not hold: to see this take the example of Remark 2.9 where α is an element of k satisfying $\alpha \neq 0$ and $\alpha^2 \neq 0$.

2.14 Remark For more results concerning the connection between invertible polynomial maps in two variables and border polynomials, we refer the reader to [37] where the authors establish a one-to-one correspondence between the invertible polynomial maps $F : k^2 \mapsto k^2$ and the matrices $(f_1(t), f_2(t)) \in M_2(k[t])$ having the property that the curves $t \mapsto f_1(t)$ and $t \mapsto f_2(t)$ only intersect at 0 and have independent tangents at 0 (k is an algebraically closed field).

2.15 The degree of the inverse of an invertible polynomial map From the definition of resultant one immediately obtains that $\deg_Y R_{X_i}(F_1 - Y_1, F_2 - Y_2) \leq \max(\deg F_1, \deg F_2)$, all i. So by Theorem 2.5 we see that $\deg G \leq \deg F$ (and hence we have equality by interchanging F and G). This is a special case of

2.16 Theorem (Gabber) *If k is a field and $F : k^n \to k^n$ is an invertible polynomial map with inverse G, then $\deg G \leq (\deg F)^{n-1}$ ($\deg F := \max \deg F_i$).*

For an elementary proof of this result we refer the reader to [46], theorem 5.1.

Theorem 2.16 forms the basis for another invertibility criterion and a new inversion formula. Let K be a field of characteristic zero and $F : k^n \to k^n$ a polynomial map with $\det JF \in k^*$. Define a sequence of polynomial maps $F^{[1]}, F^{[2]}, \ldots : k^{2n} \to k^n$ inductively

$$F^{[1]}(X, V) := (JF)^{-1}(X) \cdot V, \quad F^{[k+1]}(X, V) := \left(\frac{\partial F_j^{[k]}}{\partial X_i} \right)_{i,j=1}^n \cdot F^{[1]}(X, V).$$

2.17 Theorem (Adjamagbo, van den Essen, [4], 1988) *Let F be a polynomial map of degree d, $D = d^{n-1}$. Then F is invertible if and only if $\det JF \in k^*$ and $F^{[D+1]} = 0$. Furthermore, if F is invertible the inverse G is given by*

$$G(V) = \sum_{k=1}^{D} \frac{1}{k!} F^{[k]}(0, V - F(0)).$$

2.18 Remark An inspection of the proof of Theorem 2.17 shows that we can replace the field k by any **Q**-algebra R for which we can show the inequality of Theorem 2.16.

So one could wonder for which kind of **Q**-algebras R the inequality of Theorem 2.16 holds? As in the case of border polynomials the result of theorem 2.16 can be extended to the case that k is a reduced ring. This can be seen as follows. First observe that in case k is a ring without zero-divisors the conclusion of Theorem 2.16 still holds (by embedding k in its quotient field). Now assume k is a reduced ring. Let p be a minimal prime ideal of k and consider the ring homomorphism $\phi : k \to \overline{k} := k/p$. If F is invertible with inverse G then the induced map $\overline{F}$ is invertible with inverse $\overline{G}$. Since k/p has no zero-divisors it follows from the previous case that $\deg \overline{G} \leq (\deg \overline{F})^{n-1} \leq (\deg F)^{n-1}$. So if a is a coefficient of a monomial of G of degree $> d^{n-1}$ then $\phi(a) = 0$ i.e. $a \in p$. So a belongs to the intersection of all minimal prime ideals of k i.e. to the nilradical of k, which is the zero-ideal since k is reduced. So $a = 0$, which implies $\deg G \leq d^{n-1}$.

However, if k is not a reduced ring the conclusion of Theorem 2.16 is not true; in fact there is no bound for the degree of the inverse which depends on n and $\deg F$ only. This can be seen as follows. Let $d \in \mathbf{N}$. Take $n = 1$ and $F = X - aX^2$, where $a^d \neq 0$ and $a^{d+1} = 0$ (in some ring k). Observe that $\det JF = 1 - 2aX \in k[X]^*$ (the inverse is $1 + 2aX + (2aX)^2 + \cdots + (2aX)^d$). Let $G(F(X)) = X$. Then $G'(X - aX^2) \cdot (1 - 2aX) = 1$ (by the chain rule) so $G'(X - aX^2) = 1 + 2aX + \cdots + (2aX)^d$. So $d = \deg G'(X - aX^2) \leq 2(\deg G - 1)$, whence $\deg G \geq \frac{d}{2} + 1$. So $\deg G$ can be arbitrarely large in spite of the fact that $n = 1$ and $\deg F = 2$. The cause of the trouble is the strict inclusion $k^* \subset k[X]^*$, for if we had assumed that F is invertible and $\det JF \in k^*$ then the conclusion of Theorem 2.16 is true in case $n = 1$. So for $n = 2$ we can hope that the answer to the following question is, yes:

2.19 Question If k is a **Q**-algebra, $F : k^2 \to k^2$ is invertible and $\det JF \in k^*$, does it follow that $\deg F^{-1} \leq \deg F$?

The answer to this question is still open, in fact a positive answer to this question would imply the Jacobian Conjecture for $n = 2$. This is a special case of the following theorem of Bass, [8].

2.20 Theorem (Bass, 1982) *The Jacobian Conjecture is equivalent to: given n and d, there exists a constant $C(n, d)$ such that for any **Q**-algebra R we have, if $F : R^n \to R^n$ is invertible with $\deg F \leq d$ and $\det JF \in R^*$, then $\deg F^{-1} \leq C(n, d)$ (i.e. the degree of the inverse is bounded by a number independent of the **Q**-algebra).*

This result was used by Abhyankar and Li in [1], 1989 to open a new approach to the Jacobian Conjecture. Therefore they first generalized Theorem 2.1 to the case of polynomial rings over arbitrary commutative rings ([1], Corollary 4.3). Then the next step is to investigate the following: given a set of generators f_i of an ideal I (in a polynomial ring $R[X_1, \ldots, X_n]$, where R is a **Q**-algebra) and an admissible order on $R[X]$. Let $d = \max \deg f_i$. Does there exist a uniform bound $C(n,d)$ (i.e. independent of the **Q**-algebra R) for the degrees of the elements g_i of the reduced Gröbner basis you find? If such a bound exists, then the Jacobian conjecture would follow from Theorem 2.20 and the generalized version of Theorem 2.1 (take as input ideal $(F_1(X)-Y_1,\dots,F_n(X)-Y_n)$). However it is shown in [1] that such a bound does not exist even if the ring R is a polynomial ring in one variable over a field.

2.21 Comment Several generalizations of Theorem 2.1 have been obtained.

i) In an unpublished note André Heck (CAN, Amsterdam) has given the following improvement: let $K = k(Y)$ the quotient field of the polynomial ring $k[Y]$. Put $K[X] := K[X_1,\dots,X_n]$. Let T be the set of monomials $X_1^{i_1}\cdots X_n^{i_n}$ with $i_1,\dots,i_n \geq 0$. Choose on T an arbitrary (!) admissible order $<$. Let I be the ideal in $K[X]$ generated by the elements $Y_i - F_i(X)$. Let G be the reduced Gröbner basis of I. Then F is invertible if and only if there exist polynomials $G_i \in k[Y]$ such that $G = \{X_1 - G_1,\dots,X_n - G_n\}$. Furthermore, if F is invertible the inverse of F is given by $(G_1,\dots,G_n)$.

ii) In [51] and [52] Shannon and Sweedler and in [44] Ollivier use Gröbner bases to study the problem how to decide if a polynomial (resp. rational) map $F : k^n \to k^m$ (k a field) admits a polynomial (resp. rational) inverse. The technique is similar to the one used in [20].

2.22 Comment In 2.6 we showed that an invertible polynomial map $F : k^2 \to k^2$ can be reconstructed from its border polynomials by means of (2.7) and the formulas for λ_1 and λ_2. One could try to generalize this procedure by studying more variable resultants i.e. consider $F_1(X_1,\dots,X_n) - Y_1,\dots,F_n(X_1,\dots,X_n) - Y_n$ as polynomials in the variables $X_2,\dots,X_n$ and then compute the resultant with respect to these variables:

$$R_{X_2,\dots,X_n}(F_1(X_1,\dots,X_n) - Y_1,\dots,F_n(X_1,\dots,X_n) - Y_n),$$

which is an element in the remaining variables, so belongs to $k[Y,X_1]$. One could hope that this resultant has the form $\lambda(X_1 - G_1(Y))$ for some $\lambda \in k^*$ and $G_1 \in k[Y]$. However one can prove that in general this resultant is zero and hence contains no information at all about the inverse of F. So we are lead to

2.23 Question How can one reconstruct an invertible polynomial map from its face polynomials if $n \geq 3$?

3. The Automorphism Group of a Polynomial Ring and some Conjectures

In this last section we make some remarks about the automorphism group of a polynomial ring in several variables over a field k. If $n = 1$ the only automorphisms of $k[X]$ are of the form $X \mapsto \lambda X + \mu$ for some $\lambda \in k^*$ and $\mu \in k$.

From now on let $n \geq 2$. A polynomial map $E = (E_1,\dots,E_n) : k^n \to k^n$ is called *elementary* if there exist j such that $E_i = X_i$ for all $i \neq j$ and $E_j - X_j$ does not depend on X_j.

3.1 Theorem (Jung [24], 1942, van der Kulk [27], 1953) *Every invertible polynomial map $F : k^2 \to k^2$ is a finite product of invertible linear maps and elementary polynomial maps (we call such an F tame).*

3.2 Remark Several proofs of this theorem appeared. See [33], where a survey of all these proofs is given.

It was conjectured for a long time that the conclusion of Theorem 3.1 is also true for $n \geq 3$: the so-called tame conjecture. However in 1972, [39] Nagata constructed an example of an invertible polynomial map which is most probably not tame, namely

$$\sigma \left\{ \begin{array}{l} x \longmapsto x - 2y(xz + y^2) - z(xz + y^2)^2 \\ y \longmapsto y + z(xz + y^2) \\ z \longmapsto z \end{array} \right.$$

3.3 Remark In [5] Alev and Le Bruyn give a general method to constuct such "weird" automorphisms, by using some elementary properties of Clifford algebras.

3.4 Conjecture (Nagata) The map σ is not tame.

However it is believed that polynomial maps of degree ≤ 2 are nicer.

3.5 Conjecture (Rusek, [46], 1989). For every $n \geq 2$ an invertible polynomial map $F : k^n \to k^n$ of degree ≤ 2 is tame.

We conclude with two more conjectures.

3.6 Conjecture (Adjamagbo, van den Essen [3], 1988) If $F : k^2 \to k^2$ satisfies det $JF \in k^*$, then $\frac{d}{dX_1} R_{X_2}(F_1, F_2) \in k^*$ (this conjecture is equivalent to the Jacobian Conjecture, [3], Proposition 2.6).

3.7 Conjecture The Jacobian Conjecture is false if $n \geq 3$!

4. References

[1] S. Abhyankar, W.Li, On the Jacobian Conjecture: a New Approach via Gröbner Bases, Journal of Pure and Applied Algebra 61 (1989), 211–222.

[2] K. Adjamagbo, P. Boury, A resultant criterion and formula for the inversion of a rational map in two variables (preprint 1989).

[3] K. Adjamagbo, A. van den Essen, A resultant criterion and formula for the inversion of a polynomial map in two variables, Journal of Pure and Applied Algebra, 64 (1990), 1–6.

[4] K. Adjamagbo, A. van den Essen, A differential criterion and formula for the inversion of a polynomial map in several variables, Report 8828, Catholic University Nijmegen (to appear in J. of Pure and Appl. Algebra).

[5] J. Alev, L. Le Bruyn, Automorphisms of generic 2 by 2 matrices (preprint).

[6] H. Appelgate, H. Onishi, The Jacobian Conjecture in two variables, J. Pure Appl. Algebra 37 (1985), 215–227.

[7] H. Bass, E. Connell, D. Wright, The Jacobian Conjecture: Reduction of degree and formal expansion of the inverse, Bull. Amer. Math. Soc. 7 (1982), 287–330.

[8] H. Bass, The Jacobian Conjecture and inverse degrees, Arithmetic and Geometry, Vol II, 65–75. Progr. Math. 36, Birkhaüser, Boston, Mass, 1983.

[9] A. Bialynicki-Birula, M. Rosenlicht, Injective morphisms of real algebraic varieties, Proc. Amer. Math. Soc. 13 (1962), 200–203.

[10] S. Bochner, W. Martin, Several complex variables, Princeton Univ. Press, Princeton, N.J., 1948.

[11] N. Bourbaki, Algèbre Commutative, Chapter 3, Hermann, Paris.

[12] B. Buchberger, Gröbner bases: an algorithmic method in polynomial ideal theory. Chapter 6 in Multidimentional System Theory (edited by H.K. Bose), D. Reidel Publ. Comp., 1985.

[13] L. Campbell, A condition for a polynomial map to be invertible, Math. Ann. 205 (1973), 243–248.

[14] J. Canny, E. Kaltofen, L. Yagati, Solving systems of non–linear polynomial equations faster (preprint 1988).

[15] M. Chardin, Un algorithme pour le calcul du résultant de trois polynômes homogènes en trois variables (preprint).

[16] E. Connell, L. van den Dries, Injective polynomial maps and the Jacobian Conjecture, J. of Pure and Appl. Algebra 28 (1983), 235–239.

[17] R. Dennis, Boo Barkee, S. Wang, Automorphisms are determined by their face polynomials (preprint).

[18] L. Druzkowski, An effective approach to Keller's Jacobian Conjecture, Math. Ann. 264 (1983), 303–313.

[19] W. Engel, Ein Satz über ganze Cremona Transformationen der Ebene, Math. Ann. 130 (1955), 11–19.

[20] A. van den Essen, A criterion to decide if a polynomial map is invertible and to compute the inverse (Report 8653, Catholic Univ. Nijmegen, to appear in Communications in Algebra Vol 18, no. 10, 1990).

[21] A. van den Essen, A Note on Meisters and Olech's proof of the global asymptotic stability Jacobian Conjecture (Report 9014, Catholic Univ. Nijmegen).

[22] W. Gröbner, Sopra un teoreme di B. Segre, Atti Accad. Naz. Lincei Rend. Cl. Sci. Fis. Mat. Nat. 31 (1961), 118–122.

[23] R. Heitmann, On the Jacobian Conjecture, J. Pure Applied Algebra 64 (1990), 35–72.

[24] H. Jung, Uber ganze birationale Transformationen der Ebene, J. Reine Angew. Math. 184 (1942), 161–174.

[25] O. Keller, Ganze Cremona-Transformationen, Monatsh. Math. Phys. 47 (1939), 299–306.

[26] H. Kraft, Geometrische Methoden in der Invariententheorie, Braunschweig-Wiesbaden: Friedr. Vieweg und Sohn (1985).

[27] W. van der Kulk, On polynomial rings in two variables, Nieuw Archief voor Wiskunde (3) I (1953), 33–41.

[28] W. Li, On a problem about face Polynomials, J. of Pure and Appl. Algebra 60 (1989), 269–272.

[29] A. Magnus, On polynomial solutions of a differential equation, Math. Scand. 3 (1955), 255–260.

[30] L. Markus, H. Yamabe, Global stability criteria for differential systems, Osaka Math. J. 12 (1960), 305–317.

[31] J. McKay, S. Wang, An inversion formula for two polynomials in two variables, J. Pure Appl. Algebra 40 (1986), 245–257.

[32] J. McKay, S. Wang, On the inversion formula for two polyomials in two variables, J. Pure Appl. Algebra 52 (1988), 103–119.

[33] J. McKay, S. Wang, An elementary proof of the automorphism theorem for the polynomial ring in two variables, J. Pure Appl. Algebra 52 (1988), 91–102.

[34] G. Meisters, Jacobian problems in differential equations and algebraic geometry, Rocky Mountain J. Math. 12 (1982), 679–705.

[35] G. Meisters, C. Olech, Solution of the global asymptotic stability Jacobian Conjecture for the polynomial case, Analyse Mathématique et Applications, Gauthier-Villars, Paris 1988, 373–381.

[36] T. Moh, On the global Jacobian Conjecture and the configuration of roots, J. Reine Angew. Math. 340 (1983), 140–212.

[37] T. Moh, J. McKay, S. Wang, One face polynomials, J. Pure Appl. Algebra 52 (1988), 121–125.

[38] J. Murre, An introduction to Grothendieck's theory of the fundamental group, Tata Inst. Fundamental Research, Bombay, 1967.

[39] M. Nagata, On the automorphism group of $k[X, Y]$, Kinokuniya Book-Store, 1972.

[40] M. Nagata, Two dimensional Jacobian Conjecture, Proc. of K.I.T. Math. Workshop 1988, 77–98 & Some remarks on the two-dimensional Jacobian Conjecture, Chin. J. Math. 17 (1989), 1–7: a revised version of both papers.

[41] Y. Nakai, K. Baba, A generalization of Magnus' theorem, Osaka J. Math. 14 (1977), 403–409.

[42] A. Nowicki, On the Jacobian Conjecture in two variables, J. Pure Appl. Algebra 50 (1988), 195–207.

[43] S. Oda, The Jacobian problem and the simply-connectedness of A^n over a field k of characteristic zero, Osaka Univ., preprint 1980.

[44] F. Ollivier, Inversibility of rational mappings and structural identifiability in automatics (preprint 1989).

[45] O. Perron, Algebra I, Die Grundlagen, Walter de Gruyter & Co. Berlin, 1951.

[46] K. Rusek, Polynomial automorphisms (preprint 1989).

[47] K. Rusek, S. Cynk, Injective endomorphisms of affine algebraic varieties (in preparation).

[48] B. Segre, Corrispondenze di Mobius e Transformazioni cremoniane intere, Atti della Acc. della Scienze di Torino, Classe di Scienzo Fisiche. Mat. e. Naturel. 91 (156–57), 3–19.

[49] B. Segre, Forme differentziali e loro integrali, Vol II, Docet, Roma, 1956.

[50] B. Segre, Variazioni continua ed omotopia in geometria algebrica, Ann. Math. Pura Appl. 100 (1960), 149–186.

[51] D. Shannon, M. Sweedler, Using Gröbner bases to determine algebra membership, split surjective algebra homomorphisms and determine birational equivalence, J. Symbolic Comp. 6 (1988), 267–273.

[52] D. Shannon, M. Sweedler, Using Gröbner bases to determine subalgebra membership, preprint 1988.

[53] Y. Stein, On linear differential operators related to the Jacobian Conjecture, J. of Pure and Appl. Algebra 57 (1989), 175–186.

[54] Y. Stein, Linear differential operators related to the Jacobian Conjecture have a closed image, Journ. d'Analyse Math., 54 (1990), 237–245.

[55] A. Vitushkin, On polynomial transformations of $\mathbf{C}^n$ manifolds (Tokyo, 1973), Tokyo Univ. Press, Tokyo, 1975, 415–417.

[56] S. Wang, A Jacobian criterion for separability, J. Algebra 65 (1980), 453–494.

[57] A. Yagzhev, On Keller's problem, Siberian Math. J. 21 (1980), 747–754.

Computational Aspects of Lie Group Representations and Related Topics   45
Proceedings of the 1990 Computational Algebra Seminar
pp. 45–63 in CWI Tract 84 (1991)

Theta functions, lattices, and

statistical mechanics

Omar Foda

Institute for Theoretical Physics

University of Nijmegen

Toernooiveld 1

6525 ED Nijmegen

The Netherlands

0. Introduction

Two applications of the theta functions based on the root and weight lattices of simple Lie algebras to exactly-solvable statistical mechanical models are described. In the first part of this paper, viz. §§2-7, we reformulate Baxter's 8-vertex model in terms of the Lie group $SU(2)$, its associated root and weight lattices and the theta functions based on them. To be more precise, we will make use of the abelian subgroup of $SU(2)$ only. We will see that Baxter's model, which is the basic building block of almost everything that we know about exact solutions of statistical mechanical models, is directly related to the spin $1/2$, or vector representation of the Lie group $SU(2)$. This material has appeared, in a shorter form, in [Fo].

The second part is a report on work in progress: a study of a class of models that describe the coupling of n copies of the 8-vertex model. Statistical mechanical models are described in terms of parameters called the Boltzmann weights. The condition for exact solvability is that these weights satisfy a set of equations called the Yang-Baxter equations. The above statements will be explained in an elementary way in the following section. What we wish to mention here is that the weights obtained in the second part of this paper, are the most general that can be considered. I have not managed, as yet, to prove or disprove, that these Boltzmann weights satisfy the Yang-Baxter equations, or equivalently, that this class of models is indeed exactly solvable. In fact, it is likely that only special cases of these weights lead to exact solutions. However, I find these models sufficiently interesting to report on.

In the rest of this section, I would like to motivate both the first and the second parts of this work.

It can be argued that, in the subject of exact solutions, two major issues need to be addressed. Firstly, almost all exact solutions that we know are 2-dimensional. The only exception is the Zamolodchikov model: a solution of the tetrahedron equations: the 3-dimensional analogue of the Yang-Baxter equations. But it is not entirely satisfactory, since some of the Boltzmann weights are negative; this makes the model non-physical: the Boltzmann weights are probabilities, and furthermore, the solution cannot be extended away from criticality. (We will explain in the following section what these words mean.) How can we go beyond 2 dimensions? Recasting the 8-vertex model in the language of group theory, as described in the first part of this work, might give us ideas on how to go in this direction. After all, higher-rank groups are usually associated with transformations on higher-dimensional spaces. This is the motivation of the first part.

Next, we come to the second limitation on known exact solutions. Almost all solutions that we know are 'symmetric'. An example of a 'non-symmetric' exact solution that describes a physical system in an external symmetry-breaking field, is the 6-vertex model in an external field. There are more, but not many. Hopefully, once we learn how to solve models that correspond to coupling more than one copy of the same model, or even different models, one can consider certain limits in which one of these components 'freezes' (in the sense that its variables remain fixed in a certain direction, thus breaking the spatial symmetry of the entire system), and acts as an external field that breaks the symmetry of the other components. This is the motivation of the second part, though as we will see, we will come way short of what we wish to obtain.

The presentation is informal and elementary. It is not the intention here to give an introduction to statistical mechanics, or the relevant mathematics. Instead, references to original works and reviews are provided.

1. Exact solutions in Statistical Mechanics

All known physical phenomena that can be *theoretically* investigated, belong to one of two classes: those with a very small number of degrees of freedom, and those where the number of degrees of freedom is very large. Later, we will be more specific about what we mean by 'very small' and 'very large.' The general case of an arbitrary number of degrees of freedom is simply too complicated to handle.

Only in the above limits can we hope that a small number of features remain dominant, while all others vanish, or could be safely ignored. When that is indeed the case, then things become sufficiently simple that one can describe them in terms of an abstract model that can be mathematically investigated.

Naturally, the above scenario can work with different degrees of success: There may be situations where one ignores certain effects that are small but not vanishing. In such cases, one can regard the small but non-vanishing effect as a perturbation, and work in terms of a perturbation expansion up to a certain order in a small parameter. The most successful example of that approach is Quantum Electrodynamics: a theory that describes the electromagnetic interactions between elementary particles. No other known example of a perturbative expansion is nearly as successful. The reason is that the perturbation effects that one wishes to include are typically small, but not small enough to guarantee that the perturbation expansion converges.

There are cases where things can go even better: a very small number of features are important, all others are *strictly vanishing*; however the model remains far from trivial: one can write down a non-trivial set of equations that describe the model *exactly*. If one can find an exact and non-trivial solution to such a set of equations, then one has an exactly-solved model. Such solutions can be found in the limit where the number of degrees of freedom is three. (The cases of one and two degrees of freedom are trivial.) In these cases, things are simple because we strip all complications off the problem. Astronomers, and nuclear physicists are typically interested in such cases. Here, one talks about an exact solution of a 'few-body problem'. We will not be concerned with these in this work.

One the other hand, statistical mechanists and quantum field theorists are interested in the other limit: that of systems with a very large number of degrees of freedom. This is usually referred to as the infinite-volume limit.

In that case things become simple because *almost all complications cancel each other out.* Furthermore, there are certain systems, typically 2-dimensional, where what emerges in the infinite-volume limit can be described in terms of an exact model: an exact set of equations, for which exact and non-trivial solutions can be found.

These models typically describe 2-dimensional critical phenomena. Let us explain what we mean by that. Given the right conditions: temperature, pressure, etc., matter can change its state: a solid, such as ice, can melt into liquid: water; and liquid can evaporate into gas: vapour. Each of these transformations is an example of a 'phase transition.'

Depending on the conditions under which they occur: temperature and pressure in the case of water boiling, or external electric and magnetic fields, in the case of transitions in electric and magnetic materials, phase transitions can be 'sudden' and non-homogeneous: watching water freezing, one can actually distinguish, here and there, chunks of ice forming; or gradually and homogeneously: in that case, at no point can one say that part of the system is in one phase, while another part is in the other. Phase transitions that occur freely in nature are almost always first order. Continuous phase transitions require delicate conditions that can be achieved only in the controlled environment of the laboratory.

Sudden and non-homogeneous phase transitions are called 'first order' phase transitions, for a reason that we need not go into. Continuous and homogeneous transitions are second, or higher order phase transitions. Second and higher order phase transitions are collectively known as 'critical phenomena'. They are the subject of our interest here.

Phase transitions can be further classified from a different point of view. They can occur in the 'bulk': think of water boiling in kettle. These are 3-dimensional phase transitions: they take place in systems with a finite volume. Or, they can occur on a surface: the way that the liquid crystal display in a digital watch reacts to a change in an applied electric current, thus indicating the time of day, is an example of a surface phase transition. These are 2-dimensional phase transitions. But any physical system, no matter how thin, has a definite thickness, even a single layer of atoms has the thickness of a single atom; how could we still talk about a 2-dimensional physical system? The point is that, in discussing critical phenomena, we will be mainly interested in the way that the variables of the system fluctuate. In a very thin system, all fluctuations will take place in the two extended dimensions of the system. In other words, critical behaviour will *not* take place in the third direction. It is in that sense that we can talk about a 2-dimensional system, and 2-dimensional critical phenomena. How about one-dimensional phase transitions? : they are trivial!

In the rest of this work, we will be concerned with one solution in 2 dimensions: Baxter's model.

2. Baxter's model

Baxter's symmetric 8-vertex model [Baxt] is central to studies of exactly-solvable lattice models in two dimensions: all known off-critical solutions can be regarded as special cases or generalizations of it. For reviews of recent developments, see [JMT], [Bow].

Let us explain what we mean when we mention that a solution is 'off-critical.' We are interested in describing critical behaviour. That includes not only the behaviour of a model right at the critical point, but also the way it approaches criticality. For that last purpose, we need a solution that is valid also off criticality. There do exist exact solutions that are valid only at the critical point, such as the 3-dimensional Zamolodchikov model, referred to previously, but these are considered as incomplete. Now, back to Baxter's model.

The model is formulated on a 2-dimensional square lattice. Each site on the lattice has 4 nearest-neighbours. One-dimensional line segments, called *bonds*, extend between each pair of nearest-neighbour sites. We attach to each bond an arrow, that can point in either direction. A site, together with its 4 bonds, and the attached arrows, is called a *vertex*. One can think of an $N \times N$ square lattice: a lattice with N^2 vertices. The bonds at the edges are attached to a single site only. Each vertex can take one of 16 possible configurations. In the following, by 'a vertex' we will mean a vertex with a given configuration of arrows.

To each vertex one associates a weight: a probability that the vertex can occur; more explicitly, it is the probability that a certain site on the lattice, together with the attached 4 bonds, can have a certain arrow configuration. A vertex that has weight zero cannot occur. A configuration of the entire lattice has a weight equal to the product of the weights of the individual vertices.

To recall, we are interested in describing the critical behaviour of a model, including its behaviour as it approaches criticality. An important characteristic of approaching criticality is that certain quantities that characterize the system behave in a peculiar way.

These quantities are typically 'correlation functions.' They give us the answer to questions such as: if the variable located at the origin is in a certain state, what is the probability that the corresponding variable at a point at distance r is in the same state? At criticality, these correlation functions are inversely proportional to the distance r, raised to some power. This power is called a *critical exponent*: a number that describes the decay of the correlation functions at large distances.

The reason this behaviour is regarded as peculiar is that these critical exponents are typically *non-canonical*: they are different from what one would naively expect on the basis of classical considerations, e.g. dimensional analysis. They are also important because they can be measured in computer simulations, or even in the laboratory. An exact solution of a model means that we can *compute* quantities such as the critical exponents *exactly*. The reason why this is important is that—if we are fortunate—the models that we are dealing with can be descriptions of physical systems that can be studied in the laboratory. When this is the case, then the critical exponents can be measured, and the measurements can be compared with the predictions of the theory.

To the best of my knowledge, the theoretic predictions of the exact solutions, have always agreed with the experimental results, whenever it was possible to carry out a relevant experiment, and within the bounds of experimental accuracy.

Now back to our model on a lattice: The general 16 vertex model, where all 16 vertex configurations have non-vanishing and independent weights has not been solved. There is no guarantee that an arbitrary model can be exactly solvable. The most general exact solution, of a special case of the 16 vertex model that we have is that of the symmetric 8-vertex model, where only the 8 vertices shown in Figure 1 are allowed.

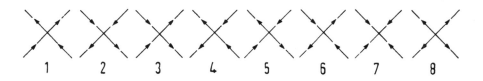

Figure 1. The vertices of the symmetric eight vertex model

The model is symmetric in the sense that vertex configurations that are related by inverting all arrows have the same weight. The fact that the non-symmetric vertex models has not been solved gives an example of what we mentioned in the above section, regarding the lack of non-symmetric exact solutions.

The weight of a vertex is called a *Boltzmann weight*. The basic step in solving a model is to find a set of Boltzmann weights that satisfy a certain set of conditions called the *Yang-Baxter equations*.

Baxter's model is important since it serves as a starting point for further generalizations. The basic observation that underlies these generalizations can be phrased as follows: the model is related to the 2-dimensional, or spin $1/2$ representation of the Lie group $SU(2)$ in the sense that each bond can take either one of two states, and these correspond to the weights of the 2-dimensional representation of $SU(2)$: spin-up and spin-down.

Accordingly, we can think of generalizations that correspond to higher dimensional representations of $SU(2)$, and beyond that to any irreducible representation of any Lie group [JMT] and [T].

Once again, a basic step towards solving a lattice model exactly is to show that one has a family of Boltzmann weights that satisfy the so-called Yang-Baxter equations. By a family of Boltzmann weights one means that the weight of a given vertex configuration depends on a continuous complex parameter, known as the *spectral parameter*, in addition to other dependences that will be considered later. The spectral parameter can be interpreted as a parametrization of the shape of the underlying lattice. In other words, it describes the deformation of the unit cells of the underlying lattice.

The reason one requires such a dependence on an extra parameter is, very briefly, as follows: Suppose we would like to generate all possible vertex configurations on a given $N \times N$ lattice. We can start from a row of N vertices at a boundary, with a given configuration of arrows, with non-vanishing weights.

We can think of this configuration as a boundary condition. To generate the rest of the lattice, we can proceed adding rows, row by row. This can be done using a certain operator that acts on the row at the boundary of the lattice to generate the next, and so on.

This operator has a matrix representation, which should be obvious from the fact that it acts on a 'row' of variables. It is called the *transfer matrix*. The elements of the transfer matrix can be expressed in terms of the Boltzmann weights, since it has to do with the arrow configurations. If the Boltzmann weights depend on a spectral parameter, then so would the transfer matrix, and we end with a family of transfer matrices. Why do we need an entire family of transfer matrices, and not just one? The reason is as follows.

The condition of exact solvability can be expressed in terms of the requirement that one has as many conservation laws as the number of degrees of freedom. In the infinite volume limit one has an infinite number of degrees of freedom, therefore one needs an infinite number of conservation laws. Where can we get these from? Let us first try to find out what exactly is being conserved.

Let us digress and give a 'space-time' interpretation to our lattice model. We are familiar with the idea of 4-dimensional space-time: 3 space dimensions and 1 time. Disregarding the fact that the metric on our lattice is Euclidean, we can think of our lattice model as a space-time with 1 space and 1 time dimensions. (In fact we can reformulate our entire discussion in terms of a Minkowskian metric, but we avoid that here.)

One can think of each row as a space-like slice, that propagates forward in time. The transfer matrix is the operator that takes care of propagating our 1-dimensional space forward in time. It is roughly the equivalent of a Hamiltonian in classical and quantum mechanics. More precisely, it is the equivalent of the exponentiated Hamiltonian, up to factors that do not concern us here. In this description, a row with a given configuration of arrows represents the state of our 1-dimensional space at a given moment in time.

A conservation law means that certain quantities remain constant as the system propagates in time. When this is the case, then the state of the system at any given moment of time: a row configuration, is the eigenvector of some operator, while the corresponding eigenvalue is the conserved quantity.

We need an infinite number of these operators. Where can we get them from? It turns out that if the transfer matrix is a function of a spectral parameter, then the coefficients of a Taylor expansion, in the spectral parameter, around a suitable value, are the operators that we are looking for.

These operators can be explicitly given as $N \times N$ matrices. Since we wish that their eigenvalues be simultaneously well defined and conserved, these matrices should be simultaneously diagonalizable. From that it follows that they should be all mutually commuting. This will be indeed the case if the two original transfer matrices, with different spectral parameters, commute.

The condition for this commutativity to take place is that the Boltzmann weights, the building blocks of the transfer matrices, satisfy the Yang-Baxter equations.

Typically, there are many more Yang-Baxter equations than Boltzmann weights. Therefore one is faced with a highly over-determined system of equations. Thus, it is no wonder that solutions could be found only in the presence of a symmetry that reduces the number of constraints by making many of them equivalent.

In this work we are interested in off-critical systems that exhibit critical behaviour in certain limits. All known off-critical solutions to the Yang-Baxter equations are given in terms of elliptic functions. Why is that so? One can say that this simply follows from the computations. But this is not satisfactory. The deeper reasons behind that fact are beyond the scope of this work. Let us accept this as a fact.

Elliptic functions are infinite series in a complex parameter q, called the *modulus* or *nome*, that parametrize the departure from criticality. In the critical limit, q tends to zero, and the Boltzmann weights reduce to trigonometric functions.

Back once again to the connection between Baxter's model and the vector representation of $SU(2)$. Baxter's original parametrization of the Boltzmann weights does not make the connection with $SU(2)$ manifest. In fact, it does not make a connection with group theory at all. However, as explained above, the connection with group theory is necessary once we attempt to study more general models.

Here, we wish to re-derive Baxter's parametrization, in a way that makes this connection clear. The purpose of the exercise is to formulate things in such a way that generalization to models based on other representations and/or other Lie groups becomes straightforward.

What we wish to do here is to rewrite Baxter's model in terms of the vector representation of $SU(2)$. To go beyond Baxter's model, we would e.g. replace the vector representation everywhere by another representation, or replace $SU(2)$ by another group.

3. The Zamolodchikov Algebra

Let us recapitulate some of the statements we made above. A necessary condition for a lattice model to be exactly solvable is that it has a number of conserved charges that is equal to the number of degrees of freedom. In the infinite-lattice limit, one should have an infinite number of conserved charges. The operators corresponding to these charges are obtained as terms in a Taylor expansion of the transfer matrix with respect to a 'spectral parameter'.

The dependence of the transfer matrix on the spectral parameter is equivalent to the presence of a one-parameter family of commuting transfer matrices. A sufficient condition to ensure the presence of a family of commuting transfer matrices, is that the Boltzmann weights of the model satisfy the Yang-Baxter equations. Obtaining new exactly-solvable models amounts to finding new solutions of the Yang-Baxter (YB) equations.

In [Z] Zamolodchikov noticed that the YB equations are related to a non-commutative algebra: Consider an algebra generated by the set $\{A_i(x)\}$, where i is a discrete index, and x is a continuous parameter. The generators satisfy the following *braiding* operation:

$$A_i(x) * A_j(y) = S_{ij}^{kl}(x - y) A_k(y) * A_l(x) \tag{1}$$

If the algebra is associative:

$$\Big(A_i(x) * A_j(y) \Big) * A_k(z) = A_i(x) * \Big(A_j(y) * A_k(z) \Big) \tag{2}$$

and all third degree monomials in the generators $\{A_i(x)\}$ can be shown to be independent with respect to variations that leave the coefficients $\{S\}$ constant, then the latter satisfy

$$S_{\alpha\alpha'}^{\gamma\gamma'}(u) S_{\gamma\alpha''}^{\beta\gamma''}(u + v) S_{\gamma'\gamma''}^{\beta'\beta''}(v) = S_{\alpha'\alpha''}^{\gamma'\gamma''}(v) S_{\alpha\gamma''}^{\gamma\beta''}(v + u) S_{\gamma\gamma'}^{\beta\beta'}(u) \tag{3}$$

which are the YB equations, once we interpret $S_{ij}^{kl}(u)$ as a Boltzmann weight, and its argument u as the spectral parameter.

Let us explain what we did above. We start from the triple product:

$$A_i(x_1) * A_j(x_2) * A_k(x_3),$$

where in the *-product of two A operators the order from left to right is *relevant*. Then we start braiding. We will do that in two different ways, and compare the results.

1. We braid the operators with arguments x_1 and x_2. Then we braid the result with the operator of argument x_3. This means braiding it firstly with an operator that has argument x_1, and then with an operator that has an argument x_2: remember that the relative positions of x_1 and x_2 have been interchanged in the first braiding.

2. We repeat the same exercise, but then in the *reverse* order: firstly we braid the operators with arguments x_2 and x_3, and then braid the result with the operator with argument x_1. That means that the latter has to go first, from left to right, through an operator that has an argument x_3, and then through another with argument x_2.

Demanding the equality of the two final results obtained above, is an expression of the associativity of the braiding operation, or equivalently, the Zamolodchikov algebra. However, the final results have the form of a sum of terms, each consisting of the product of 3 A operators, with a coefficient that consists of the product of 3 S coefficients, one from each time that an A operator was braided with another A operator. Now here comes a complication: If these coefficients were numerical constants, then one could use the fact that triple products of A operators, all with different indices are all independent, and equate the coefficients of identical terms on each side. This would give us directly, the Yang-Baxter equations in (3). However, the S coefficients, or S matrices, depend on the parameters that appear in the A operators. Therefore, one has to work harder in order to extract the Yang-Baxter equations. We will indicate below, once we work in terms of an explicit representation of the A operators, one way of doing this.

We can find new solutions to the Yang-Baxter equations by looking for new realizations of the Zamolodchikov algebra (1). Although in principle one can think of the Yang-Baxter equations as functional equations and proceed to find solutions to them, it should be easier to find new candidates for associative Zamolodchikov algebras.

4. Cherednik's Representation

In [Ch] Cherednik proposed a realization of the Zamolodchikov algebras in terms of theta functions, that leads to off-critical Boltzmann weights satisfying the YB equations. Let us begin with a few definitions.

4.1 Theta functions

Our main reference on theta functions is [KP]. The classical theta functions $\Theta_{\mu,m}$ of degree m, parameter q, characteristic μ, and complex argument z are defined as

$$\Theta_{\mu,m}(z) = \sum_{\gamma \in \mathbf{Z}+\mu/m} q^{m\gamma^2} e^{-2\pi i m \gamma \cdot z} \tag{4}$$

The parameter q is the modulus, or the nome. It can also be rewritten as $q = e^{i\pi\tau}$, where τ is a complex number, with positive definite imaginary part, called the period matrix. In the rest of this work, we will only consider τ with $\text{Im } \tau > 0$, so that the theta functions in (4) have a very fast rate of convergence. (See page 1 of [M] for a discussion; [M] is recommended as an introduction to the subject of theta functions.)

Notice that the definition given in (4), is different from the standard one used in [M], [Fa]: we have only one characteristic rather than two, since the second can always be absorbed in z. (Our functions are those of characteristic $(\mu/m, 0)$ in [M].) For fixed $m \in \mathbf{N}$ and $\beta \in \mathbf{C}$, define $H_{m,\beta}$ to be the vector space of all analytic complex functions f satisfying $f(z + 1) = f(z)$ and $f(z + \tau) = e^{-2\pi i m z - \pi i \beta}$. Then $H_{m,\beta}$ has dimension m. Moreover, for $\beta = \tau m$ then the space $H_{m,\beta}$ contains the theta functions $\Theta_{\mu,m}$ ($\mu \in \{0, \ldots, m - 1\}$); they form a basis.

4.2 A realization of the Zamolodchikov algebras

Next we turn to Cherednik's realization of the Zamolodchikov algebra [Ch]. Since Cherednik's work is quite technical, we will follow the clear exposition given in Appendix II of [TF], with modifications that suit our purposes.

Consider the operators that act on $H_{m,\beta}$ as follows:

$$A_{i,n}(x)f(z) = \Theta_{i,n}(z - x)f(z - \eta). \tag{5}$$

That is, they act on f by shifting the argument by a constant η, and multiplication by a degree n theta function. This results in an operator $A_{i,n} : H_{m,\beta} \to H_{m+n,n(\tau-2x)+\beta-2\eta m}$. This can be verified directly by use of the definition of $H_{m,\beta}$ or by observing that the result of multiplying two degree m_1 and m_2 theta functions can be expanded in terms of degree $m_1 + m_2$ theta functions:

$$\Theta_{\mu_1,m_1}(z_1)\Theta_{\mu_2,m_2}(z_2) = \sum_{\gamma \in \mathbf{Z}/(m_1+m_2)\mathbf{Z}} d_\gamma \Theta_{\mu_1+\mu_2+m_1\gamma, m_1+m_2}(z_1 + z_2), \tag{6}$$

where

$$d_\gamma = \Theta_{m_2\mu_1 - m_1\mu_2 + m_1 m_2\gamma, m_1 m_2(m_1+m_2)}(z_1 - z_2). \tag{7}$$

For, applying (6), (7) with $z_1 = z - x$ and $z_2 = z - \eta$, we see that d_γ does not depend on z, and that the argument of the theta functions depending on z is $2z - x - \eta$.

Clearly, the action of $A_{i,m}(x)$, as explained above, is not the most general that one can consider, but it is what we need in this work. Next, we consider the compositions:

$$\begin{aligned} &A_{i,m}(x)A_{j,m}(y)\Theta_{\mu,m}, \\ &A_{k,m}(y)A_{l,m}(x)\Theta_{\mu,m}. \end{aligned} \tag{8}$$

Both operations map $H_{\mu,\tau m}$ into $H_{3\mu, 2m(\tau-x-y)+(\tau-6\eta)m}$. As the images lie in each other's span, we can relate them by a matrix:

$$A_{i,m}(x)A_{j,m}(y)\Theta_{\mu,m} = S_{ij}^{kl}(x - y, \eta)A_{k,m}(y)A_{l,m}(x)\Theta_{\mu,m}. \tag{9}$$

The justification for the choice of arguments in the matrix S follows form the equation below, which is gotten from (9) by some obvious rewritings.

$$\Theta_{i,m}(x)\Theta_{j,m}(y+\eta) = S_{ij}^{kl}(x-y,\eta)\Theta_{i,m}(y)\Theta_{j,m}(x+\eta) \qquad (10)$$

To derive the Yang-Baxter equations in this formalism we consider the action of the triplet $A_{i,m}(w)A_{j,m}(x)A_{k,m}(y)$, braid them in two different ways as discussed above, then consider the action of each result on the state $\Theta_{\mu,m}$, expressed in terms of theta functions.

Next we wish to show that the structure constants $S_{ij}^{kl}(x-y)$ satisfy the Yang-Baxter equations. The basic idea is to make use of the linear independence of the triple products of theta functions with different characteristics, which follows from the independence of the single theta functions. But then the problem, as we mentioned above, is that the S coefficients are not entirely constant but depend on the variables x, y, z and η. However, we can use the fact that the S coefficients depend only on differences of the arguments x, y, z. This together with a study of the behaviour of the various terms under discrete shifts in η allows us to separate the various terms in the sums obtained, and prove the Yang-Baxter equations.

The S matrices obtained above are given in terms of theta functions and, therefore, are candidates for the Boltzmann weights of an off-critical model. This was Cherednik's realization of the Zamolodchikov algebra. But how can we obtain the Boltzmann weights of a *specific* lattice model? Let us consider Baxter's symmetric eight vertex model. The allowed vertices are shown in Figure 1.

At this point, we can make use of another idea, also due to Zamolodchikov: one can think of each vertex as a description of a scattering process between two particles. Recall our space-time description of a lattice model: think of a vertex as a picture that describes two particles, each carrying a spin variable: an attribute, that can take one of two values. They approach each other, collide, then proceed ahead. All that can happen during the collision, is that particles exchange their spins, or change it. It is also possible that nothing happens at all.

We refer to the two particles coming in, and before they participate in a collision, as the *incoming states*. We refer to the two particles that go their separate ways after the collision, as the *outgoing states*. Of course, each outgoing state of a collision later becomes one of the incoming states of another, and so forth.

We wish to associate theta functions with the incoming states i and j, and the outgoing k and l, for definite values of the indices, then compute the Boltzmann weight from (10). Since each index has two values, we wish to have a 2-dimensional vector space of theta-functions. For that we take $m = 2$ in (4). The rest of the computation is straightforward, and has been outlined in [TF].

We wish to redo this computation in a way that makes the connection with the spin $1/2$ representation of $SU(2)$ explicit. For that we propose to use a Cherednik-type representation of the Zamolodchikov algebra based on theta functions that are related to $SU(2)$. We will see that they reduce to the theta functions used above. However, as we have mentioned before, we expect that the relationship with Lie groups allows one to extend the derivation to more general vertex models.

5. Theta functions based on $SU(2)$ lattices

There is a direct generalization of the classical theta functions (4) to functions based on symmetric quadratic forms $\gamma \mapsto \gamma Q^L \gamma$ (cf. [Sch]). Following the notation of [KP], these are defined as

$$\Theta^L_{\mu,m}(z) = \sum_{\gamma \in L + \frac{\mu}{m}} q^{m(\gamma Q^L \gamma)} e^{-2\pi i m(\gamma Q^L z)} \qquad (11)$$

where L is an r-dimensional lattice, μ and z are r-dimensional vectors, and the quadratic form Q^L acts as a metric in the space of the lattice L.

An important class of theta functions are those based on quadratic forms associated to Lie groups. Here we are interested in those related to $SU(2)$.

5.1 The weight and root lattices of $SU(2)$

Our main references on lattices associated with Lie groups are [Serre], [CS]. Here we wish to recall some simple facts, and phrase them in a very elementary language. In a matrix representation of a rank r Lie group, r torus generators can be simultaneously diagonalized. They form the 'Cartan subalgebra' of the corresponding Lie algebra. For $SU(2)$ we have $r=1$, and only one generator can be diagonalized. The states that form the irreducible representations of the group are eigenvectors of the diagonalized generators. The corresponding eigenvalues are the 'weights' associated with the representation.

For a rank r group, the weights form r-dimensional vectors, and can be represented as vertices of an r-dimensional lattice called the weight lattice of the group. For $SU(2)$ the lattice is one dimensional.

The normalization of the weights will be explained below. The weights of the adjoint representation—for $SU(2)$ this is the spin 1, or 3-dimensional representation—are called the 'roots'. Any root is an integral linear combinations of r 'simple' roots; they generate a 'root lattice'.

We shall only consider the irreducible root systems in which the squared norm of each simple root equals 2 (these are the root systems with the so-called simply-laced diagrams). The weight lattice can be shown to be dual to the root lattice: it is generated by the 'fundamental weights', which are defined as the duals to the simple roots. Notice that the root lattice is a sublattice of the weight lattice.

The inner product of the vectors that generate a lattice defines a matrix. The matrix corresponding to the root lattice is the Cartan matrix. The matrix of the weight lattice is the inverse Cartan matrix. In the case of $SU(2)$, these are one-by-one matrices.

We can write down a theta function based on a quadratic form as in (11). In this case, the characteristics would take values in the dual lattice modulo the lattice corresponding to the quadratic form. It is therefore natural to write down theta functions based on the root lattice of a group with characteristics taking values in the weight lattice modulo the roots.

We can do that for the lattices based on $SU(2)$, and obtain a parametrization of the eight-vertex model that way, since the unit cell of the $SU(2)$ root lattice contains two sites from the weight lattice. However, the characteristics do not take values in the weights of the spin $1/2$ representation. Therefore, we wish to proceed differently. We start with theta functions based on L^*, the *weight* lattice of $SU(2)$, with characteristics taking values in the root lattice L. But since L is only a sub-lattice of L^*, we will have to work with level $m > 1$ theta functions, where the characteristics take values in L mod mL^*, and choose m such that there are precisely two independent characteristics. This way, the characteristics, and consequently the incoming and outgoing states in a vertex, can be directly related to the weights of the spin $1/2$ representation of $SU(2)$.

6. The Boltzmann weights of the eight-vertex model

In the normalization where the squared norm of the simple roots is 2, the Cartan matrix of $SU(2)$ is simply the scalar 2. The inverse Cartan matrix is $1/2$. The level m theta functions based on the weight lattice of $SU(2)$ are:

$$\Theta_{\mu,m}(z) = \sum_{\gamma \in Z + \frac{\mu}{m}} q^{m\gamma \cdot \frac{1}{2} \cdot \gamma} e^{-2\pi i m \gamma \cdot \frac{1}{2} \cdot z}.$$

The above is identical to (4), up to the 'inverse Cartan matrices', which are simply factors of $1/2$. In this case, this can be absorbed in the other parameters, but we wish to leave it this way, to remind us that in more general cases, if we deal with theta functions based on groups of a higher rank, full matrices will show up.

The only possibility that leads to a 2-dimensional space of theta functions, where the characteristics have the correct periodicity properties, is $m = 4$. In this case, the characteristics, that take values in L mod $4L^*$, can be chosen as $\{-1/2, 1/2\}$ or $\{0, 1\}$. The two choices are equivalent, since they differ by shifts of the origin of the weight lattice, and the first coincides with the weights of the spin $1/2$ representation.

To simplify the computations, we will make use of the invariance of the theta functions under shifts by vectors in the weight lattice, so that the characteristics can be in the second set $\{0, 1\}$, and write our theta functions as

$$\Theta^L_{\mu,4}(z) = \sum_{\gamma \in L + \mu/2} q^{2\gamma^2} e^{-4\pi i \gamma z}.$$

Note that these are identical to what one obtains starting with theta functions based on the root lattice and $m = 1$. These are precisely the theta functions used in [TF] to compute the weights of the symmetric eight-vertex model.

Next we proceed with the derivation of the Boltzmann weights. For each vertex, we associate theta functions with the incoming states, take their product, and expand it in terms of a basis of weight $2m$ theta functions using equation (6). We do the same for the outgoing states, and relate the two expansions using equation (10). Then, we solve for the Boltzmann weights, using the orthogonality relation

$$\int \Theta^L_{\mu,m}(z)\overline{\Theta^L_{\mu',m}(z)}dz \sim \delta_{L+\mu,L+\mu'}.$$

where the proportionality factor will not concern us. This above orthogonality relation can be proven quite simply using the series expansions of the theta functions involved.

The S coefficients can be obtained starting from (10), with all allowed values of indices. In each equation, taking the product of the theta functions on each side, one obtains the analogue of a vector equation in theta functions of degree 2 (those whose arguments are the *sum* of the arguments of the initial thetas that entered the product).

Using the fact that these are orthogonal, and that all other terms are constants with respect to their arguments, we find that each equation separates into two independent linear algebraic equations in two S coefficients, that we can solve. The answer is

$$S^{00}_{00}(z) = S^{11}_{11}(z) = \left(\Theta_0(-z+\eta)\Theta_0(z+\eta) - \Theta_2(-z+\eta)\Theta_2(z+\eta)\right)/d_1$$

$$S^{11}_{00}(z) = S^{00}_{11}(z) = \left(\Theta_0(-z+\eta)\Theta_2(z+\eta) - \Theta_0(z+\eta)\Theta_2(-z+\eta)\right)/d_1$$

$$S^{10}_{10}(z) = S^{01}_{01}(z) = \left(\Theta_1(-z+\eta)\Theta_1(z+\eta) - \Theta_3(-z+\eta)\Theta_3(z+\eta)\right)/d_2$$

$$S^{01}_{10}(z) = S^{10}_{01}(z) = \left(\Theta_1(-z+\eta)\Theta_3(z+\eta) - \Theta_1(z+\eta)\Theta_3(-z+\eta)\right)/d_2$$

where

$$d_1 = \Theta^2_0(-z+\eta) - \Theta^2_2(-z+\eta),$$
$$d_2 = \Theta^2_1(-z+\eta) - \Theta^2_3(-z+\eta).$$

This is not manifestly equivalent to Baxter's parametrization [Baxt], but one can show that it is, cf. [TF].

7. What next?

The purpose of the above exercise was to elucidate Cherednik's realization of the Zamolodchikov algebra, and to parametrize the weights of the symmetric eight-vertex model in a way that makes the connection with Lie group theory clear. In fact, we wanted to do things in such a way that a generalization to other models becomes straightforward. The next obvious step is to generate parametrizations of extended models based on higher representations of $SU(2)$, and beyond that to models based on arbitrary representations of Lie groups of type A_n, D_n, E_n.

In the rest of this paper we will look at another direction for generalizing Baxter's model: We remain with the fundamental representation of $SU(2)$, but consider Boltzmann weights that describe the coupling of n copies of the basic 8-vertex model.

8. Coupled vertex models

In the previous sections, we discussed Baxter's model: a vertex model that has 2 states per bond. Thinking of a vertex as a scattering process, where two particles come in, collide, then go their separate ways, we have represented the scattering states: the incoming and outgoing states in terms of theta functions that belong to a 2-dimensional vector space of theta functions.

We used the two elements of the basis of that vector space to represent the two possibilities for incoming and outgoing states: states with spin-up or spin-down.

These theta functions are genus-1 theta functions: their period matrices are 1×1 complex matrices, i.e., complex scalars. More generally, there are theta functions of genus n: their period matrices are $n \times n$ complex symmetric matrices. Can we obtain statistical mechanical models that generalize Baxter's model, where the genus-n theta functions play the same role that the genus-1 thetas played in Baxter's model?

Consider a vertex model with 2^n states per bond. We propose a representation of the scattering states in terms of the level-2 n-loop theta functions. Here we wish to consider the $n = 2$ case in some detail. It should be evident that the discussion generalizes directly to all n.

Just as we did above, we represent the scattering states by operators $\{A_i\}$ that act as

$$A_i(x)\Theta_j(z) = \Theta_i(z - x)\Theta(z - \eta). \tag{12}$$

We will restrict our attention from now on to the multiplicative factor of the action of the $\{A_i\}$ operators on the states Θ_i. Up to the shift in the argument by η, it contains all the information we need: keeping track of the anisotropy introduced by η, these theta functions will stand for the bond states.

The vector space of level-2 2-loop theta functions is $2 \times 2 = 4$ dimensional. Therefore we can associate the basis elements with the bond states of a 4-state model. Representing these by 2 arrows on each bond, and using the notation $\Theta[\mu_1, \mu_2]$ for the theta functions, where μ_i is the ith characteristic, we associate the basis theta functions with the bond states as follows:

[spin-down, spin-down] $\sim \Theta[0, 0]$, [spin-up, spin-down] $\sim \Theta[1, 0]$

[spin-down, spin-up] $\sim \Theta[0, 1]$, [spin-up, spin-up] $\sim \Theta[1, 1]$

There are $4^2 = 16$ possible pairs of initial/final states. As a consequence of the product relation (6), the set of all initial states divides into four subsets, the elements of each sharing the same subspace of intermediate states, exclusively.

Therefore, we can divide the set of all scattering processes, into 4 distinct ones. Giving only the characteristics that denote the bond states, these are:

$$[00][00] = S_{00\ 00}^{00\ 00}[00][00] + S_{00\ 00}^{10\ 10}[10][10] + S_{00\ 00}^{01\ 01}[01][01] + S_{00\ 00}^{11\ 11}[11][11]$$

$$[10][10] = S_{10\ 10}^{00\ 00}[00][00] + S_{10\ 10}^{10\ 10}[10][10] + S_{10\ 10}^{01\ 01}[01][01] + S_{10\ 10}^{11\ 11}[11][11]$$

$$[01][01] = S_{01\ 01}^{00\ 00}[00][00] + S_{01\ 01}^{10\ 10}[10][10] + S_{01\ 01}^{01\ 01}[01][01] + S_{01\ 01}^{11\ 11}[11][11]$$

$$[11][11] = S_{11\ 11}^{00\ 00}[00][00] + S_{11\ 11}^{10\ 10}[10][10] + S_{11\ 11}^{01\ 01}[01][01] + S_{11\ 11}^{11\ 11}[11][11]$$

$$[10][00] = S_{10\ 00}^{10\ 00}[10][00] + S_{10\ 00}^{00\ 10}[00][10] + S_{10\ 00}^{11\ 01}[11][01] + S_{10\ 00}^{01\ 11}[01][11]$$

$$[00][10] = S_{00\ 10}^{10\ 00}[10][00] + S_{00\ 10}^{00\ 10}[00][10] + S_{00\ 10}^{11\ 01}[11][01] + S_{00\ 10}^{01\ 11}[01][11]$$

$$[11][01] = S_{11\ 01}^{10\ 00}[10][00] + S_{11\ 01}^{00\ 10}[00][10] + S_{11\ 01}^{11\ 01}[11][01] + S_{11\ 01}^{01\ 11}[01][11]$$

$$[01][11] = S_{01\ 11}^{10\ 00}[10][00] + S_{01\ 11}^{00\ 10}[00][10] + S_{01\ 11}^{11\ 01}[11][01] + S_{01\ 11}^{01\ 11}[01][11]$$

$$[01][00] = S_{01\ 00}^{01\ 00}[01][00] + S_{01\ 00}^{11\ 10}[11][10] + S_{01\ 00}^{00\ 01}[00][01] + S_{01\ 00}^{10\ 11}[10][11]$$

$$[11][10] = S_{11\ 10}^{01\ 00}[01][00] + S_{11\ 10}^{11\ 10}[11][10] + S_{11\ 10}^{00\ 01}[00][01] + S_{11\ 10}^{10\ 11}[10][11]$$

$$[00][01] = S_{00\ 01}^{01\ 00}[01][00] + S_{00\ 01}^{11\ 10}[11][10] + S_{00\ 01}^{00\ 01}[00][01] + S_{00\ 01}^{10\ 11}[10][11]$$

$$[10][11] = S_{10\ 11}^{01\ 00}[01][00] + S_{10\ 11}^{11\ 10}[11][10] + S_{10\ 11}^{00\ 01}[00][01] + S_{10\ 11}^{10\ 11}[10][11]$$

$$[11][00] = S_{11\ 00}^{11\ 00}[11][00] + S_{11\ 00}^{01\ 10}[01][10] + S_{11\ 00}^{10\ 01}[10][01] + S_{11\ 00}^{00\ 11}[00][11]$$

$$[01][10] = S_{01\ 10}^{11\ 00}[11][00] + S_{01\ 10}^{01\ 10}[01][10] + S_{01\ 10}^{10\ 01}[10][01] + S_{01\ 10}^{00\ 11}[00][11]$$

$$[10][01] = S_{10\ 01}^{11\ 00}[11][00] + S_{10\ 01}^{01\ 10}[01][10] + S_{10\ 01}^{10\ 01}[10][01] + S_{10\ 01}^{00\ 11}[00][11]$$

$$[00][11] = S_{00\ 11}^{11\ 00}[11][00] + S_{00\ 11}^{01\ 10}[01][10] + S_{00\ 11}^{10\ 01}[10][01] + S_{00\ 11}^{00\ 11}[00][11]$$

To obtain the S matrix elements that appear in the above equations, we consider each in turn. Let us illustrate the procedure for the first. We begin by writing it explicitly:

$$\Theta[00](x)\Theta[00](y+\eta) = S_{00\ 00}^{00\ 00}\Theta[00](y)\Theta[00](x+\eta)$$
$$+ S_{00\ 00}^{10\ 10}\Theta[10](y)\Theta[10](x+\eta)$$
$$+ S_{00\ 00}^{01\ 01}\Theta[01](y)\Theta[01](x+\eta)$$
$$+ S_{00\ 00}^{11\ 11}\Theta[11](y)\Theta[11](x+\eta)$$

This corresponds to the scattering process in Figure 2.

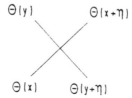

Figure 2. A two-particle scattering process

Notice that it is the presence of a non-vanishing η that leads to non-trivial scattering. We expand the product of level-2 theta functions in terms of level-4 functions using (6), the coefficients of each level-4 function must vanish separately, since the latter form a basis. This leads to the following 4 equations:

$$
\begin{bmatrix}
\Theta[00] \\
\Theta[20] \\
\Theta[02] \\
\Theta[22]
\end{bmatrix}_f
=
\begin{bmatrix}
\Theta[00] & \Theta[20] & \Theta[02] & \Theta[22] \\
\Theta[20] & \Theta[00] & \Theta[22] & \Theta[02] \\
\Theta[02] & \Theta[22] & \Theta[00] & \Theta[20] \\
\Theta[22] & \Theta[02] & \Theta[20] & \Theta[00]
\end{bmatrix}_i
\begin{bmatrix}
S^{00\ 00}_{00\ 00} \\
S^{10\ 10}_{00\ 00} \\
S^{01\ 01}_{00\ 00} \\
S^{11\ 11}_{00\ 00}
\end{bmatrix}
\tag{13}
$$

where the argument of the initial states with subscript i, is $(y - x - \eta)$, and that of the final states with subscript f is $(x - y - \eta)$. Notice that the S matrix elements depend only on the difference of the variables x and y, up to shifts by the parameter η. This is the difference property, as in the 8-vertex model. The matrix of theta functions in (13) has non-vanishing determinant; this can be seen from the fact that the components of each column are independent theta functions, and that subsequent columns are formed by independent permutations of the components of the first. Thus, the S matrix elements in (13) can be computed explicitly.

Notice that though we have 64 S matrix elements to consider, they are not all independent: the representation of the scattering states is given in terms of n-loop theta functions that are based on a product of n copies of the weight lattice of $SU(2)$. Since each such lattice is $\mathbf{Z}_2$ symmetric, our solutions possess $(\mathbf{Z}_2)^n$-symmetry. These are symmetries under flipping all spins that belong to each copy of the n-coupled vertex models independently. In our $n = 2$ example these are:

$$
S^{k_1 k_2\ \ell_1 \ell_2}_{i_1 i_2\ j_1 j_2} = S^{\tilde{k}_1 k_2\ \tilde{\ell}_1 \ell_2}_{i_1 i_2\ j_1 j_2} = S^{k_1 \tilde{k}_2\ \ell_1 \tilde{\ell}_2}_{i_1 \tilde{i}_2\ j_1 j_2}
\tag{14}
$$

where $\tilde{k}_1 = (k_1 + 2) \bmod 4$, etc. This reduces the number of S matrix elements that we need to compute explicitly by a factor of $2 \times 2 = 4$.

Let us end this section with an outline of the procedure for general n:
1. Each bond is assigned n arrows. Thus we have 2^n states per bond.
2. Associate to each bond a level-2 n-loop theta function, the ith characteristic being 0 or 1, depending on the direction of the ith arrow.
3. Relate the 2^{2n} possible final pairs of states to the initial in terms of S matrix elements. A given final state is related with non-vanishing S matrix elements to 2^n initial states only, due to the $(Z_2)^n$ symmetries (14).
4. Expanding the products of level-2 theta functions in terms of level-4 functions, only 2^n of the latter contribute. This can be deduced from (6), and the symmetries (14). Thus we obtain 2^n equations in 2^n unknowns that can be solved since the matrix of coefficients is invertible: the column vectors are independent permutations of 2^n independent level-4 theta functions.

9. Interpretation and discussion

An interesting aspect of the Boltzmann weights that we have obtained is that the spectral and crossing parameters are multi-component vectors. How do we interpret that? A clue is obtained from the fact that in the limit where all off-diagonal terms in the period matrix vanish, an n-loop theta function degenerates into the product of n 1-loop theta functions (cf. [M]). Consequently our weights degenerate into a product of n solutions that are based on 1-loop theta functions, and these correspond to the 8-vertex model.

That is the reason we interpret the multi-loop weights as coupled 8-vertex models. The coupling between two copies i and j is proportional to the off-diagonal elements of the period matrix.

In our approach, the basic building blocks of a vertex model are not the vertices — these are regarded as composite objects — but rather the scattering states associated with the bonds. Consequently, one does not start by looking for a set of Boltzmann weights by solving an overdetermined set of YB equations, that can be complicated; but for a representation of the scattering states with an associative algebra. Once we settle on an acceptable representation, the Boltzmann weights are obtained using simple algebra.

We have reported on a derivation of the Boltzmann weights of Baxter's model that makes the relationship with the group $SU(2)$ very explicit. We can explicitly show that the Boltzmann weights obtained do satisfy the Yang-Baxter equations. Furthermore, we have presented a class of models, that can be considered as direct generalizations of Baxter's model, but based on higher genus theta functions. What has not been shown is whether the Yang-Baxter equations remain satisfied.

It is very likely that only a restricted class of these higher-genus models, where the Boltzmann weights are restricted by extra conditions, are exactly solvable.

10. Acknowledgements

I wish to thank Bert van Geemen and Emma Previato for discussions, and Professor Arjeh Cohen for the invitation to present this material.

11. References

[AM]   H. Au-Yang, B.M. McCoy, J.H.H. Perk, S. Tang and M.-H. Yan, *Commuting transfer matrices in the chiral Potts models: solutions of star-triangle equations with genus >1*, Physics Letters, **A 123**(1987), 219–223.

[BPA]   R. J. Baxter, J.H.H. Perk and H. Au-Yang, *New solutions of the star-triangle relations for the chiral Potts model*, Phys. Letters, **A 128**(1988), 138–142.

[Baxt]   R. J. Baxter, *Exactly-solved models in statistical mechanics*, Academic Press, London, 1982.

[Bel]   A.A. Belavin, *Dynamical symmetry of integrable quantum systems*, Nucl. Phys., **B180 (FS2)**(1980), 189–200.

[Bow]   L. Ehrenpreis and R. C. Gunning (eds.), *Theta Functions – Bowdoin 1987*, Proceedings of Symposia in Pure Mathematics, vol. 49, part I, 1989.

[CC]   D.V. Chudnovsky & D.V. Chudnovsky, *The construction of factorized S-matrices – The relationships between the Baxter model and "Zamolodchikov algebras"*, Phys. Letters, **B 98**(1981), 83–88.

[Ch]   I.V. Cherednik, *Some S-matrices connected with Abelian varieties (in Russian)*, Dokl. Akad. Nauk. SSSR, **249**(1979), 1095–1098.

[CS]   J.H. Conway & N.J.A. Sloane, *Sphere Packings, Lattices and Groups*, Grundlehren der Mathematischen Wissenschaften 290, Springer Verlag, 1988.

[Fa]   J.D. Fay, *Theta functions on Riemann surfaces*, Lecture Notes in Mathematics 352, Springer Verlag, 1973.

[Fo]   O. Foda, *SU(2) parametrization of Baxter's model*, J. of Physics, **A23**(1990), L739-L745.

[JMT]   M. Jimbo, T. Miwa and A. Tsuchiya (eds.), *Integrable systems in quantum field theory and statistical mechanics*, Advanced Studies in Pure Mathematics 19, Academic Press, 1989.

[KP]   V. G. Kac & D. H. Peterson, *Infinite-dimensional Lie algebras, theta functions and modular forms*, Adv. in Math., **53**(1984), 125–264.

[KRS]   P. P. Kulish, N. Yu. Reshetikhin, E.K. Sklyanin, *Yang-Baxter equation and representation theory, I*, Letters Math. Phys., **5**(1981), 393–403.

[M]   D. Mumford, *Tata Lectures on Theta, I*, Progress in Math. 28, Birkhäuser, Boston, 1983.

[OH]   H.C. Öttinger & J. Honerkamp, *Note on the Yang-Baxter equations for generalized Baxter models*, Phys. Letters, **A88**(1982), 339–343.

[Serre]   J.-P. Serre, *A Course in Arithmetic*, Graduate Text in Math. 7, Springer Verlag, 1973.

[Sch]   B. Schoeneberg, *Elliptic Modular Functions*, Springer Verlag, Berlin, 1974.

[T]   C.A. Tracy, *Complete Integrability in Statistical Mechanics and the Yang-Baxter Equations*, Physica, **14D**(1985), 253–264.

[TF]   L.A. Takhtadzhan & L. D. Faddeev, *The quantum method of the inverse problem nd the Heisenberg XYZ model*, Russian Math. Surveys 34, **5**(1979), 11–68.

[V]   H.J. de Vega, *Yang-Baxter algebras, conformal invariant models and quantum groups*, pp. 567–640 in: Integrable systems in quantum field theory and statistical mechanics (eds.: M. Jimbo, T, Miwa, A. Tsuchiya), Advanced Studies in Pure Math. 19, Academic Press, 1989.

[Z1]   A.B. Zamolodchikov, *Exact two-particle S-matrix of quantum solitons of the sine-Gordon model*, JETP Letters, **25**(1977), 468-471.

[Z2]   A.B. Zamolodchikov & Al. B. Zamolodchikov, *Relativistic factorized S-matrix in two dimensions having O(N) isotopic symmetry*, Nuclear Phys., **B133**(1978), 525–535.

[Z3]   A.B. Zamolodchikov & Al. B. Zamolodchikov, *Factorized S-matrices in two dimensions as the exact solutions of certain relativistic quantum field theory models*, Ann. Phys., **120**(1979), 253–291.

Computational Aspects of Lie Group Representations and Related Topics   65
Proceedings of the 1990 Computational Algebra Seminar
pp. 65–88 in CWI Tract 84 (1991)

The Robinson-Schensted and

Schützenberger algorithms

and interpretations

Marc A. A. van Leeuwen

Rijksuniversiteit Utrecht

Budapestlaan 6

Utrecht

The Netherlands

0. Introduction

The subject of this paper has a history that is somewhat unusual within the field of computational mathematics. Instead of the usual order of events that an algorithm is devised in order to answer effectively a problem arising in some field of mathematics, we have here the case of a pair of well known combinatorial algorithms, whose properties have been extensively studied for their own sake, which have been found to occur as solutions of certain mathematical questions of relatively recent study. The algorithms referred to are an algorithm first formulated by G. de B. Robinson in 1938 [Rob], and independently rediscovered in 1961 by C. Schensted [Sche], which is now known as the Robinson-Schensted algorithm, and a related algorithm formulated by M. P. Schützenberger in 1963 [Schü1], which we shall call the Schützenberger algorithm. The related mathematical questions have arisen in the study of the unipotent variety of the general linear group GL_n, and the relationship with the Robinson-Schensted algorithm was found by R. Steinberg in 1976 [Stb1]; statement and proof of this relationship can be found in [Spa II 9.8] and [Stb2].

In the latter article part of the material of the present paper is treated in a
very succinct form. The relationship with the Schützenberger algorithm does
not appear to have been noted before, although it is quite natural in view of
the known combinatorial relation to the Robinson-Schensted algorithm. Because of the historic order of discovery, we shall consider the mathematical
questions involved, and their solutions, as 'interpretations' of the indicated algorithms. Although they are certainly not the only problems that are related to
the Robinson-Schensted algorithm, we believe the interpretations to be rather
fundamental, since they actually give more insight into the combinatorial properties of the algorithms.

Our paper is organised into two sections, the first giving the combinatorial
definitions and properties (without proofs) of the algorithms, the second section
giving the indicated interpretations with proofs, which effectively also proves
the combinatorial properties stated in the first section.

1. The Robinson-Schensted and Schützenberger algorithms

In this section we present the algorithms under consideration in a purely
combinatorial fashion. First, the combinatorial concepts such as partitions,
Young diagrams and Young tableaux are introduced, in terms of which the
algorithms operate. Next the Robinson-Schensted is given, which establishes a
bijection between pairs (P, Q) of Young tableaux of equal shape on one hand,
and permutations on the other hand. From the representation theory (over $\mathbf{C}$)
of the group S_n of permutations of n symbols it is known that its irreducible representations are parametrised by partitions of n, and for such a partition λ the
corresponding representation has a dimension equal to the number of Young
tableaux of shape λ. Therefore the bijective correspondence defined by the
Robinson-Schensted algorithm can be considered as a combinatorial realisation
in this particular case of the general fact that the sum of squares of the dimensions of the irreducible representations of a finite group equals the order of
the group. Finally we introduce the Schützenberger algorithm, which defines
a shape preserving bijection from the set of Young tableaux to itself. The correspondences defined by these two algorithms are related in many ways: their
definitions are quite similar, they can be characterised by simple recurrence
relations, for both an identity can be proved that exhibits a symmetry which
is not at all obvious from the definition, and most importantly, there is an
identity that interrelates them in a very strong way.

1.1. Partitions and tableaux.

In this subsection we introduce some combinatorial concepts for later use.

A *partition* λ of some $n \in \mathbf{N}$ is a weakly decreasing sequence $\lambda_1 \geq \lambda_2 \geq \cdots$
of natural numbers, that ends with zeros, and whose sum $|\lambda| = \sum_i \lambda_i$ equals n;
the terms λ_i of this sequence are called the *parts* of the partition. Although
conceptually partitions are infinite sequences, the trailing zeros are usually
suppressed, so we write $\lambda = (\lambda_1, \ldots, \lambda_m)$ if $\lambda_i = 0$ for $i > m$. We denote by $\mathcal{P}_n$
the (obviously finite) set of all partitions of n, and by $\mathcal{P}$ the union of all $\mathcal{P}_n$ for
$n \in \mathbf{N}$.

We associate to each $\lambda \in \mathcal{P}_n$ an n-element subset of $\mathbf{N}_{>0} \times \mathbf{N}_{>0}$, namely its *Young diagram* $Y(\lambda)$, defined by $(i, j) \in Y(\lambda) \iff j \leq \lambda_i$. The elements of a Young diagram will be called its *squares*, and we may correspondingly depict the Young diagram: the square (i, j) will be drawn in row i and in column j; e.g., for $\lambda = (6, 4, 4, 2, 1) \in \mathcal{P}_{17}$ we have

$$Y(\lambda) = \quad$$ 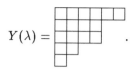 $$.$$

Clearly any partition $\lambda \in \mathcal{P}$ is completely determined by $Y(\lambda)$, and it is often convenient to mentally identify the two; in this spirit we shall use certain set theoretical notation for partitions, which is defined by passing to their Young diagrams, e.g., $\lambda \subseteq \mu$ for $\lambda, \mu \in \mathcal{P}$ means $Y(\lambda) \subseteq Y(\mu)$. The set $\mathbf{N}_{>0} \times \mathbf{N}_{>0}$ has a natural partial ordering given by $(i, j) \leq (i', j')$ whenever $i \leq i'$ and $j \leq j'$. A finite subset S of $\mathbf{N}_{>0} \times \mathbf{N}_{>0}$ is a Young diagram if and only if for any square $s \in S$ we also have $s' \in S$ for all $s' \leq s$. From this characterisation it is clear that the set of all Young diagrams is closed under transposition of all of their squares (written $(i, j)^t = (j, i)$), hence we have an involution on each $\mathcal{P}_n$ (also called transposition and written $\lambda \mapsto \lambda^t$) defined by $Y(\lambda^t) = Y(\lambda)^t$. The parts of λ^t can be interpreted as the column lengths of $Y(\lambda)$, from which we get $\lambda_j^t = \#\{ i \mid \lambda_i \geq j \}$ (the operator '#' denotes the number of elements of a finite set).

When $\mu \subseteq \lambda$ and $|\mu| = |\lambda| - 1$, the difference $Y(\lambda) - Y(\mu)$ consists of a single square, which lies both at the end of a row and of a column of $Y(\lambda)$, while it lies one position beyond both the end of a row and of a column of $Y(\mu)$. We call such a square a *corner* of λ, and a *cocorner* of μ (so for $\lambda = (6, 4, 4, 2, 1)$ whose diagram is displayed above, we have as corners $(1, 6)$, $(3, 4)$, $(4, 2)$, and $(5, 1)$, and as cocorners $(1, 7)$, $(2, 5)$, $(4, 3)$, $(5, 2)$, and $(6, 1)$). There is a corner in column j of $Y(\lambda)$ if and only if j occurs as a non-zero part of λ, while there is a cocorner in column j if and only if $j - 1$ occurs as a part of λ (here we allow zero); consequently, the number of cocorners exceeds that of the corners by 1.

The principal reason for referring to the elements of a Young diagram $Y(\lambda)$ as squares (rather than as points), is that it allows one to represent maps $f: Y(\lambda) \to \mathbf{N}$ by filling each square $s \in Y(\lambda)$ with the number $f(s)$. We shall call such a filled Young diagram a *Young tableau* (or simply a tableau) of shape λ if it satisfies the following two conditions*: all numbers are distinct, and they increase along each row and column. This is equivalent to requiring that the map $f: Y(\lambda) \to \mathbf{N}$ be injective and monotonous (a morphism of partially ordered sets). If T is a Young tableau of shape λ we write $\lambda = \operatorname{sh} T$. Any tableau T' that can be obtained from T by renumbering the entries in an order

---

* The term Young tableau is used by different authors for quite different classes of filled Young diagrams, and several adjectives are used to indicate certain subclasses, in particular *standard*; unfortunately its meaning is not standard. Our use of the term is quite common in the literature about the Robinson-Schensted algorithm.

preserving way is called similar to T (written $T' \sim T$) (for the corresponding maps $f, f' : Y(\lambda) \to \mathbf{N}$ this means $f' = g \circ f$ for some monotonous $g : \mathbf{N} \to \mathbf{N}$), and we call T *normalised* if its set of entries (i.e., Im f) equals $\{1, 2, \ldots, |\lambda|\}$. Clearly '$\sim$' is an equivalence relation, and every equivalence class contains a unique normalised element; let $\mathcal{T}_\lambda$ denote the set of normalised Young tableaux of shape λ.

Another way to characterise tableaux among the filled Young diagrams is by the following recursive predicate P. Let T consist of a diagram $Y(\lambda)$ filled with numbers, then $P(T)$ holds if either $\lambda = (0)$ or the highest occurring entry appears in a unique square s, which is a corner of λ, and the restriction T' of T to $Y(\lambda) - \{s\}$ satisfies $P(T')$. An elementary verification shows that indeed $P(T)$ holds if and only if T is a tableau. We introduce operators $\lceil \cdot \rceil$ and $\downarrow$ on non-empty tableaux, by defining $\lceil T \rceil$ as the corner of sh T containing the highest entry of T, and $T^\downarrow$ as the tableau obtained by removing that square from T (so in the above definition of P we have $s = \lceil T \rceil$ and $T' = T^\downarrow$). Repeatedly applying the operator $\downarrow$ to T until reaching the empty tableau, we obtain a sequence of tableaux whose shapes form a decreasing chain

$$\mathrm{ch}\, T \stackrel{\mathrm{def}}{=} \left(\mathrm{sh}\, T \supset \mathrm{sh}\, T^\downarrow \supset \mathrm{sh}\, T^{\downarrow\downarrow} \supset \cdots \supset (0)\right) \tag{1}$$

in $\mathcal{P}$. Conversely, from any chain $\lambda \supset \lambda' \supset \lambda'' \supset \cdots \supset (0)$ in $\mathcal{P}$ with $|\lambda^{(i)}| = n - i$ for all i, a tableau $T \in \mathcal{T}_\lambda$ may be constructed for which the sequence equals ch T, namely by assigning the number $|\lambda|$ to the unique square in $Y(\lambda) - Y(\lambda')$, and filling the squares of $Y(\lambda')$ in the same way according to the chain $\lambda' \supset \lambda'' \supset \cdots \supset (0)$. It is also clear that for an arbitrary tableau T, this construction applied to ch T will yield the normalised tableau similar to T. To illustrate the correspondence, consider the tableaux

$$T = \begin{array}{|c|c|c|}\hline 3 & 6 & 11 \\\hline 5 & 8 \\\cline{1-2} 7 \\\cline{1-1} 19 \\\cline{1-1}\end{array} \quad \sim \quad T' = \begin{array}{|c|c|c|}\hline 1 & 3 & 6 \\\hline 2 & 5 \\\cline{1-2} 4 \\\cline{1-1} 7 \\\cline{1-1}\end{array} \in \mathcal{T}_{(3,2,1,1)},$$

both of which correspond to the chain

$$\mathrm{ch}\, T = \mathrm{ch}\, T' = \left(\;\square\square\square \supset \square\square\square \supset \square\square \supset \square\square \supset \square\square \supset \square\square \supset \square \supset \emptyset\;\right).$$

So $\mathcal{T}_\lambda$ corresponds bijectively to the set of maximal strictly decreasing chains in $\mathcal{P}$ that start in λ.

1.2. The Robinson-Schensted algorithm.

We shall now define the Robinson-Schensted correspondence in its traditional form. It should be noted that in the literature there exist many different definitions of this correspondence, often seemingly without much resemblance, except that they all are of an algorithmic nature. Indeed, the oldest definition, in a paper by Robinson [Rob, §5] (where it appears as a special case of a rather obscurely defined construction used in a proof of the Littlewood-Richardson rule) is so unlike the algorithm given independently by Schensted almost a quarter century later [Sche], that it was not recognised for quite a few years that two algorithms had been defined giving rise to essentially the same correspondence. Schensted's definition, which we shall reproduce, may be considered to be the basic one since it is doubtlessly the easiest one to understand and to perform by hand.

The algorithm is based on a procedure to insert a new number into a Young tableau, displacing certain entries and eventually leading to a tableau with one square more than the original one. More precisely, there is a pair of mutually inverse procedures that convert into each other the following sets of data: on one hand a tableau P and a number m not occurring as entry of P, and on the other hand a non-empty tableau T and a specified corner s of sh T. The procedures are such that the following always holds: the set of entries of T is that of P together with the number m, and the shape of P is that of T with the corner s removed.

Given a tableau P and a number m, the insertion procedure I computes the pair $(T, s) = I(P, m)$ as follows. The first step is to insert m into the first row of P, where it either replaces the smallest entry larger than m, or, if no such entry exists, it is simply appended at the end of the row, and the procedure stops. Then, in case a number has been replaced, the following (similar) step is repeated until it tells you to stop: the entry replaced by another in the previous step is inserted into the row succeeding its original row, where it either replaces the smallest entry larger than itself, or, if no such entry exists, it is appended at the end of that row and the procedure stops. If an empty row is encountered during this process, a one-square row is created and the procedure stops, so termination is guaranteed in all cases; the tableau then obtained is T, while the square occupied in the last step is the corner s.

The inverse procedure E extracts a number from a tableau T, clearing a specified corner s, and yielding $(P, m) = E(T, s)$ as follows. The first step is to remove the square s and the number it contains from T, then repeat the following step until it tells you to stop: if the number removed or replaced in the previous step was in the first row then m is that number, P is the current tableau, and the procedure stops; otherwise the number is moved to the row preceding its original row, where it replaces the largest entry smaller than itself (such an entry exists, since the number originally directly above it is certainly smaller). A more formal and elaborate description of these algorithms can be found in the excellent exposition [Kn2].

Although we have yet to show that after each of these procedures has acted the tableau properties still hold, it can be verified immediately that the two procedures are inverses of each other in the sense that the effect of one can be undone by applying the other (even if the intermediate array of numbers were no tableau). We illustrate the rules by an example that involves four steps. We show the intermediate stages of the procedure I; for an example of the procedure E, read from right to left.

$m = 7, P =$

2	5	6	8
3	10	12	
9	13	15	

2	5	6	7
3	10	12	
9	13	15	

2	5	6	7
3	8	12	
9	13	15	

2	5	6	7
3	8	12	
9	10	15	

2	5	6	7
3	8	12	
9	10	15	
13			

$= T, s = (4, 1)$

At each stage except the rightmost there is one number missing: this is the entry that has been superseded but not yet inserted into another row.

Before we prove that the arrays of numbers returned by the procedures will always be tableaux, provided that the input is as specified, we establish a recurrence relation that the results of these procedures satisfy. We compare the computation of $I(P, m)$ with that of $I(P^{\downarrow}, m)$, under the assumption that the highest entry h of P exceeds m. The presence of h can only affect the insertion steps if at some point it is the *only* entry in its row that exceeds a number being inserted into that row. If this occurs then the next step will be the final one of the computation of $I(P, m)$ (since h can replace no other element) while in absence of h (as in the computation of $I(P^{\downarrow}, m)$) the insertion procedure already terminates without this last step. Therefore if T is the result of inserting h into P, then inserting h into $P^{\downarrow}$ will yield $T^{\downarrow}$. More formally, we may write

$$\text{if } I(P, m) = (T, s) \text{ then } I(P^{\downarrow}, m) = (T^{\downarrow}, s') \text{ for some square } s'. \qquad (2)$$

The relation between s and s' can be expressed as follows. In the first place we must have

$$\{s, \lceil P \rceil\} = \{s', \lceil T \rceil\} \qquad (3)$$

because both sets are equal to $Y(\mathrm{sh}\, T) - Y(\mathrm{sh}\, P^{\downarrow})$; in case $s' \neq \lceil P \rceil$ this already implies that $s = s'$ and $\lceil T \rceil = \lceil P \rceil$, which is in agreement with the case that h is not displaced during the insertion. The remaining case that h is displaced is fixed by the additional condition

$$\text{if } s' = \lceil P \rceil \text{ then } s \text{ lies one row below } s'. \qquad (4)$$

For $E(T, s)$ we get a recurrence by replacing (2) by the equivalent

$$\text{if } E(T, s) = (P, m) \text{ then } E(T^{\downarrow}, s') = (P^{\downarrow}, m) \text{ for some square } s', \qquad (5)$$

where again s and s' are related by (3) and (4), although in this case it is more natural to replace the condition $s' = \lceil P \rceil$ in (4) by $s = \lceil T \rceil$, which is equivalent by (3). Recall that for (2) we excluded the case that m exceeds all entries in P; we must correspondingly exclude in (5) the case that $s = \lceil T \rceil$ and this square lies in the first row.

Now we prove that the insertion procedure preserves the tableau properties, i.e., that if P is a tableau and $(T, s) = I(P, m)$, then T is also a tableau.
First consider the set of squares that are occupied by numbers during the insertion process; this changes only in the last step. Since the number appended to
some row in the last step is higher than all other entries in that row, it cannot
have been displaced from a square directly above any of them, which excludes
the possibility that this row has become longer than its predecessor; therefore
the shape will remain a Young diagram. Now by the recursive characterisation
of tableaux in the previous subsection, to prove that T is a tableau it remains
to show that $T^{\downarrow}$ is a tableau. By our remarks above this follows by a trivial
induction, for if m exceeds all entries of P then $T^{\downarrow} = P$, which is a tableau by
assumption, while otherwise $T^{\downarrow}$ may be obtained by inserting m into $P^{\downarrow}$, and
therefore is a tableau by induction. The proof for the extraction procedure is
easier still, since the shape will remain a diagram simply because s is required
to be a corner of sh T. Then P is a tableau because either $P = T^{\downarrow}$ (in the
case excluded above) or $P^{\downarrow}$ can be obtained by extraction from $T^{\downarrow}$, hence is a
tableau by induction.

Having verified the proper behaviour of the auxiliary procedures, we can
now define the full Robinson-Schensted algorithm. This establishes a bijection
between the group S_n of permutations and the set $\bigcup_{\lambda \in \mathcal{P}_n} \mathcal{T}_\lambda \times \mathcal{T}_\lambda$ of pairs (P, Q)
of normalised tableaux with sh $P = $ sh $Q \in \mathcal{P}_n$. Given a permutation $\sigma \in S_n$,
represented as a sequence $(\sigma_1, \ldots, \sigma_n)$ of distinct numbers (so σ maps $i \mapsto \sigma_i$),
we build up the pair (P, Q) in n stages as follows. Let (P_{i-1}, Q_{i-1}) be the
pair at the beginning of stage i (we put $P_0 = Q_0$ equal to the empty tableau),
and compute $(P_i, s) = I(P_{i-1}, \sigma_i)$; then Q_i is obtained from Q_{i-1} by adding
the number i in the position of square s. Since the number added to Q_{i-1} is
the highest until then, it is clear that each Q_i is a (normalised) tableau; the
set of entries of P_i is $\{\sigma_1, \ldots, \sigma_i\}$, so the last one P_n is a normalised tableau.
Also, the shapes of the two tableaux will be the same after each stage, in
particular it holds for $(P, Q) = (P_n, Q_n)$, so that P and Q are as required. Like
the auxiliary procedures, this algorithm too can be directly reversed: starting
with $(P_n, Q_n) = (P, Q)$ repeatedly transform (P_i, Q_i) into (P_{i-1}, Q_{i-1}) (for $i =
n, \ldots, 2, 1$), meanwhile determining the numbers $p_n, \ldots, p_1$, namely $Q_{i-1} = Q_i^{\downarrow}$
and $(P_{i-1}, \sigma_i) = E(P_i, \lceil Q_i \rceil)$. We illustrate the algorithm by an example; again
one may read from right to left for an example of the inverse process.

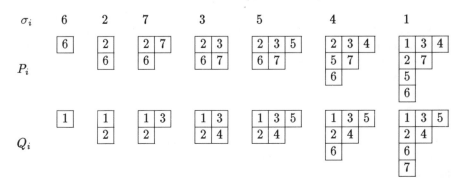

If by these bijections the permutation $\sigma \in S_n$ corresponds to the pair of normalised tableaux (P, Q), we write $\sigma = R(P, Q)$ and $(P, Q) = R^{-1}(\sigma)$ (so we let R stand for the function defined using the extraction algorithm, mainly because functions with multiple arguments are notationally more convenient than those with multiple results). The procedures I and E have obvious transposed counterparts I^t and E^t, whose definition can be obtained by replacing all occurrences of the word 'row' by 'column'. These transposed procedures can be used to define another bijection $R^t \colon \bigcup_{\lambda \in \mathcal{P}} T_\lambda \times T_\lambda \xrightarrow{\sim} S_n$ in exactly the same way that R is defined; it obviously satisfies $R^t(P, Q) = R(P^t, Q^t)$.

We now turn to the first of the "remarkable properties" announced above. Recall that the set S_n of permutations forms a group, so its elements can be inverted; in terms of sequences of numbers, the inverse σ^{-1} of $\sigma = (\sigma_1, \ldots, \sigma_n)$ is the sequence $(\sigma^{-1}{}_1, \ldots, \sigma^{-1}{}_n)$ whose term $\sigma^{-1}{}_i$ is the unique index j such that $\sigma_j = i$.

1.2.1. Theorem For all $(P, Q) \in \bigcup_\lambda T_\lambda \times T_\lambda$

$$R(Q, P) = R(P, Q)^{-1}.$$

In view of the asymmetry between P and Q in the definition of R, this is unexpected indeed. This theorem was first stated (without proof) in [Rob], and first proved in [Schü1]. A better proof (and of a slightly more general statement) can be found in [Kn1] while an elementary proof may be given using the recursion relation for E given above; however, the theorem will also follow from the interpretation given in the second section of this paper.

We defer the statement of other properties of the Robinson-Schensted correspondence to the next subsection, as they require other definitions not yet introduced. However, to give some indication, we mention a fact that will follow from a stronger statement given later. Let I_m denote the operation of inserting a number m into a tableau P not containing it, where only the tableau yielded is considered (so if $I(P, m) = (T, s)$ then $T = I_m(P)$); also let I_m^t be its transposed counterpart. Then every I_m commutes with every $I_{m'}^t$, i.e., for $m \neq m'$ and every tableau P not containing m or m' we have $I_m(I_{m'}^t(P)) = I_{m'}^t(I_m(P))$. Since moreover the operations I_m and I_m^t are interchangeable when applied to the empty tableau, we have that reversing the order of the sequence of numbers of a permutation has the effect that the left tableau ('P') obtained by applying R^{-1} will be the transpose of the original one (but nothing is said about the right tableau). Historically, it is this fact that led to the formulation of the Schützenberger algorithm described in the next subsection.

We close this subsection by describing a convenient method of performing the Robinson-Schensted algorithm, especially useful for computer programming. It is an iterative procedure, but it is based on the recursion relations for I and E. For this purpose tableaux are represented not by 2-dimensional arrays, but rather by linear ones: the i-th entry of the array describes the position of the square whose entry is i (or has a special value if no such square exists). A very convenient circumstance is that it is sufficient to record the row numbers of the squares, since the tableau property guarantees that the

c-th occurrence from left to right of some number r corresponds to a square in column c of row r. In fact the array of numbers must satisfy an extra condition in order to denote a tableau, namely, if $r > 1$ then the c-th occurrence of $r - 1$ must precede the c-th occurrence of r (for all applicable r, c). The number 0 can be used to denote an absent square. We call such an array of numbers a *row-encoded tableau*; in the literature they are known under the hardly informative names 'lattice permutations' and '*mots de Yamanouchi*'.

The computation of $(T, s) = I(P, m)$ is performed by modifying a row-encoded tableau P with entries $P[i]$ for $1 \leq i \leq n$, into the row-encoded-tableau T. This is done by making an increasingly large subtableau correspond to T rather than to P; an index i indicates up to which number the entries have been incorporated, and a variable r records the row number of the square s by which the shape of the subtableau has been extended due to the insertion. The according to (2) all that is needed when the index i is increased by 1 is to possibly update the values of $P[i]$ and r. By (3) nothing needs to be done if $P[i] \neq r$, and if $P[i] = r$ then by (4) both values should be increased by 1. Therefore, it suffices to put $r := 0$, and then repeat the following for $i = m, \ldots, n$ in that order: if $P[i] = r$ then increase both $P[i]$ and r by 1 (otherwise do nothing). Note that the condition $P[i] = r$ is satisfied the first time, since we assume that m does not occur in P initially; the final value of r represents the row of the square s. The complete computation of $R^{-1}(\sigma)$ for $\sigma \in S_n$ consists of initialising P to all zeros and then performing the above loop successively for $m = \sigma_1, \ldots, \sigma_n$ in that order, each time inserting the final value of r into the next position of a row-encoded tableau Q. The procedure can be reversed in an obvious way (but the number of iterations of the inner loop can not be predicted in this case: it stops when r becomes 0, which will not fail to happen if we start with proper values for P and Q). In the limit of huge n these procedures are theoretically less efficient on the average than a straightforward 2-dimensional approach, but their extreme simplicity probably makes them more favourable in most practical situations.

1.3. The Schützenberger algorithm.

In this subsection we introduce an algorithm due to Schützenberger that is intimately related to the Robinson-Schensted algorithm. The Schützenberger algorithm defines a shape preserving transformation of normalised tableaux, i.e., for each $\lambda \in \mathcal{P}$ it defines a map $S: \mathcal{T}_\lambda \to \mathcal{T}_\lambda$. Like the Robinson-Schensted algorithm, it is based on the repeated application of a basic procedure that modifies a given tableau in a specific manner. In the current case we shall call this the "deflation" procedure D, since it starts by emptying the square in the upper left-hand corner, and the proceeds to rearrange the remaining squares to form a proper tableau. Like the other procedures we have seen, D can be reversed step by step, giving rise to an "inflation" procedure D^{-1}. More precisely, these procedures convert into each other the following sets of data: on one hand a non-empty tableau P, and on the other hand a tableau T, a specified cocorner s of sh T, and a number m. These are such that sh P is obtained by extending sh T with s, and the entries of T are those of P with the smallest entry m left out.

Given a tableau P, the deflation procedure computes $(T, s, m) = D(P)$ as follows. The first step is to put m equal to the smallest entry of P, and remove that entry, leaving an empty square in position $(1, 1)$. Then the following step is repeated until the empty square is a corner of the shape sh P of the original tableau: move into the empty square the smaller one of the entries located directly to the right of and below it (if only one of these positions contains an entry, move that entry). Because the empty square moves down or to the right in each step, termination is evidently guaranteed; s is defined to be the final position of the empty square, and T consists of the remaining non-empty squares. The latter is indeed a tableau, since at each stage of the process the entries of the non-empty squares remain increasing along each row and column. In fact, when there are entries both to the right and below the empty square, the choice to move the smaller one is dictated by the tableau property.* By the same consideration it is also clear that each intermediate state of the tableau determines the previous position of the empty square, and hence the previous state: this position is directly to the left of or above the empty square, whichever contains the *larger* entry. Consequently, given T, s, and m the deflation procedure can be run in reverse to determine P, and this defines D^{-1}. We demonstrate these procedures by an example:

$$P = \begin{array}{|c|c|c|c|}\hline 1&2&5&10\\\hline 3&4&9\\\cline{1-3} 6&7&11\\\cline{1-3} 8\\\cline{1-1}\end{array} \quad \begin{array}{|c|c|c|}\hline 2&5&10\\\hline 3&4&9\\\hline 6&7&11\\\hline 8\\\cline{1-1}\end{array} \quad \begin{array}{cccc} 2&&5&10\\ 3&4&9\\ 6&7&11\\ 8 \end{array} \quad \begin{array}{|c|c|c|c|}\hline 2&4&5&10\\\hline 3&&9\\ 6&7&11\\ 8 \end{array} \quad \begin{array}{|c|c|c|c|}\hline 2&4&5&10\\\hline 3&7&9\\ 6&&11\\ 8 \end{array}$$

$$\begin{array}{|c|c|c|c|}\hline 2&4&5&10\\\hline 3&7&9\\ 6&11\\ 8 \end{array} \quad \text{so that we have} \quad T = \begin{array}{|c|c|c|c|}\hline 2&4&5&10\\\hline 3&7&9\\ 6&11\\ 8 \end{array}, \; s = (2,2), \; m = 1.$$

There are recursion relations for D and D^{-1} similar to those for I and E. For any tableau P with at least two squares we compare the computation of $D(P)$ with that of $D(P^{\downarrow})$. Since the highest entry h of P lies at some corner of sh P, it can only be moved in the final step; like in the case of I we conclude that if applying D to P yields a tableau T, then applying D to $P^{\downarrow}$ will yield $T^{\downarrow}$. This may be formalised as

$$\text{if } D(P) = (T, s, m) \text{ then } D(P^{\downarrow}) = (T^{\downarrow}, s', m) \text{ for some square } s'. \quad (6)$$

As in the case of I the relation between s and s' is expressed by a pair of requirements, of which the first is

$$\{s, \lceil T \rceil\} = \{s', \lceil P \rceil\} \quad (7)$$

---

* The rule stating which square to displace during the insertion procedure of the Robinson-Schensted algorithm cannot be characterised in such a way, since displacing the last *smaller* entry might equally well preserve the tableau property; the definition given in [Schü1] of that insertion procedure is therefore incorrect.

since both sets are equal to $Y(\operatorname{sh} P) - Y(\operatorname{sh} T^{\downarrow})$. For the second requirement we use the notation $x \parallel y$ to express the fact that the squares x and y are adjacent, either horizontally or vertically; to be precise $x \parallel (r,c)$ holds if either $x = (r-1,c)$ or $x = (r,c-1)$ (it is not necessary to include the case that x lies to the right or below y). Then if $s' \parallel \lceil P \rceil$ no additional condition is needed, since $s = \lceil P \rceil$ is forced because s' is no corner of $\operatorname{sh} P$. It therefore suffices to require

$$\text{if } s' \nparallel \lceil P \rceil \text{ then } s = s'. \tag{8}$$

The recurrence relation for D^{-1} is obtained by taking

$$\text{if } D^{-1}(T, s, m) = P \text{ then } D^{-1}(T^{\downarrow}, s', m) = P^{\downarrow} \text{ for some square } s', \tag{9}$$

where again s and s' are related by (7) and (8), and T should not be empty.

As is the case for the Robinson-Schensted algorithm, the full Schützenberger algorithm essentially consists of repetition of the basic procedure. To compute $S(P)$ for $P \in T_{\lambda}$ with $\lambda \in P_n$, put $P_0 = P$, and for $i = 1, \ldots, n$ compute $(P_i, s_i, m_i) = D(P_{i-1})$; we will have $m_i = i$ and P_n will be the empty tableau. The sequence of shapes $\lambda = \operatorname{sh} P_0 \supset \operatorname{sh} P_1 \supset \cdots \supset \emptyset$ equals $\operatorname{ch} P^*$ for a unique $P^* \in T_{\lambda}$, and we define $S(P) = P^*$. Note that while the smallest entries of P are removed first, it is the largest entries of P^* whose position is determined first, as we have $\lceil P^* \rceil = s_1$, $\lceil P^{*\downarrow} \rceil = s_2$ etcetera. The values m_i, being entirely predictable, play no role whatsoever; they were only introduced to make the procedure D fully invertible. In fact the concrete values of the entries are more a nuisance than that they are of any help for this procedure, as it essentially deals with chains of partitions only. The inverse algorithm S^{-1} of S is obviously the following: set P_n equal to the empty tableau, and successively compute $P_{i-1} = D^{-1}(P_i, P^*[n+1-i], i)$ for $i = n, \ldots, 1$, where $P^*[j]$ denotes the square with entry j in P^*; then $S^{-1}(P^*) = P_0$. Again we give an example; here we display the successive stages $P = P_0, P_1, P_2, \ldots,$ and meanwhile the entries of P^* that are determined up to this point. Reading from right to left for the inverse algorithm, those entries of P^* that have already served their purpose are erased.

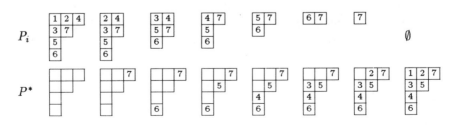

It is obvious from the definition that S commutes with transposition: $S(P^t) = S(P)^t$; however, like the Robinson-Schensted algorithm, it also has an unexpected symmetry, which is expressed by the following

1.3.1. Theorem   *The Schützenberger algorithm S defines an involution, i.e.,*

$$S(T) = S^{-1}(T)$$

for all $T \in \bigcup_\lambda \mathcal{T}_\lambda$.

This fact was first stated and proved by Schützenberger in [Schü1 §5], but the proof is indirect, being based on the relation of the Schützenberger algorithm with the Robinson-Schensted algorithm that we shall formulate below. We do not now of any published direct proof of this fact, although such a proof can be given on the basis of the recursion relations for D and D^{-1}. We shall see that the fact also comes about quite naturally in our interpretation of S. The most important combinatorial fact about the Robinson-Schensted and Schützenberger algorithms that we shall discuss is the interrelation, expressed by the following far reaching

1.3.2. Theorem   *Let $\lambda \in \mathcal{P}_n$ and $P, Q \in \mathcal{T}_\lambda$, and let $\sigma \in S_n$ be determined by*

$$\sigma = R(P, Q).$$

Then we also have

$$\tilde{w}\sigma = R^t(S(P), Q) \tag{10}$$
$$\sigma\tilde{w} = R^t(P, S(Q)) \tag{11}$$
$$\tilde{w}\sigma\tilde{w} = R(S(P), S(Q)) \tag{12}$$

where $\tilde{w} \in S_n$ is the "order reversing" permutation given by $\tilde{w}_i = n + 1 - i$.

The permutation $\sigma\tilde{w}$ has as sequence of numbers the reverse of that of σ, so (11) generalises our earlier statement that this reversal of terms leads to transposition of the left tableau. That statement about the left tableau was proved by Schensted [Sche Lemma 7], while the remainder of the identity is proved in [Schü1 §5]; from (11) one immediately deduces 1.3.1, and using 1.2.1 one also obtains (10) and (12). The current formulation of the theorem (more or less) is due to D. E. Knuth, and can be found in [Kn2 Theorem D]. He expresses the remarkable character of these facts as follows (p. 60)

> "The reader is urged to try out these processes on some simple examples. The unusual nature of these coincidences might lead us to suspect that some sort of witchcraft is operating behind the scenes! No simple explanation for these phenomena is yet known; there seems to be no obvious way to prove even that case $\{(12)\}$ corresponds to tableaux having the same *shape* as P and Q."

There are more interesting properties of these algorithms, such as the following (due to Schensted): the first part of the partition $\text{sh}\,P = \text{sh}\,Q$ is equal to the length of a maximal increasing sequence of numbers obtainable by deleting 0 or more terms from $(\sigma_1, \ldots, \sigma_n)$. We do not go into any such properties here, which generally interpret only partial information about the tableaux, although it may be interesting to reconsider them in the light of the geometric interpretations to be given in the next section. We conclude this first section with remarking that there exists an apparently completely different approach to the Robinson-Schensted and Schützenberger algorithms, which is followed in [Schü2]. It is based on a generalised version of the deflation procedure that is *non-deterministic*, i.e., there is an element of choice in the prescription of the actions to be performed. In this approach most of the results we mentioned become almost trivial, but the hard part is to prove that the correspondences are well defined, namely that the final outcome is not affected by any of the choices made. Although Schützenberger does not mention how his alternative definitions have come about, we deem it likely that this non-deterministic scheme could be deduced from the theorems given above, in combination with more obvious properties of the correspondences involved, such as that truncating the sequence of σ to an initial subsequence will imply truncation of the right ('Q') tableau to a subtableau.

2. Interpretations

The combinatorial facts of the previous section are quite remarkable, even if they can be proved in a fairly straightforward combinatorial manner. In this section we present a geometric construction, encountered in the study of the general linear group GL_n, in which partitions, Young tableaux and permutations have natural interpretations. The algorithms of the first section emerge in this setting as procedures for computing certain geometric correspondences. In this interpretation the combinatorial identities given above become quite natural.

More precisely stated, we have the following. Partitions of n parametrise unipotent conjugacy classes in GL_n, and for any unipotent u in the class parametrised by a partition λ, there is a corresponding subvariety $\mathcal{F}_u$ of the flag variety of GL_n, whose irreducible components are parametrised by normalised Young tableaux of shape λ. Also there is a concept of relative positions between elements of the flag variety, which associates to each pair of flags a permutation. Now the Schützenberger algorithm describes the effect of passing to the dual vector space on the set of irreducible components of $\mathcal{F}_u$, and the Robinson-Schensted algorithm computes the relative position between a pair of flags generically chosen in a specified pair of irreducible components of $\mathcal{F}_u$. The transpose Robinson-Schensted algorithm has a similar interpretation in case one of the irreducible components is specified in the ordinary way, and the other is given in terms of the dual flag variety; this provides an interpretation for theorem 1.3.2.

2.1. The group GL_n, unipotent elements.

Our intended interpretations of the Robinson-Schensted and Schützenberger algorithms involve certain geometric structures related to the general linear group GL_n over some field. As we shall be using the Zariski topology on algebraic varieties defined over this field, a natural choice for it is any algebraically closed field; however, all that matters is that such varieties have a well-defined dimension, such that the complement of any subvariety of codimension ≥ 1 is dense, and therefore the milder requirement that the field is infinite will suffice.

Let V be a vector space of dimension n, and view GL_n as the group of automorphisms of V. An element $u \in GL_n$ is called *unipotent* if all of its eigenvalues (over the algebraic closure of the ground field) all are 1, or equivalently if $\eta = u - \mathbf{1}$ is *nilpotent*, i.e., $\eta^n = 0$. By the theory of Jordan normal forms, V can then be decomposed into a direct sum of *Jordan blocks* for u, i.e., u-stable subspaces each of which admits a basis $x_1, \ldots, x_d$ (for varying d) such that $\eta(x_1) = 0$ and $\eta(x_i) = x_{i-1}$ for $1 < i \leq d$. This decomposition is generally not unique, but the multiset of dimensions of the blocks (i.e., disregarding order but counting multiplicities) is determined uniquely by u. Arranging these dimensions in weakly decreasing order, we obtain a partition of n, that we call the *Jordan type* of u, denoted $J(u)$.

Denote by $\mathbf{P}(V)$ the projective space of V; its elements are lines through the origin in V. For $l \in \mathbf{P}(V)$ the conditions $u[l] = l$, $\eta[l] \subseteq l$ and $\eta[l] = 0$ are equivalent (since η is nilpotent), so the set of fixed points of u in $\mathbf{P}(V)$ is $\mathbf{P}(\mathrm{Ker}\,\eta)$. For such fixed points l, there is a transformation $u_{[l]}$ induced by u in the quotient space V/l, and it is also unipotent; we also define $\eta_{[l]} = u_{[l]} - \mathbf{1}$ which is nilpotent. We have $J(u_{[l]}) \subset J(u)$ by the following argument. If $p \colon V \to V/l$ denotes the natural projection then we have by definition $\mathrm{Im}\,\eta_{[l]}^j = p[\mathrm{Im}\,\eta^j]$. Putting $\lambda = J(u)$ we have $\lambda_j^t = \dim(\mathrm{Im}\,\eta^{j-1}) - \dim(\mathrm{Im}\,\eta^j)$, as each Jordan block of dimension $\geq j$ contributes 1 to this number. Comparing this to the same formula for $\mu = J(u_{[l]})$, we find that $\mu_j^t = \lambda_j^t$ unless $l \in \mathbf{P}(\mathrm{Im}\,\eta^{j-1}) - \mathbf{P}(\mathrm{Im}\,\eta^j)$, in which case $\mu_j^t = \lambda_j^t - 1$. This establishes $\mu \subset \lambda$, and moreover determines the square by which $Y(\mu)$ differs from $Y(\lambda)$. Since by assumption $l \in \mathbf{P}(\mathrm{Ker}\,\eta)$, we are led to define for $j > 0$ subspaces $W_j = \mathrm{Im}\,\eta^{j-1} \cap \mathrm{Ker}\,\eta$ of V, and subvarieties $U_j = \mathbf{P}(W_j) - \mathbf{P}(W_{j+1})$ of the projective space $\mathbf{P}(V)$; then there is a unique j for which $l \in U_j$, and it is the column number of abovementioned square in $Y(\lambda) - Y(\mu)$. The centraliser Z_u in GL_n of u acts on each variety U_j, and using linear algebra it can be shown that these actions are transitive; therefore the non-empty sets among the U_j are in fact the orbits in $\mathbf{P}(\mathrm{Ker}\,\eta)$ under the action of Z_u. The number of these orbits is finite; in fact one easily shows that U_j is non-empty if and only if j occurs as a part of $J(u)$.

To determine for a hyperplane $H \subset V$ the Jordan type $J(u|_H)$, we may reason similarly using the dual vector space V^*. Since the decomposition of V into Jordan blocks induces a similar decomposition of V^*, we have $J(u^*) = J(u)$ for the (unipotent) transformation u^* induced by u in V^* (sometimes called the transpose of u); we define $W_j^* \subseteq V^*$ and $U_j^* \subseteq \mathbf{P}(V^*)$ analogously to W_j and U_j, but using u^* instead of u. Denote by H° the subspace of V^* of linear forms vanishing on H; since H is a hyperplane, $\dim H^\circ = 1$ and therefore $H^\circ \in \mathbf{P}(V^*)$. In the same way as above, the unique $j > 0$ for which $H^\circ \in U_j^*$ determines the square by which $Y(J(u|_H))$ differs from $Y(J(u))$.

2.2. Flags.

A (complete) **flag** f in V is a chain $f_0 \subset f_1 \subset \cdots \subset f_n = V$ of subspaces, where $\dim f_i = i$; the individual spaces f_i are called the *parts* of f. We define $\mathcal{F}$ to be the set of all such flags, called the *flag variety* of V, which is a (projective) variety on which GL_n acts; the subset of flags fixed by u is denoted

$\mathcal{F}_u$. There are (GL_n-equivariant) maps $\alpha\colon \mathcal{F} \to \mathbf{P}(V)$ and $\omega\colon \mathcal{F} \to \mathbf{P}(V^*)$ given by $\alpha\colon f \mapsto f_1$ and $\omega\colon f \mapsto f_{n-1}°$. For $l \in \mathbf{P}(V)$, each flag $f \in \alpha^{-1}[l]$ determines a flag $f^\downarrow$ in V/l by $f_i^\downarrow = p[f_{i+1}]$ for $0 \le i < n$, where as before $p\colon V \to V/l$ is the natural projection; it is easily seen that this defines an isomorphism between $\alpha^{-1}[l]$ and the flag variety of V/l. Similarly for each hyperplane $H \subset V$, the inverse image $\omega^{-1}[H°]$ is isomorphic to the flag variety of H, where the image f^- of $f \in \mathcal{F}$ is obtained by simply forgetting the largest part $f_n = V$ of f.

In the case of flags $f \in \mathcal{F}_u$ we have $l = \alpha(f) \in \mathbf{P}(\mathrm{Ker}\,\eta)$ and $f^\downarrow$ lies in the subvariety $\mathcal{F}_{u_{[l]}}$ of the flag variety of V/l. We may repeat this process for $f^\downarrow$ in place of f, and thus obtain a sequence of flags f, $f^\downarrow$, $f^{\downarrow\downarrow}$, ... in the spaces V, V/f_1, V/f_2, ..., which flags are fixed by the unipotent transformations u, $u_{[f_1]}$, $u_{[f_2]}$ ... respectively induced by u in these spaces. Taking Jordan types we obtain a decreasing chain of partitions $J(u) \supset J(u_{[f_1]}) \supset J(u_{[f_2]}) \supset \cdots$, which determines a normalised Young tableau $q_u(f)$ of shape $\lambda = J(u)$. The column number j of any entry d of this tableau is determined as above by the position of the 1-dimensional part of the flag $f^{\downarrow\cdots\downarrow}$ in the space V/f_{n-d} relative to the nilpotent transformation $u_{[f_{n-d}]} - \mathbf{1}$ of that space. Using restriction to hyperplanes instead of dividing out lines, we similarly define flags f, f^-, f^{--}, ... in the spaces $V = f_n$, f_{n-1}, f_{n-2}, ..., which flags are fixed by the unipotents u, $u|_{f_{n-1}}$, $u|_{f_{n-2}}$, ... respectively; from this we obtain a decreasing chain of partitions $\lambda = J(u)$ $J(u|_{f_{n-1}})$, $J(u|_{f_{n-2}})$, ..., determining a tableau $r_u(f) \in T_\lambda$. Defining for each flag $f \in \mathcal{F}$ a dual flag f^* in the flag variety of V^* by $f_i^* = f_{n-i}°$, we obviously have $q_u(f) = r_{u^*}(f^*)$. The two tableau-valued functions q_u and r_u on $\mathcal{F}_u$ can be used to distinguish a finite number of subsets of $\mathcal{F}_u$: for $T \in T_\lambda$ we define

$$\mathcal{F}_{u,T} = \{\, f \in \mathcal{F}_u \mid r_u(f) = T \,\} \quad \text{and} \quad \mathcal{F}_{u,T}^* = \{\, f \in \mathcal{F}_u \mid q_u(f) = T \,\};$$
$$\text{(13a, b)}$$

these sets are non-empty by a simple inductive argument. Note that we have "switched preferences" by using r_u rather than q_u for the unstarred notation; this follows the notation in [Stb2], but [Spa II.5.3] effectively uses q_u, not r_u. The advantage of using r_u is that it is somewhat easier to define (using restrictions rather than quotients), and the numbers in the tableau $r_u(f)$ relate more directly to the parts of f (for instance, $J(u|_{f_i})$ is the shape of the sub-tableau of $r_u(f)$ containing entries $\le i$); moreover the interpretation of the Robinson-Schensted algorithm comes out more naturally. A disadvantage however is that when studying r_u in an inductive way, we generally have to work in $\mathbf{P}(V^*)$ rather than in $\mathbf{P}(V)$ (as we have already seen), and this can be more cumbersome. Where possible we shall take the "best of both ways" by stating properties for both $\mathcal{F}_{u,T}$ and $\mathcal{F}_{u,T}^*$, but proving them for $\mathcal{F}_{u,T}^*$ only. In any case we shall see that our results enable a translation between the two conventions.

2.2.1. Proposition
(a) For each $T \in T_\lambda$ the sets $\mathcal{F}_{u,T}$ and $\mathcal{F}_{u,T}^*$ are irreducible.
(b) $\dim \mathcal{F}_{u,T} = \dim \mathcal{F}_{u,T}^* = \sum_i (i-1)\lambda_i$ independently of $T \in T_\lambda$.

Proof. We give the proof for $\mathcal{F}_{u,T}^*$, by induction on $|\lambda| = \dim V$. Fitst note that by construction each set $\mathcal{F}_{u,T}^*$ is Z_u-stable. For each non-empty U_j the set $\alpha^{-1}[U_j]$ is the union of the sets $\mathcal{F}^*_{u,T}$ for those tableaux $T \in \mathcal{T}_\lambda$ whose entry n occurs in column j. If T is such a tableau, then for any $l \in U_j$ the isomorphism $f \mapsto f^\downarrow$ of $\alpha^{-1}[l]$ with the flag variety of V/l maps $\mathcal{F}^*_{u,T} \cap \alpha^{-1}[l]$ isomorphically to $\mathcal{F}^*_{u_{[l]},T^\downarrow}$, which is irreducible by induction. Because U_j is a Z_u-orbit and connected, and therefore already is an orbit for the connected component Z°_u of Z_u, we find that $\mathcal{F}^*_{u,T}$ is irreducible, as it is the surjective image of the irreducible set $Z^\circ_u \times (\mathcal{F}^*_{u,T} \cap \alpha^{-1}[l])$ by the map $(z,f) \mapsto z \cdot f$; this proves part (a). (In fact for GL_n every unipotent centraliser Z_u is connected, so $Z^\circ_u = Z_u$, but we can do without that knowledge here.) We also have $\dim \mathcal{F}^*_{u,T} = \dim U_j + \dim \mathcal{F}^*_{u_{[l]},T^\downarrow}$, so to prove (b) it suffices to show that $\dim U_j = i - 1$, where i is the row number of the entry n in T. But this is clear since i is the number of parts $\geq j$ of $J(u)$, which equals $\dim W_j$, while U_j is a dense part of $\mathbf{P}(W_j)$. □

It follows from the proposition that the set of irreducible components of $\mathcal{F}_u$ can be described as the set of the closures $\overline{\mathcal{F}_{u,T}}$ for $T \in \mathcal{T}_\lambda$, but equally well as the set of closures $\overline{\mathcal{F}^*_{u,T}}$ for $T \in \mathcal{T}_\lambda$. We shall show below that the Schützenberger correspondence relates these two descriptions to each other:

$$\overline{\mathcal{F}^*_{u,T}} = \overline{\mathcal{F}_{u,S(T)}}. \tag{14}$$

To illustrate these parametrisations of the irreducible components of $\mathcal{F}_u$, we consider the simplest case where there is more than one such component, which occurs for GL_3 with $J(u) = (2,1)$; we have $\mathcal{T}_{(2,1)} = \{T, T'\}$ where

$$T = \begin{array}{|c|c|} \hline 1 & 2 \\ \hline 3 \\ \cline{1-1} \end{array} \quad \text{and} \quad T' = \begin{array}{|c|c|} \hline 1 & 3 \\ \hline 2 \\ \cline{1-1} \end{array}.$$

To be specific, we take

$$u = \begin{pmatrix} 1 & 1 & 0 \\ 0 & 1 & 0 \\ 0 & 0 & 1 \end{pmatrix}.$$

Calling the standard basis vectors e_1, e_2, e_3 we have $W_1 = \langle e_1, e_3 \rangle$, $W_2 = \langle e_1 \rangle$, and $W_j = 0$ for $j > 2$. There are two orbits of Z_u on $\mathbf{P}(\text{Ker } \eta) = \mathbf{P}(W_1)$, namely U_1, which is the projective line $\mathbf{P}(W_1)$ with the exception of the single point $\langle e_1 \rangle$, and $U_2 = \{\langle e_1 \rangle\}$. For any $l \in U_1$ and flag $f \in \mathcal{F}_u \cap \alpha^{-1}[l]$ we have $f_1 = l$, and since $f_2 \supset f_1$ must be u-stable, there is no choice but to take $f_2 = W_1 = \langle e_1, e_3 \rangle$, and of course $f_3 = V$. Therefore $\mathcal{F}_u \cap \alpha^{-1}[l]$ consists of just one flag for any $l \in U_1$, and $\mathcal{F}^*_{u,T}$ is the union of these for all $l \in U_1$, whence it is isomorphic as a variety to U_1. On the other hand for $l \in U_2$ (i.e., $l = \langle e_1 \rangle$) and $f \in \mathcal{F}_u \cap \alpha^{-1}[l]$, we may take for f_2 any plane containing the line l, since $\eta[f_2]$ will certainly be contained in $\text{Im } \eta = \langle e_1 \rangle$ and hence in f_2. This gives a projective line of choice, and it follows that $\mathcal{F}^*_{u,T'}$ is isomorphic to a full projective line. Observe that $\mathcal{F}^*_{u,T}$ and $\mathcal{F}^*_{u,T'}$ both have dimension 1, as stated by the proposition. Of the flags in $\mathcal{F}^*_{u,T'}$ there is one that lies in the closure of $\mathcal{F}^*_{u,T}$, namely the one that has $f_2 = \langle e_1, e_3 \rangle$. Therefore, the whole variety $\mathcal{F}_u$ can be depicted as

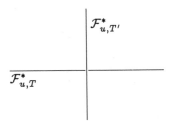

The map $\alpha\colon \mathcal{F}_u \to \mathbf{P}(\mathrm{Ker}\,\eta)$ corresponds to a vertical projection onto a projective line in this picture. On the other hand the map ω, which discriminates upon the part f_2 of flags only, corresponds to a horizontal projection in the picture. Therefore the set $\mathcal{F}_{u,T}$ is the vertical line in the picture, but without the intersection point, and $\mathcal{F}_{u,T'}$ is the horizontal line including that point. Since $S(T) = T'$ we have agreement with (14); the example also shows that the closures taken in (14) cannot be omitted.

2.3. Interpretation of the Schützenberger algorithm.

In this subsection we prove (14), using the recurrence relation for the "deflation" procedure D. The crucial ingredient is the following lemma which gives an interpretation of that procedure. Thos procedure may produce non-normalised tableaux; for such a tableau P we therefore define $\mathcal{F}_{u,P}$ to be equal to $\mathcal{F}_{u,P_N}$, where P_N is the normalised tableau similar to P.

2.3.1. Lemma   *Let P be a non-empty tableau, from which we compute $(T, s, m) = D(P)$ by the deflation procedure, and let j be the column number of the square s. Then there exists a dense Z_u-stable subset $\mathcal{D}$ of $\mathcal{F}_{u,P}$ such that $\alpha[\mathcal{D}] \subseteq U_j$, and $f^\downarrow \in \mathcal{F}_{u_{[\alpha(f)]},T}$ for all $f \in \mathcal{D}$. Moreover for any $l \in U_j$ the set $\{ f^\downarrow \mid f \in \mathcal{D} \cap \alpha^{-1}[l] \}$ is dense in $\mathcal{F}_{u_{[l]},T}$.*

Proof. In the proof we shall be considering the line and hyperplane part of the same flag; we make the following preliminary remarks. For $n \geq 2$ and $f \in \mathcal{F}_u$, let $l = f_1$ and $H = f_{n-1}$. Then $l \subseteq H$ and u induces a unipotent transformation in H/l, which can be obtained either as $(u|_H)_{[l]}$ or $u_{[l]}|_{H/l}$; we shall denote it simply by $u_{H/l}$. The flag induced by f in H/l is $f^{-\downarrow} = f^{\downarrow -}$. For the analogue α_H of α on the flag variety of H we have $\alpha_H(f^-) = \alpha(f) = f_1$. We shall also need the analogues of the spaces W_j and U_j defined for the hyperplane H and using $u|_H$ instead of u; these shall be written as $W_j(H) \subseteq H$ and $U_j(H) \subseteq \mathbf{P}(H)$.

We now prove the first statement of the lemma by induction on the number of squares of P. If P has just one square it is trivially true. Otherwise, let c be the column number of $\lceil P \rceil$; we have $\omega[\mathcal{F}_{u,P}] = U_c^*$. By (6) we have $D(P^\downarrow) = (T^\downarrow, s', m)$ with s' satisfying (7) and (8); let j' be the column number of s'. We proceed to formulate the induction hypothesis applied to $P^\downarrow$ in place of P. Let $H \subset V$ be a hyperplane with $H^\circ \in U_c^*$; for any $f \in \mathcal{F}_{u,P} \cap \omega^{-1}[H^\circ]$ we have $f^- \in \mathcal{F}_{u|_H,P^\downarrow}$. The induction hypothesis now implies that by restricting f to lie in a dense subset $\mathcal{D}_H$ of $\mathcal{F}_{u,P} \cap \omega^{-1}[H^\circ]$, we can achieve that the line $l = \alpha(f)$ lies in $U_{j'}(H)$ and that the flag $f^{-\downarrow}$ lies in $\mathcal{F}_{u_{H/l},T^\downarrow}$; the latter may be rephrased as: $r_{u_{H/l}}(f^{\downarrow -}) = T^\downarrow$.

We claim that if we can prove for f in a dense subset of $\mathcal{D}_H$ that $l \in U_j$, then we are done. First of all, the statement can then be extended by the Z_u-action to f in a dense subset of $\{\, z \cdot f \mid z \in Z_u, f \in \mathcal{D}_H \,\}$, which is Z_u-stable and dense in $\mathcal{F}_{u,P}$. Secondly, the statement $f^{\downarrow} \in \mathcal{F}_{u_{[l]},T}$ to be proved is equivalent to $r_{u_{[l]}}(f^{\downarrow}) = T$, and of the chain of Jordan types encoded in $r_{u_{[l]}}(f^{\downarrow})$, all but the first are in order by the induction hypothesis; so it remains to prove only $J(u_{[l]}) = \operatorname{sh} T$. But since $Y(\operatorname{sh} T)$ differs from $Y(\operatorname{sh} P)$ by the square s which appears in column j, this will follow directly from $l \in U_j$, which proves our claim.

The induction hypothesis gives us for $f \in \mathcal{D}_H$ that $l \in U_{j'}(H)$, and we wish deduce, for a dense subset of those f, that $l \in U_j$. To this end it will be sufficient that a dense part of $U_{j'}(H)$ is contained in U_j, because the map $\alpha_H : \mathcal{D}_H \to U_{j'}(H)$ is open, so that inverse images of dense subsets are dense. (The openness of α_H follows from its equivariance for the centraliser $Z_{u|_H}$ of $u|_H$ in $GL(H)$, which acts on $\mathcal{D}_H$ via its isomorphism with $\{\, f^- \mid f \in \mathcal{D}_H \,\}$, and which acts transitively on $U_{j'}(H)$; in the sequel similar arguments will be tacitly assumed.) We now consider the relation between the spaces of the form $U_i(H)$ and the spaces U_i. As it is given that $H^\circ \in U_c^*$, we easily see that $W_i(H) = W_i$ for all $i \neq c$, while $W_c(H)$ has codimension 1 in W_c. Now if $j' \notin \{c-1,c\}$, then we cannot have $s' \parallel \lceil P \rceil$, so that $j = j'$ by (8), while $U_j(H) = U_j$, and we are done. When $j' = c$ on the other hand we must have $s' \parallel \lceil P \rceil$ (vertically), and hence $j = c$ by (7); in this case $U_j(H)$ is a subvariety of codimension 1 of U_j, and we are done as well. When $j' = c-1$ we may or may not have $s' \parallel \lceil P \rceil$ (horizontally). In the first case we have $j = c = j' + 1$ and $W_{j'}(H) = W_{j-1} = W_j \neq W_{j+1}$ (because columns $j-1$ and j of P must have equal length that exceeds that of column $j+1$), and it follows that $U_{j'}(H) \subseteq U_j$. Only in our final case $j' = c-1$ and $s' \nparallel \lceil P \rceil$ do we have to resort to a dense subset of $U_{j'}(H)$. Indeed $j = j'$ and $W_j(H) = W_j$, and U_j is strictly a subset of $U_j(H)$, since its complement in $\mathbf{P}(W_j)$ is one dimension higher; nevertheless U_j, being non-empty, is dense in $\mathbf{P}(W_j)$ and hence a fortiori in $U_j(H)$.

This proves the first statement of the lemma, the last statement follows most easily by a dimension consideration (although it can also be proved directly similarly to the first statement). All fibres $\mathcal{D} \cap \alpha^{-1}[l]$ for $l \in U_j$ are isomorphic by the Z_u-action, whence they must have dimension $\dim \mathcal{D} - \dim U_j$, and since $\mathcal{D}$ is dense in $\mathcal{F}_{u,P}$ this is equal to $\dim \mathcal{F}_{u_{[l]},T}$. The map $f \mapsto f^{\downarrow}$ is an isomorphism on each $\mathcal{F}_u \cap \alpha^{-1}[l]$, and its image of $\mathcal{D} \cap \alpha^{-1}[l]$ is therefore dense in $\mathcal{F}_{u_{[l]},T}$. $\qquad\square$

The main theorem of this section follows easily.

2.3.2. Theorem   Let $P \in \mathcal{T}_\lambda$, and let $Q = S(P)$ be obtained from it by the Schützenberger algorithm, then the intersection $\mathcal{F}_{u,P}^* \cap \mathcal{F}_{u,Q}$ is dense in both $\mathcal{F}_{u,P}^*$ and $\mathcal{F}_{u,Q}$.

Proof.   By induction on the size of the tableaux, the case of empty tableaux being trivial. Applying the lemma and the definition of the algorithm S, we see that $J(u_{[f_1]}) = \operatorname{sh} T = \operatorname{sh} Q^{\downarrow}$ and $f^{\downarrow} \in \mathcal{F}_{u_{[f_1]},T}$ for all $f \in \mathcal{D} \subseteq \mathcal{F}_{u,P}$ (using the notation of the lemma). Of those f, a dense subset has $f^{\downarrow} \in \mathcal{F}_{u_{[f_1]},Q^{\downarrow}}^*$ by the induction hypothesis, and this implies $f \in \mathcal{F}^*_{u,Q}$. Using the second part of the lemma (or a dimension argument), this set is also dense in $\mathcal{F}^*_{u,Q}$. □

The theorem immediately implies (14). Since $f \in \mathcal{F}_{u,P} \iff f^* \in \mathcal{F}^*_{u^*,P}$ and $f^{**} = f$, it also implies 1.3.1.

2.4. Relative positions.

The interpretation of the Robinson-Schensted algorithm we intend to give also uses the correspondence of tableaux to irreducible components of $\mathcal{F}_u$, but in addition needs the concept of relative positions of flags. It is obvious that a pair of flags $f, f' \in \mathcal{F}$ can be in a number of qualitatively different positions with respect to each other, depending on for instance whether f_1 is or is not contained in f'_2 and similar questions. The relative position of f and f' is completely determined if for all $0 < i, j < n$ the values $\dim (f_i \cap f'_j)$ are given (and vice versa), but these numbers are not entirely independent; it is therefore convenient to encode a relative position in a different way, namely by a permutation of n, which we shall denote $\pi(f, f')$. Since $\pi(f, f')$ does not depend on a choice of basis for V, we have $\pi(g \cdot f, g \cdot f') = \pi(f, f')$ for all $g \in GL_n$. On the other hand if f is the standard flag for the basis $e_1, \ldots, e_n$, given by $f_i = \langle e_1, \ldots, e_i \rangle$ for $0 \leq i \leq n$, and f' is the standard flag for this basis permuted by some $\sigma \in S_n$, i.e., $f'_i = \langle e_{\sigma_1}, \ldots, e_{\sigma_i} \rangle$, then $\pi(f, f')$ is defined to be equal to σ. From Bruhat's lemma for GL_n it follows that these two rules uniquely define $\pi(f, f')$ for all $f, f' \in \mathcal{F}$.

We give some examples. For every $f \in \mathcal{F}$ we have $\pi(f, f) = \mathbf{e}$, the identity permutation. The other extreme occurs when f, f' are generically chosen: then $f_i \cap f'_j$ is zero whenever possible, i.e., whenever $i + j \leq n$; in that case $\pi(f, f')$ is the permutation $\tilde{w} \in S_n$ of 1.3.2. In the above GL_3 example with $\mathcal{F}_u$ consisting of two intersecting lines, we have $\pi(f, f') = (2, 1, 3)$ for any pair of distinct $f, f' \in \mathcal{F}_{u,T}$ (since only their 1-dimensional parts differ), and $\pi(f, f') = (2, 3, 1)$ for any $f \in \mathcal{F}_{u,T}$ and any $f' \in \mathcal{F}_{u,T'}$ except the flag at the intersection of the two components of $\mathcal{F}_u$ (since $f_1 \neq f'_1 \subseteq f_2$ but $f_1 \not\subseteq f'_2$). It is clear from this definition that $\pi(f', f) = \pi(f, f')^{-1}$ for all $f, f' \in \mathcal{F}$, and also that $\pi(f^*, f'^*) = \tilde{w}\pi(f, f')\tilde{w}$ (the latter identity comes from the fact that the dual f^* of the standard flag is given by $f^*_i = \langle e^*_{n+1-i}, \ldots, e^*_n \rangle$ on the dual standard basis).

We can describe $\sigma = \pi(f, f')$ more explicitly in two ways. First, in terms of the numbers $a_{i,j} = \dim (f_i \cap f'_j)$ for $0 \leq i, j \leq n$ the permutation σ is given by $\sigma_j = \min\{ i \mid a_{i,j} > a_{i,j-1} \}$, and its permutation matrix by

$$\delta_{i,\sigma_j} = a_{i,j} - a_{i,j-1} - a_{i-1,j} + a_{i-1,j-1} \qquad \text{for } 1 \leq i, j \leq n. \tag{15}$$

Secondly, $\pi(f, f')$ can be determined by a recursive formula, and it is this form that we shall be using in the sequel. This formula on one hand explicitly gives the final term in the sequence of σ:

$$\sigma_n = \min\{ i \mid f_i \not\subseteq f'_{n-1} \}. \tag{16}$$

Since this number σ_n depends only on f and the hyperplane part $H = f'_{n-1}$ of f', we shall also denote it by $\pi(f, H)$, the relative position of f and H. The remaining values of σ are computed from the relative position of a pair of flags in the subspace H, namely $f|_H$ and f'^{-}, where $f|_H$ is defined as follows. For those i for which $f_i \subseteq H$ we put $(f|_H)_i = f_i$, and for those for which $f_{i-1} \not\subseteq H$ we put $(f|_H)_{i-1} = f_i \cap H$. (One part f_i in not used—in the present case this is f_{σ_n}—since for that part $f_i \cap H = f_{i-1}$.) Now let $\sigma' \in S_{n-1}$ be the relative position $\pi(f|_H, f'^{-})$, then the remaining values of σ are defined by

$$\sigma_i = \begin{cases} \sigma'_i & \text{if } \sigma'_i < \sigma_n \\ \sigma'_i + 1 & \text{if } \sigma'_i \geq \sigma_n \end{cases} \qquad (\text{for } i < n). \tag{17}$$

Note how adding 1 in the second case ensures that we get a proper permutation, and that in each case the part $(f|_H)_{\sigma'_i}$ was obtained from f_{σ_i}. The latter remark implies that if we would endow the parts of flags derived from f with numeric labels to indicate which part of f they stem from (setting the label equal to the dimension for parts of f itself, but keeping the label unaltered when restricting to a hyperplane) and change the right hand side of (16) so that it returns the label of f_i rather than its dimension i, then a recursive definition of $\pi(f, f^{\downarrow})$ could be given in which (17) would simply read $\sigma_i = \sigma'_i$ $(i < n)$ (but the recursive calls of π would yield sequences such as σ' that are not necessarily permutations).

The correctness of both explicit descriptions of $\pi(f, f')$ can be verified easily in the basic case of the definition of $\pi(f, f')$, in which f and f' are respectively the standard and permuted standard flag. Incidentally, there is yet another recursive description of $\pi(f, f')$ that starts by giving $\sigma_1 = \min\{\, i \mid f_i \supseteq f'_1 \,\}$, and uses $\pi(f_{[f'_1]}, f'^{\downarrow})$ for suitably defined $f_{[f'_1]}$ to find the remaining values of σ; however, we shall not use such a description.

2.5. Interpretation of the Robinson-Schensted algorithm.

In terms of relative positions the Robinson-Schensted algorithm has a geometric interpretation analogous to that of the Schützenberger algorithm. We need some additional notation. Since the function π on $\mathcal{F} \times \mathcal{F}$ takes only a finite number of values, we have for every irreducible subset X that π is constant on a dense subset of X; the value it takes on that subset will be denoted $\gamma(X)$, and is called the generic relative position on X. The geometric interpretation of the Robinson-Schensted algorithm now states that the generic relative positions on the irreducible components of $\mathcal{F}_u \times \mathcal{F}_u$ can be expressed as follows:

$$\gamma(\overline{\mathcal{F}_{u,P}} \times \overline{\mathcal{F}_{u,Q}}) = R(P, Q) \tag{18}$$

$$\gamma(\overline{\mathcal{F}^*_{u,P}} \times \overline{\mathcal{F}_{u,Q}}) = \tilde{w}R^t(P, Q) \tag{19}$$

$$\gamma(\overline{\mathcal{F}_{u,P}} \times \overline{\mathcal{F}^*_{u,Q}}) = R^t(P, Q)\tilde{w} \tag{20}$$

$$\gamma(\overline{\mathcal{F}^*_{u,P}} \times \overline{\mathcal{F}^*_{u,Q}}) = \tilde{w}R(P, Q)\tilde{w} \tag{21}$$

By (14) and the properties of $\pi(f, f')$, the last two identities follow from the first two, so it is those first two identities that we shall focus on. Note that the last equation implies that to obtain a nice interpretation of the Robinson-Schensted algorithm using the notation of [Spa], relative positions have to be conjugated by $\tilde{w}$.

Like in the case of the Schützenberger algorithm, most of the work is required in proving an interpretation of the basic step, in the current case the "extraction" procedures E and E^t. In the following lemmas $Z_{u,H}$ denotes the stabiliser in Z_u of H.

2.5.1. Lemma   Let $\lambda = J(u)$ and let a tableau $T \in T_\lambda$ and a corner s of λ be given; put c equal to the column number of s and let $(P, m) = E(T, s)$ be computed by the extraction procedure. Then for all hyperplanes $H \subseteq V$ with $H^\circ \in U_c^*$ there exists a dense $Z_{u,H}$-stable subset $\mathcal{D}_H$ of $\mathcal{F}_{u,T}$ such that for all $f \in \mathcal{D}_H$ we have $\pi(f, H) = m$ and $f|_H \in \mathcal{F}_{u|_H, P}$.

2.5.2. Lemma   Let $\lambda = J(u)$ and let a tableau $T \in T_\lambda$ and a corner s of λ be given; put c equal to the column number of s and let $(P, m) = E^t(T, s)$ be computed by the transpose extraction procedure. Then for all hyperplanes $H \subseteq V$ with $H^\circ \in U_c^*$ there exists a dense $Z_{u,H}$-stable subset $\mathcal{D}_H$ of $\mathcal{F}_{u,T}^*$ such that for all $f \in \mathcal{D}_H$ we have $\pi(f, H) = n + 1 - m \; (= \tilde{w}_m)$ and $f|_H \in \mathcal{F}_{u|_H, P}^*$.

The proofs of these two lemmas are somewhat similar, and we prove here only the latter, leaving the proof of the former as an exercise to the reader (a proof can also be obtained from [Stb2] whose lemma 1.2 is essentially equivalent to our lemma 2.5.1).

Proof of 2.5.2.   We use the notations $W_i(H)$ and $U_i(H)$ as in the proof of 2.3.1; as we have seen there we have $W_i(H) = W_i$ unless $i = c$, and $W_c(H)$ has codimension 1 in W_c. Let $f \in \mathcal{F}_{u,T}$ and $l = f_1$; we examine in which circumstances we can have $l \not\subseteq H$, which is equivalent to $\pi(f, H) = 1$. If the square $\lceil T \rceil$ is in column j, then $l \subseteq W_j \subseteq W_1$, so unless $j = c = 1$ it follows that $l \subseteq W_1(H) \subseteq H$. When $j = c = 1$ on the other hand, $U_1 \cap \mathbf{P}(H) = U_1(H)$, which is either empty or of codimension 1 in U_1, so for f in a dense subset of $\mathcal{F}_{u,T}$ we will have $\pi(f, H) = 1$; this is as claimed by the lemma since in this case $E^t(T, s) = (T^\downarrow, n)$. Furthermore, for such f we may decompose $V = l \oplus H$ as direct sum of u-stable subspaces, so there is an isomorphism $H \xrightarrow{\sim} V/l$ that transforms $u|_H$ into $u_{[l]}$, and also $f|_H$ into $f^\downarrow$; therefore it follows from $q_{u_{[l]}}(f^\downarrow) = T^\downarrow$ that $q_{u|_H}(f|_H) = T^\downarrow$, completing the proof for the case $j = c = 1$.

The proof of the lemma is by induction on $|\lambda|$, and for $|\lambda| = 1$ we are always in the case $j = c = 1$ already treated. In the remaining cases we wish to find the numbers j' and c' such that $l \in U_{j'}(H)$ and $H^\circ \in U_{c'}^*(l^\circ)$, where $l^\circ \subset V^*$ is the hyperplane of functions vanishing on the line l (which is canonically isomorphic to $(V/l)^*$), and $U_i^*(l^\circ)$ is defined in analogy to U_i^*, but using $u^*|_{l^\circ}$ instead of u^*. Because j' is the column number of the square in $Y(J(u|_H)) - Y(J(u_{H/l}))$, and c' is the column number of the square in $Y(J(u_{[l]})) - Y(J(u_{H/l}))$, we must always have $\{c, j'\} = \{c', j\}$, so either one of j', c' determines the other. Moreover, if $j \neq c$ then we must have $j' = j$ and $c' = c$ (this can also be deduced directly from $U_j(H) \supseteq U_j$ and $U_c^*(l^\circ) \supseteq U_c^*$). When $j = c$ we have that $W_j(H)$ has codimension 1 in W_j while $W_j \subseteq W_{j-1} = W_{j-1}(H)$, so a dense part of U_j lies in $U_{j-1}(H)$, and for f in a dense subset of $\mathcal{F}_{u,T}$ we will have $j' = c' = j - 1$.

From the transpose counterpart of (5) we know that $E^t(T^\downarrow, s') = (P^\downarrow, m)$ for some corner s' of $\operatorname{sh} T^\downarrow$, that is together with $\lceil P \rceil$ uniquely determined from s and $\lceil T \rceil$ by (3) and the transpose counterpart of (4). But we have just established that those conditions are met if we take for s' the corner of $\operatorname{sh} T^\downarrow$ in column j', and for $\lceil P \rceil$ the corner in column c' of $\operatorname{sh} P$. Now we apply the induction hypothesis, replacing V, u, s, c, T and H by V/l, $u_{[l]}$, s', c', $T^\downarrow$ and H/l respectively. We obtain that fixing any $l \in U_j \cap U_{j'}(H)$ as determined above, and for $f^\downarrow$ in a dense subset of $\mathcal{F}^*_{u_{[l]},T^\downarrow}$ we have $\pi(f^\downarrow, H/l) = n - m$ and $f^\downarrow|_{H/l} \in \mathcal{F}^*_{u|_{H/l},P^\downarrow}$. Using that $\pi(f^\downarrow, H/l) = \pi(f, H) - 1$ (since dimensions are decreased by 1 in descending from f to $f^\downarrow$) and $f^\downarrow|_{H/l} = (f|_H)^\downarrow$, together with $l = f_1 \in U_{j'}(H)$, the conclusions $\pi(f, H) = n + 1 - m$ and $f|_H \in \mathcal{F}^*_{u|_H,P}$ of the lemma follow. The denseness and $Z_{u,H}$-stability of the set $\mathcal{D}_H$ of all f for which these conclusions are valid are obvious. $\square$

Contrary to what was the case for the interpretation of the Schützenberger algorithm, the main results do not follow immediately from the lemma's here; this is due to the fact that in general the set $\{ f|_H \mid f \in \mathcal{D}_H \}$ is not dense in its component of $\mathcal{F}_{u|_H}$, despite the fact that $\mathcal{D}_H$ is dense in its component of $\mathcal{F}_u$. We resolve the difficulty here in the same way as in [Stb2], using the invertibility of the Robinson-Schensted algorithm and the following

2.5.3. Fact   For each $\sigma \in S_n$ there are unique $\lambda \in \mathcal{P}_n$ and $P, Q \in \mathcal{T}_\lambda$ such that for any unipotent $u \in GL_n$ with $J(u) = \lambda$ we have $\sigma = \gamma(\overline{\mathcal{F}_{u,P} \times \mathcal{F}_{u,Q}})$.

This fact comes from the general study of the unipotent variety, see [Spr1 3.8], [Spr2 4.4.1] or [Stb1 3.5, 3.6]. We also use the fact that the closure of a subset $\mathcal{F}^2_\sigma = \{ (f, f') \mid \pi(f, f') = \sigma \}$ of $\mathcal{F} \times \mathcal{F}$ is the union of similar subsets $\mathcal{F}^2_\tau$ for certain $\tau \in S_n$; putting $\sigma \geq \tau$ for these permutations then defines a partial order on S_n called the Bruhat order (in fact $\sigma \geq \tau$ holds if and only if the numbers $a_{i,j}$ associated to σ as in the previous subsection are all greater than or equal to the corresponding numbers for τ). It is then clear that the generic relative position on some irreducible component of $\mathcal{F}_u \times \mathcal{F}_u$ is also maximal on that component in the Bruhat order.

2.5.4. Theorem   Let $P, Q \in \mathcal{T}_\lambda$, and let $\sigma = R(P, Q)$ be obtained from them by the Robinson-Schensted algorithm, then for (f, f') in a dense subset of $\mathcal{F}_{u,P} \times \mathcal{F}_{u,Q}$ one has $\pi(f, f') = \sigma$.

Proof.   We prove first that on a dense subset $\pi(f, f') \leq \sigma$ holds in the Bruhat order, which implies that it holds on all of $\mathcal{F}_{u,P} \times \mathcal{F}_{u,Q}$. This is done by induction on $|\lambda|$, comparing the definition of $R(P, Q)$ with the recursive formula for $\pi(f, f')$. Let c be the column number of $\lceil Q \rceil$, we have $\omega[\mathcal{F}_{u,Q}] = U^*_c$, so we may choose any hyperplane H with $H^\circ \in U^*_c$ and restrict ourselves to the case $f'_{n-1} = H$. We now apply lemma 2.5.1 with $s = \lceil Q \rceil$ and find for f in a dense subset $\mathcal{D}_H$ of $\mathcal{F}_{u,P}$ that $\pi(f, H) = \sigma_n$ and $f|_H \in \mathcal{F}_{u|_H,T}$, where $(T, \sigma_n) = E(P, s)$. Here T differs from its normalised counterpart T_N in that all entries $\geq \sigma_n$ are increased by 1 in T. Invoking the induction hypothesis for $T_N, Q^\downarrow$ we find that $\pi(f|_H, f^-) \leq R(T_N, Q^\downarrow)$ for all $(f, f') \in \mathcal{D}_H \times \omega^{-1}[H^\circ]$; by (17) and the definition of R this implies $\pi(f, f') \leq R(P, Q)$, completing the proof of our initial claim. To prove that in fact $\pi(f, f^\downarrow) = R(P, Q)$ for generically chosen f, f', consider the values $\gamma(\overline{\mathcal{F}_{u,P} \times \mathcal{F}_{u,Q}})$ and $R(P, Q)$ as (P, Q) traverses $\bigcup_{\lambda \in \mathcal{P}_n} \mathcal{T}_\lambda \times \mathcal{T}_\lambda$. On one hand, by 2.5.3 and the invertibility of R, both values traverse S_n meeting each permutation exactly once; on the other hand the former is always less than or equal to the latter. This is only possible if both values are equal for each pair (P, Q), which proves the theorem. $\square$

2.5.5. Theorem *Let $P, Q \in T_\lambda$, and let $\sigma = R^t(P, Q)$ be obtained from them by the transpose Robinson-Schensted algorithm, then for (f, f') in a dense subset of $\mathcal{F}^*_{u,P} \times \mathcal{F}_{u,Q}$ one has $\pi(f, f') = \tilde{w}\sigma$.*

This is entirely analogous to the previous proof, using lemma 2.5.2 instead of 2.5.1. $\square$

Remark The way we have completed the proofs of these theorems is not the only possible one: there is another approach that is in some ways more satisfactory than the current one, although it needs a longer proof. That approach is to prove that, although $\{ f|_H \mid f \in \mathcal{D}_H \}$ may not be dense, we do obtain a dense subset from it by applying the action of $Z_{u|_H}$ to it (note that this is different from applying the action of $Z_{u,H}$—which indeed has no effect—since not all elements of $Z_{u|_H}$ lift to Z_u). Roughly speaking one attempts to realise a given flag f' in H as $f|_H$ for $f \in \mathcal{F}_{u,P}$ by adapting not only f but also u to the situation, while keeping $u|_H$ fixed. Full details shall be given elsewhere; this technique is also used in a more complicated situation in [vLee 4.6]. This alternative method makes no use of 2.5.3 or the invertibility of R, and it implies that either of these facts may be deduced from the other.

2.6. Conclusion.

The above theorems obviously prove equations (18)–(21). Together with (14) these equations imply the combinatorial statements of 1.3.2. As 1.3.1 and 1.2.1 are also immediate from the given geometric interpretations, and the invertibility of R is directly related to the geometric fact 2.5.3, we may conclude that these are quite natural interpretations of the Robinson-Schensted and Schützenberger algorithms (not only of the resulting correspondences, but also of the procedures they are built-up from), and indeed we may claim to have revealed (at least one sort of) the "witchcraft operating behind the scenes" of those algorithms. The parallel between the recursive definitions of the algorithms and the proofs of our interpretations is so close that, had the algorithms not been known long before the questions about $\mathcal{F}_u$ were studied, they could have been deduced from that study of $\mathcal{F}_u$. In fact, the varieties $\mathcal{F}_u$ have their analogues for other algebraic groups than GL_n (see [Spa]), and in his thesis [vLee], the author has studied the question of computing generic relative positions for them in the case of the other classical groups (Sp_{2n} and O_n), and using analogous methods to those above has derived algorithms similar to the Robinson-Schensted algorithm to compute the desired quantities.

3. References

[Kn1]   D. E. Knuth, "Permutations, matrices and generalised Young tableaux", *Pacific Journal of Math.* **34** (1970), 709–727.

[Kn2] D. E. Knuth, "The art of Computer programming, Vol. III Sorting and Searching", *Addison-Wesley* (1975), Tableaux and involutions, p. 48–72.

[vLee] M. A. A. van Leeuwen, "A Robinson-Schensted algorithm in the geometry of flags for Classical Groups", *Thesis (Rijksuniversiteit Utrecht, the Netherlands)* (1989).

[Rob] G. de B. Robinson, "On representations of the symmetric group", *American Journal of Math.* **60** (1938), 745–760.

[Sche] C. Schensted, "Longest increasing and decreasing subsequences", *Canadian Journal of Math.* **13** (1961), 179–191.

[Schü1] M. P. Schützenberger, "Quelques remarques sur une construction de Schensted", *Math. Scandinavica* **12** (1963), 117–128.

[Schü2] M. P. Schützenberger, "La correspondence de Robinson", *in Lecture Notes in Mathematics* **579** Combinatoire et représentation du groupe symétrique (1976), 59–113.

[Spa] N. Spaltenstein, "Classes Unipotentes et Sous-groupes de Borel", *Lecture Notes in Mathematics* **946** (1982).

[Spr1] T. A. Springer, "Geometric questions arising in the study of unipotent elements", *in Proceedings of Symposia in Pure Mathematics* **37** The Santa Cruz conference on Finite Groups (1980), 255–264.

[Spr2] T. A. Springer, "Conjugacy classes in Algebraic Groups", *in Lecture Notes in Mathematics* **1185** Group Theory, Beijing 1984, 175–209.

[Stb1] R. Steinberg, "On the desingularisation of the unipotent variety", *Inventiones Math.* **36** (1976), 209–224.

[Stb2] R. Steinberg, "An Occurrence of the Robinson-Schensted Correspondence", *Journal of Algebra* **113** (1988), 523–528.

Computational Aspects of Lie Group Representations and Related Topics   89
Proceedings of the 1990 Computational Algebra Seminar
pp. 89–106 in CWI Tract 84 (1991)

Good filtrations, decomposition rules

and standard monomial theory

Peter Littelmann

Mathematisches Institut der Universität Basel

Rheinsprung 21

CH–4051 Basel

Switzerland

0. Introduction

Let G be a simply connected, split semisimple algebraic group defined over a field k. Fix a maximal split torus T and a Borel subgroup B containing T. For a B–character μ let $\mathcal{L}_\mu$ be the associated line bundle on G/B (1.1), and if μ is a dominant character, then denote by V_μ the G–module $H^0(G/B, \mathcal{L}_\mu)$ of highest weight μ.

If k is an algebraically closed field of characteristic zero, then the modules V_μ are simple (Borel–Weil theorem), and every finite dimensional G–module is isomorphic to a direct sum of them (Weyl's complete reducibility theorem). This is not true in general. The notion of a good filtration of a G–module can be seen as a substitute for semisimple modules. Here we say that a G–stable filtration of a G–module M is *good* if all the subquotients are isomorphic to V_μ for some dominant B–character μ.

Consider the G–module $V_{\lambda,\mu} := V_\lambda \otimes V_\mu$. If k is algebraically closed, then the existence of good filtrations for $V_{\lambda,\mu}$ has been proved in [2,13,20] (in the first two papers certain restrictions are made on the characteristic of k). For arbitrary fields, a proof is given in [17] for the case where G has no simple component of type F_4, E_7, E_8.

The aim of this paper is to give for $G = Sl_{n+1}(k)$ an explicit construction of a good filtration of $V_{\lambda,\mu}$. We wish to give an outline of the construction: The main tool is the basis of V_μ given by the standard monomials (see section 2). These monomials are T–eigenvectors, they are indexed by standard Young tableaux, and we denote by $-\nu(T)$ the weight of a standard monomial $p(T)$. Using the geometrical properties of the standard monomials, we define a B–stable complete flag

$$0 \subset F_1 \subset \cdots \subset F_m = V_\mu,$$

such that the F_i have as basis a subset of the standard monomials. Enumerate the tableaux such that F_i is generated by the standard monomials $p(T_j)$, $j \leq i$. Now let λ be another dominant B–character. In [10] we introduced a special subclass of tableaux, the λ–dominant tableaux (see section 2). Let $T_{i_1}, \ldots, T_{i_r}$ be the λ–dominant standard tableaux, and consider the corresponding subflag $0 \subset F_{i_1} \subset \cdots \subset F_{i_r} = V_\mu$. Denote by $\mathcal{F}_{i_j}$ the vector bundle on G/B associated to the B–module F_{i_j}. We show that the induced G–stable filtration

$$V_0 := 0 \subset V_1 := H^0(G/B, \mathcal{L}_\lambda \otimes \mathcal{F}_{i_1}) \subset \cdots \subset V_r := H^0(G/B, \mathcal{L}_\lambda \otimes \mathcal{F}_{i_r}) \simeq V_{\lambda,\mu}$$

is a good filtration. Moreover, $V_j/V_{j-1} \simeq V_{\lambda+\nu(T_{i_j})}$, so this gives at the same time for char $k = 0$ a decomposition rule for the tensor product:

$$V_{\lambda,\mu} = V_\lambda \otimes V_\mu \simeq \bigoplus_{j=1}^{r} V_{\lambda+\nu(T_{i_j})}.$$

In fact, it is easy to see that the notion of a λ–dominant tableau corresponds to the notion of a lattice permutation in the usual formulation of the Littlewood–Richardson rule, so the good filtration constructed above gives also a proof of the Littlewood–Richardson rule.

Moreover, we study the following more general situation: Let $Q \supset B$ be a parabolic subgroup of G, denote by $L \supset T$ its Levi subgroup, and let Y be a union of Schubert varieties in G/B. Denote by $\mathcal{H}^0(Y, \mathcal{L}_\mu)$ the bundle (see 1.1) on Q/B associated to the B–module $H^0(Y, \mathcal{L}_\mu)$. Suppose that λ is Q–dominant (see 1.3). We are going to construct a good filtration of the Q–module $H^0(Q/B, \mathcal{L}_\lambda \otimes \mathcal{H}^0(Y, \mathcal{L}_\mu))$, i.e., the subquotients of this filtration are isomorphic to $H^0(Q/B, \mathcal{L}_\nu)$ for some Q–dominant weight ν. For char $k = 0$, a decomposition rule for the L–module $H^0(Q/B, \mathcal{L}_\lambda \otimes \mathcal{H}^0(Y, \mathcal{L}_\mu))$ ensues. In particular, we get a decomposition rule for V_μ considered as L–module.

A standard monomial theory has been also developed for other simple groups (see [6,7,8,9,18]). We give a short introduction into this theory in section 3. Using the notion of a standard Young tableau in the sense of Seshadri et al., the notion of a λ–dominant tableau has then a straightforward generalization. In fact, the results for $G = Sl_{n+1}(k)$ hold also for all simple groups for which a standard monomial theory has been developed. We state the results in 3.13 and 3.14 without proof. We refer to [11] for a detailed proof.

Acknowledgements The author would like to thank the CWI in Amsterdam for the invitation and for its hospitality.

1. Schubert varieties

1.0 The aim of this section is to introduce some notation and to recall the vanishing theorem for the higher cohomology of certain line bundles on (generalized) Schubert varieties. To motivate our interest in Schubert varieties, we would like to consider first the following example:

Let λ, μ be dominant B–characters and let $Y \subset G/B$ be a Schubert variety, i.e. Y is a B–stable irreducible subvariety of G/B (see 1.2). By Theorem 1.3, the restriction map $V_\mu = H^0(G/B, \mathcal{L}_\mu) \to H^0(Y, \mathcal{L}_\mu)$ is surjective, so we get a short exact sequence of B–modules:

$$0 \longrightarrow Ker \longrightarrow V_\mu = H^0(G/B, \mathcal{L}_\mu) \longrightarrow H^0(Y, \mathcal{L}_\mu) \longrightarrow 0.$$

To see how this sequence induces a filtration of $V_{\lambda,\mu}$, let $\mathcal{H}^0(G/B, \mathcal{L}_\mu)$ be the vector bundle (cf. 1.1) on G/B associated to the B–module $V_\mu = H^0(G/B, \mathcal{L}_\mu)$. But V_μ is a G–module, so the bundle $\mathcal{H}^0(G/B, \mathcal{L}_\mu)$ is in fact a trivial bundle (see 1.1) and we have

$$H^0(G/B, \mathcal{L}_\lambda \otimes \mathcal{H}^0(G/B, \mathcal{L}_\mu)) \simeq H^0(G/B, \mathcal{L}_\lambda) \otimes H^0(G/B, \mathcal{L}_\mu) = V_{\lambda,\mu}.$$

By use of this isomorphism we can view $V_{\lambda,\mu}$ as the global sections of the vector bundle $\mathcal{L}_\lambda \otimes \mathcal{H}^0(G/B, \mathcal{L}_\mu)$ on G/B. Next consider the vector bundles $\mathcal{K}$ and $\mathcal{H}^0(Y, \mathcal{L}_\mu)$ on G/B associated to the B–modules Ker and $H^0(Y, \mathcal{L}_\mu)$ in the short exact sequence above. We get a short exact sequence of vector bundles:

$$0 \longrightarrow \mathcal{L}_\lambda \otimes \mathcal{K} \longrightarrow \mathcal{L}_\lambda \otimes \mathcal{H}^0(G/B, \mathcal{L}_\mu) \longrightarrow \mathcal{L}_\lambda \otimes \mathcal{H}^0(Y, \mathcal{L}_\mu) \longrightarrow 0.$$

Now by Corollary 1.4 and Theorem 1.3, the associated long exact cohomology sequence is in fact a short exact sequence of G–modules:

$$0 \to H^0(G/B, \mathcal{L}_\lambda \otimes \mathcal{K}) \to V_{\lambda,\mu} = H^0(G/B, \mathcal{L}_\lambda \otimes \mathcal{H}^0(G/B, \mathcal{L}_\mu))$$
$$\to H^0(G/B, \mathcal{L}_\lambda \otimes \mathcal{H}^0(Y, \mathcal{L}_\mu)) \longrightarrow 0.$$

The next task will be then to investigate the structure of the B–modules Ker and $H^0(Y, \mathcal{L}_\mu)$. This will be done in the next section with the help of the standard monomial theory.

1.1 We shall first recall the construction of the associated fibre bundle. Let Z be a B–variety. We define a right B–action on $G \times Z$ by $(g, z) \circ b := (gb, b^{-1}z)$. This is a free B–action, and we denote by $G \times^B Z$ the orbit space $(G \times Z)/B$. Since the left action of G on $G \times Z$, defined by $g \cdot (g', z) := (gg', z)$, commutes with the right action of B, the orbit space $G \times^B Z$ has in a natural way the structure of a G–variety. The projection $G \times Z \to G$ commutes with the right action of B on G and induces a natural map $G \times^B Z \to G/B$. In fact, this map makes $G \times^B Z$ into a fibre bundle on G/B with fibre Z (see [4], I, 5.14).

Recall that any character $\lambda : T \to k^*$ extends (trivially) to a character of B, so the character groups $X(T)$ and $X(B)$ can be identified. For $\lambda \in X(T)$ let M_λ be the one–dimensional B–module corresponding to the representation $\lambda : B \to GL(M_\lambda) \simeq k^*$. We denote by $\mathcal{L}_\lambda$ the line bundle $G \times^B M_{-\lambda}$ on G/B.

If $Q \supset B$ is a parabolic subgroup of G and Z is a B–variety, then we denote by $Q \times^B Z$ the associated fibre bundle on Q/B (same construction as above). By abuse of notation we write also $\mathcal{L}_\lambda$ for the line bundle $Q \times^B M_{-\lambda}$ on Q/B.

Note if the B–action on Z comes from a Q–action on Z, then the canonical map

$$Q \times^B Z \to Q/B \times Z, \quad (q, z) \mapsto (qB, qz)$$

is an isomorphism of Q–varieties (where Q acts on the right side via the diagonal action). For example $\tilde{X} := Q \times^B G/B \simeq Q/B \times G/B$. Let p_1, p_2 be the projection maps. We denote by $\mathcal{L}_{\lambda,\mu}$ the line bundle $p_1^* \mathcal{L}_\lambda \otimes p_2^* \mathcal{L}_\mu$ on $\tilde{X}$ ($\simeq Q/B \times G/B$), where $p_1 : \tilde{X} \to Q/B$ and $p_2 : \tilde{X} \to G/B$ are the projection maps.

1.2 Let $\mathrm{Nor}_G(T)$ be the normalizer of T in G and denote by $W := \mathrm{Nor}_G(T)/T$ the Weyl group of G. For $w \in W$ let $n_w \in \mathrm{Nor}_G T$ be a representative and denote by e_w the point $n_w B$ in G/B (which is independent of the choice of n_w). By the Schubert variety $X(w)$ we mean the closure of the orbit $B \cdot e_w$ in G/B. By the Schubert variety $\tilde{X}(w)$ in $\tilde{X} = Q \times^B G/B$ we mean the closed subvariety $Q \times^B X(w)$. (Of course, if $Q = B$, then $\tilde{X}(w) = X(w)$). Note that the isomorphism $Q \times^B G/B \to Q/B \times G/B$ induces an isomorphism of $\tilde{X}(w)$ onto the closure of the Q–orbit $Q \cdot (e_1, e_w)$ in $Q/B \times G/B$.

1.3 Let $L \subset Q$ be the Levi subgroup of Q containing T. Fix a W–invariant scalar product $(\cdot, \cdot)$ on $X(T) \otimes_{\mathbf{Z}} \mathbf{Q}$ and set $\langle \lambda, \mu \rangle := 2(\lambda, \mu)/(\mu, \mu)$. We say that $\lambda \in X(T)$ is Q–dominant if $\langle \lambda, \alpha \rangle \geq 0$ for all simple roots α of G contained in the root system of L.

Theorem ([5,11,12,14,16]) *Let* $\lambda, \mu \in X(T)$ *be such that* λ *is* Q–*dominant and* μ *is dominant. For a union of Schubert varieties* Y *in* G/B *let* $\tilde{Y}$ *be the union of Schubert varieties* $Q \times^B Y$ *in* $\tilde{X}$.

(i) $H^i(\tilde{Y}, \mathcal{L}_{\lambda,\mu}) = 0$ *for all* $i > 0$.

(ii) *The restriction map* $H^0(\tilde{X}, \mathcal{L}_{\lambda,\mu}) \to H^0(\tilde{Y}, \mathcal{L}_{\lambda,\mu})$ *is surjective.*

About the proof For $Q = B$, this is just a reformulation of Theorem 2 in [16]. For $Q = G$ this has been proved in [5] for char $k = 0$, and for char $k > 0$ in [12] and [14]. The proofs in [12] and [14] easily generalize to the situation above (see [11]). $\square$

1.4 Suppose that λ is Q–dominant and μ is dominant. Let Y be a union of Schubert varieties in G/B and let $\tilde{Y}$ be as above. The cohomology groups $H^i(\tilde{Y}, \mathcal{L}_{\lambda,\mu})$ can be calculated as the cohomology groups of a vector bundle on Q/B (cf. 1.0 for the case $Y = G/B$):

Consider the bundle map $\pi : \tilde{Y} \to Q/B$. Since π is a Q–equivariant map and Q/B is a homogeneous Q–space, to calculate the higher direct images $R^i \pi_* \mathcal{L}_{\lambda,\mu}$ (see [3], III, §8) of $\mathcal{L}_{\lambda,\mu}$ it suffices to calculate the stalk at the point $1 \cdot B \in Q/B$. Now the fibre of π over $1 \cdot B$ is Y, and $\mathcal{L}_{\lambda,\mu} = p_1^* \mathcal{L}_\lambda \otimes p_2^* \mathcal{L}_\mu$. But the restriction of $p_1^* \mathcal{L}_\lambda$ to Y is a trivial bundle on which B acts via the character $-\lambda$, and the restriction of $p_2^* \mathcal{L}_\lambda$ is the line bundle $\mathcal{L}_\mu$. Since $H^i(Y, \mathcal{L}_\mu) = 0$ for $i > 0$ (Theorem 1.3), it follows that $R^i \pi_* \mathcal{L}_{\lambda,\mu} = 0$ for $i > 0$, and $\pi_* \mathcal{L}_{\lambda,\mu} = Q \times^B (M_{-\lambda} \otimes H^0(Y, \mathcal{L}_\mu))$ (see [3], III, Corollary 12.9). So $\pi_* \mathcal{L}_{\lambda,\mu}$ is the tensor product of $\mathcal{L}_\lambda$ and the vector bundle $\mathcal{H}^0(Y, \mathcal{L}_\mu)$ associated to the B–module $H^0(Y, \mathcal{L}_\mu)$. Since the higher direct images of $\mathcal{L}_{\lambda,\mu}$ vanish, we get the following isomorphism in cohomology (see [3], III, Exercise 8.1):

Corollary $H^i(Q \times^B Y, \mathcal{L}_{\lambda,\mu}) \simeq H^i(Q/B, \mathcal{L}_\lambda \otimes \mathcal{H}^0(Y, \mathcal{L}_\mu))$.

2 Standard monomial theory and the Littlewood–Richardson rule.

2.0 The aim of this section is to show the close connection between the standard monomial theory and decomposition rules for the group $G = Sl_{n+1}(k)$. The aim of standard monomial theory (SMT) can be described as follows: Let G be a simply connected, simple split algebraic group and denote by $\omega_1, \ldots, \omega_n$ the fundamental weights. Let $X(w) \subset G/B$ be a Schubert variety.

The first step in SMT is to construct for $i = 1, \ldots, n$ a basis $f_{i,1}, \ldots, f_{i,d(i)}$ of $H^0(X(w), \mathcal{L}_{\omega_i})$. If $\mu = \sum_{i=1}^n a_i \omega_i$ is a dominant weight, then the canonical map

$$H^0(X(w), \mathcal{L}_{\omega_1})^{\otimes a_1} \otimes \cdots \otimes H^0(X(w), \mathcal{L}_{\omega_n})^{\otimes a_n} \longrightarrow H^0(X(w), \mathcal{L}_\mu)$$

is surjective ([15]), so $H^0(X(w), \mathcal{L}_\mu)$ is spanned by the monomials $\prod f_{i,i_j}$, $i = 1, \ldots, n$, $j = 1, \ldots, a_i$. The second step in SMT is now to give a rule for which monomials to choose to obtain a basis of $H^0(X(w), \mathcal{L}_\mu)$. These monomials are then called the *standard monomials*.

In this section G will always denote the special linear group $Sl_{n+1}(k)$. We keep the other notation introduced in the preceding section.

2.1 Let $\mathbf{p} = (p_1, \ldots, p_n)$ with $p_1 \geq p_2 \geq \cdots \geq p_n$ be a partition of a natural number m. We identify $\mathbf{p}$ with its associated Young diagram, which consists of left justified rows of boxes with p_1 boxes in the first column, p_2 boxes in the second column, ..., and p_n boxes in the nth column.

By a Young tableau $\mathcal{T}$ of shape $\mathbf{p}$ we mean a filling of the boxes of the corresponding diagram with positive integers. We identify a row or a column of a Young tableau with the sequence of integers filled in the boxes of the corresponding row or column.

The Young tableau $\mathcal{T}$ is called *row standard* if the integers are strictly increasing in the rows and are smaller than or equal to $n + 1$. We say that $\mathcal{T}$ is *standard* if $\mathcal{T}$ is row standard and the integers are non–decreasing in the columns (from the top to the bottom). Here we enumerate the rows of a tableau from the bottom to the top. For $1 \leq l \leq p_1$ we denote by $\mathcal{T}(l)$ the

Young tableau obtained from T by omitting the $(l+1)$st row up to the top row.

Below we give an example of a standard tableau T of shape $(5,2,1)$ and of the truncated tableaux $T(1)$, $T(2)$, $T(3)$ and $T(4)$:

$$
T = \begin{array}{|c|c|c|}
\hline 1 & 2 & 4 \\
\hline 2 & 4 \\
\cline{1-2} 3 \\
\cline{1-1} 4 \\
\cline{1-1} 4 \\
\cline{1-1}
\end{array}
\quad , \quad
T(1) = \boxed{4} \ , \quad
T(2) = \begin{array}{|c|} \hline 4 \\ \hline 4 \\ \hline \end{array} , \quad
T(3) = \begin{array}{|c|} \hline 3 \\ \hline 4 \\ \hline 4 \\ \hline \end{array} , \quad
T(4) = \begin{array}{|c|c|} \hline 2 & 4 \\ \cline{1-1} 3 \\ \cline{1-1} 4 \\ \cline{1-1} 4 \\ \cline{1-1} \end{array}
$$

If i is a positive integer, then we denote by $c_T(i)$ the number of boxes in T filled in with the number i. In the example above, we have $c_T(1) = 1$, $c_T(2) = 2$, $c_T(3) = 1$ and $c_T(4) = 4$.

2.2 For $i = 1, \ldots, n$ let $\omega_i = \epsilon_1 + \cdots + \epsilon_i$ be the i-th fundamental weight. We associate to a dominant weight $\mu = \sum_{i=1}^{n} a_i \omega_i$ the partition $\mathbf{p}(\mu) = (p_1, \ldots, p_n)$ with $p_i := \sum_{j=i}^{n} a_j$. For simplicity we will sometimes write that a Young tableau is of shape μ instead of $\mathbf{p}(\mu)$. If T is a row standard Young tableau of shape μ, then we define the *weight* of T as

$$\nu(T) := c_T(1)\epsilon_1 + \cdots + c_T(n+1)\epsilon_{n+1}.$$

For $1 \leq l \leq p_1$ denote by $\nu_l(T)$ the weight $\nu(T(l))$.

For the tableau T in 2.1 we have $\nu_1(T) = \epsilon_4$, $\nu_2(T) = 2\epsilon_4$, $\nu_3(T) = \epsilon_3 + 2\epsilon_4$, $\nu_4(T) = \epsilon_2 + \epsilon_3 + 3\epsilon_4$ and $\nu(T) = \nu_5(T) = \epsilon_1 + 2\epsilon_2 + \epsilon_3 + 4\epsilon_4$.

Definition Let λ be a Q–dominant weight. A standard Young tableau of shape μ is called (Q, λ)–*dominant*, if all the weights $\lambda + \nu_l(T)$, $l = 1, \ldots, p_1$, are Q–dominant. If $Q = G$, then we say just that T is λ–dominant, and if $\lambda = 0$ we just say that T is Q–dominant.

If we consider the example above, (where $G = Sl_4(k)$), then T is not ω_2 dominant since $\omega_2 + \nu_1(T) = \epsilon_1 + \epsilon_2 + \epsilon_4$ is not a dominant weight. But it is easy to see that T is $(6\epsilon_1 + 4\epsilon_2 + 3\epsilon_3)$–dominant.

2.3 In this section we assume k to be an algebraically closed field of characteristic zero. For a dominant weight λ denote by V_λ the simple G–module $H^0(G/B, \mathcal{L}_\lambda)$, and for a Q–dominant weight η denote by U_η the simple L–module $H^0(Q/B, \mathcal{L}_\eta)$.

Littlewood–Richardson rule.

(i) *Let $T_1, \ldots, T_l$ be the λ–dominant standard Young tableaux of shape μ. Then the decomposition of the tensor product $V_\lambda \otimes V_\mu$ is given by*

$$V_\lambda \otimes V_\mu = \bigoplus_{j=1}^{l} V_{\lambda + \nu(T_j)}.$$

(ii) Let $T_1, \ldots, T_l$ be the Q–dominant standard Young tableaux of shape μ. The decomposition of V_μ into simple L–modules is given by

$$\mathrm{res}_L V_\lambda = \bigoplus_{j=1}^{l} U_{\nu(T_j)}.$$

2.4 We wish to show that these decomposition rules can be seen as special cases of a more general decomposition rule. We shall first recall a few facts about standard monomial theory. In the following, k is again an arbitrary field.

Let P_i, $i = 1, \ldots, n$, be the maximal parabolic subgroup of G associated to the fundamental weight ω_i, let W_i be the Weyl group of P_i, and let $\pi_i : W \to W/W_i$ be the projection. Recall that W is isomorphic to the symmetric group S_{n+1}, and $W_i \simeq S_i \times S_{n+1-i}$ is the stabilizer of ω_i in W.

For $\tau \in W/W_i$ let $1 \leq j_1 < \cdots < j_i \leq n+1$ be such that $\tau(\omega_i) = \epsilon_{j_1} + \cdots + \epsilon_{j_i}$. We associate to τ the sequence $(j_1, \ldots, j_i)$. It is easy to see this induces a bijection

$$W/W_i \longrightarrow I(i, n+1) := \{(j_1, \ldots, j_i) \mid 1 \leq j_1 < \cdots < j_i \leq n+1\}.$$

In the following, we will identify W/W_i with $I(i, n+1)$. Moreover, on $I(i, n+1)$ we have a canonical partial order: $(j_1, \ldots, j_i) \leq (j'_1, \ldots, j'_i)$ if $j_l \leq j'_l$ for $l = 1, \ldots, i$. Note that this partial order coincides with the usual Bruhat order on W/W_i under the bijection above. Further, if $\tau = (j_1, \ldots, j_i)$, then $\tau(\omega_i) = \epsilon_{j_1} + \cdots + \epsilon_{j_i}$.

2.5 Let $Y = X(w_1) \cup \cdots \cup X(w_r)$ be a union of Schubert varieties in G/B. Denote by I_Y the set of elements $\tau \in I(i, n+1)$ such that $\tau \leq \pi_i(w_j)$ for some $j = 1, \ldots, r$. The following theorem can be found in [19], or [9], Theorem 3.15.

First Basis Theorem *There exists a basis $\{p(\tau)\}$ of $H^0(G/B, \mathcal{L}_{\omega_i})$, indexed by the elements of $I(i, n+1)$, such that $p(\tau)$ is a T–weight vector of weight $-\tau(\omega_i)$. The restriction $p(\tau)|_Y$ of $p(\tau)$ to Y is not identically zero if and only if $\tau \in I_Y$, and the set $\{p(\tau)|_Y \mid \tau \in I_Y\}$ is a basis for $H^0(Y, \mathcal{L}_{\omega_i})$.*

In what follows, we refer to this basis as the *standard basis* of $H^0(G/B, \mathcal{L}_{\omega_i})$.

2.6 Suppose that $\mu = \sum_{i=1}^{n} a_i \omega_i$ is a dominant weight, and let T be a row standard Young tableau of shape $\mathbf{p}(\mu) = (p_1, \ldots, p_n)$. For $1 \leq l \leq p_1$ let $1 \leq i_l \leq n$, $1 \leq j_l \leq a_{i_l}$ be such that $l = a_1 + \cdots + a_{i_l - 1} + j_l$. The lth row τ_{i_l, j_l} of T can then be considered as an element of $I(i_l, n+1)$. Denote by $p(\tau_{i_l, j_l}) \in H^0(G/B, \mathcal{L}_{\omega_{i_l}})$ the corresponding section. By the monomial $p(T)$ of type $\mathbf{p}(\mu)$ we mean the product

$$p(T) := \prod_{l=1}^{p_1} p(\tau_{i_l, j_l}) \in H^0(G/B, \mathcal{L}_\mu).$$

For simplicity we denote by $p(T)$ also the restriction of this section to a union of Schubert varieties Y. To give a basis of $H^0(Y, \mathcal{L}_\mu)$, we need first the notion of a defining chain for a row standard tableau T.

2.7 Let μ be a dominant weight and let T be a row standard Young tableau of shape $\mathbf{p}(\mu)$. Denote by τ_l the lth row of T. We have already seen that we can consider τ_l as an element of $I(i_l, n+1)$. For $l = 1, \ldots, p_1$ let $\Gamma_l \in W$ be such that $\pi_{i_l}(\Gamma_l) = \tau_l$. The sequence $(\Gamma_1, \ldots, \Gamma_{p_1})$ is called a *defining chain* for T, if

$$\Gamma_1 \geq \Gamma_2 \geq \cdots \geq \Gamma_{p_1}.$$

One can prove that T is standard if and only if such a defining chain exists ([7]). Moreover, if T is standard, then there exists a unique minimal defining chain $(\Gamma_1, \ldots, \Gamma_{p_1})$; i.e., if $(\Gamma'_1, \ldots, \Gamma'_{p_1})$ is any other defining chain for T, then $\Gamma_1 \leq \Gamma'_1, \ldots, \Gamma_{p_1} \leq \Gamma'_{p_1}$ in the Bruhat order on W.

Definition Let $Y = X(w_1) \cup \cdots \cup X(w_r)$ be a union of Schubert varieties, and let T be a row standard Young tableau of shape $\mathbf{p}(\mu)$. The tableau T is called *standard on Y* if $\Gamma_1 \leq w_j$ for some $j = 1, \ldots, r$ for the minimal defining chain $(\Gamma_1, \ldots, \Gamma_{p_1})$ of T. The monomial $p(T)$ of type $\mathbf{p}(\mu)$ is called *standard*, if the tableau T is standard. If T is standard on Y, then $p(T)$ is called *standard on Y*.

The following theorem is taken from [9], Corollary 9.8. In fact, it is stated there only for Schubert varieties. But the (scheme theoretic) intersection of Schubert varieties is a union of Schubert varieties ([16]). Now an easy induction on the number of irreducible components of maximal dimension proves the following generalization.

Second Basis Theorem Let $\mu = \sum_{i=1}^{n} a_i \omega_i$ be a dominant weight. The standard monomials on Y of type $\mathbf{p}(\mu)$ form a basis of T–eigenvectors of $H^0(Y, \mathcal{L}_\mu)$. The weight of $p(T)$ is $-\nu(T)$.

2.7 Using the basis given by the standard monomials, we wish now to define a complete flag in $H^0(Y, \mathcal{L}_\mu)$. Recall that we identify W/W_i with $I(i, n+1)$, and that we can view a row in a standard tableau also as a coset in W/W_i for some $i = 1, \ldots, n$. Let now $l(\cdot)$ be the length function on W/W_i, and fix a total ordering "$\prec$" on W/W_i such that $l(\delta_1) < l(\delta_2)$ implies $\delta_1 \prec \delta_2$. Denote by "$<$" the corresponding lexicographic order on the set of standard Young tableaux of shape μ, i.e., $T_1 < T_2$ if there exists a number l, $1 \leq l \leq p_1$, such that the first $(l-1)$ rows of the tableaux are equal, and the lth row of T_2 is greater than the lth row of T_1. Let now $T_1, \ldots, T_m$ be the standard Young tableaux on Y of shape μ, enumerated such that $T_1 > T_2 > \cdots > T_m$. Denote by F_i the subspace of $H^0(Y, \mathcal{L}_\mu)$ spanned by the monomials $p(T_j)$, $j \leq i$.

Theorem 2.8

(i) *The complete flag $F_0 := 0 \subset F_1 \subset \cdots \subset F_m = H^0(Y, \mathcal{L}_\mu)$ is B–stable.*

(ii) *Suppose that $\lambda \in X(T)$ is Q–dominant and let $T_{i_1}, \ldots, T_{i_s}$, $1 \leq i_1 \leq \cdots \leq i_s \leq m$, be the subset of (Q, λ)–dominant tableaux. Denote by $\mathcal{F}_{i_1}, \ldots, \mathcal{F}_{i_s}$ the vector bundles on Q/B associated to the B–modules F_{i_j}, $j = 1, \ldots, s$. Set $M_j := H^0(Q/B, \mathcal{L}_\lambda \otimes \mathcal{F}_{i_j})$. The filtration of Q–modules*

$$M_0 := 0 \subset M_1 \subset \cdots \subset M_m \simeq H^0(Q \times^B Y, \mathcal{L}_{\lambda,\mu})$$

is good, and $M_j/M_{j-1} \simeq H^0(Q/B, \mathcal{L}_{\lambda+\nu(T_{i_j})})$.

2.9. The Littlewood–Richardson rule

Before we prove the theorem note that (ii) implies the Littlewood–Richardson rule: Suppose now that k is an algebraically closed field, char $k = 0$. Set first $Q = G$ and $Y = G/B$. Since $H^0(G/B, \mathcal{L}_\mu)$ is a G–module, we get by Corollary 1.4:

$$H^0(G \times^B G/B, \mathcal{L}_{\lambda,\mu}) \simeq H^0(G/B, \mathcal{L}_\lambda \otimes H^0(G/B, \mathcal{L}_\mu)) \simeq$$

$$\simeq H^0(G/B, \mathcal{L}_\lambda) \otimes H^0(G/B, \mathcal{L}_\mu).$$

Now by (ii) the tensor product is a direct sum $\bigoplus_{j=1}^l H^0(G/B, \mathcal{L}_{\lambda+\nu(T_{i_j})})$, where $T_{i_1}, \ldots, T_{j_l}$ are the λ–dominant standard Young tableaux of shape μ.

If $\lambda = 0$ and $Y = G/B$, then we see similarly that

$$H^0(Q \times^B G/B, \mathcal{L}_{0,\mu}) \simeq H^0(G/B, \mathcal{L}_\mu),$$

and by (ii) this module decomposes into the direct sum $\bigoplus_{j=1}^l H^0(Q/B, \mathcal{L}_{\nu(T_{i_j})})$, where $T_{i_1}, \ldots, T_{j_l}$ are the Q–dominant standard Young tableaux of shape μ.

2.10 Proof of the theorem

The proof of (i) is by induction on $|\mu| = \sum_{i=1}^n a_i$. For simplicity we assume that $a_1 > 0$ (otherwise one has to replace a_1, ω_1, etc. by a_{i_0}, ω_{i_0} etc., where i_0 is such that $a_{i_0} > 0$ and $a_i = 0$ for $i < i_0$).

Enumerate the elements in I_Y such that $\tau_0 \succ \tau_1 \succ \cdots \succ \tau_p$. Let Y_i be the union of all Schubert varieties $X(w)$ in Y such that $\pi_1(w) = \tau_i$. If we set $Z_i := \bigcup_{j \geq i} Y_j$, then $Z_p \subset Z_{p-1} \subset \cdots \subset Z_0 = Y$.

Let U_i be the kernel of the restriction map $H^0(Y, \mathcal{L}_\mu) \to H^0(Z_{i+1}, \mathcal{L}_\mu)$. We obtain a B–stable flag

$$U : U_{-1} = 0 \subset U_0 \subset \cdots \subset U_{p-1} \subset U_p = H^0(Y, \mathcal{L}_\mu).$$

Let $p(T) = p(\tau_j)p'$ be a standard monomial in $H^0(Y, \mathcal{L}_\mu)$ where p' is an element of $H^0(Y, \mathcal{L}_{\mu-\omega_1})$. If $j \leq i$, then $\tau_j \not\leq \tau_l$ for all $l \geq i+1$, so $p(\tau_j)$ vanishes on Z_{i+1}, and $p(T) \in U_i$. On the other hand, if $j > i$, then let $(\Gamma_1, \ldots, \Gamma_{p_1})$ be the minimal defining chain for T. Now $X(\Gamma_1) \subset Y$ and $\pi(\Gamma_1) = \tau_j$, so $X(\Gamma_1) \subset Y_j \subset Z_{i+1}$ and $p(T)$ is standard on Z_{i+1}. Hence the set of standard monomials $p(T) \in H^0(Y, \mathcal{L}_\mu)$ of the form $p(T) = p(\tau_j)p'$, $j \leq i$, forms a basis of U_i, and the flag U is a subflag of the complete flag F in the theorem.

Let R_{i+1} denote the scheme theoretic intersection $Y_i \cap Z_{i+1}$ (which is a union of Schubert varieties by [16]). The same arguments as above show that the kernel N_i of the restriction map $H^0(Y_i, \mathcal{L}_\mu) \to H^0(R_{i+1}, \mathcal{L}_\mu)$ has as basis the standard monomials $p(\mathcal{T})$ in $H^0(Y_i, \mathcal{L}_\mu)$ such that $p(\mathcal{T}) = p(\tau_i)p'$. So the restriction map $H^0(Y, \mathcal{L}_\mu) \to H^0(Y_i, \mathcal{L}_\mu)$ induces an isomorphism $N_i \simeq U_i/U_{i-1}$.

Now put $p(\mathcal{T}) = p(\tau_i)p' \in N_i$. Consider the map $f_i : N_i \to H^0(Y_i, \mathcal{L}_{\mu-\omega_1})$, where $f_i(p(\mathcal{T})) := p'$. The map is well defined and injective. Moreover, if $p' \in H^0(Y_i, \mathcal{L}_{\mu-\omega_1})$, then $p(\tau_i)p'$ is a standard monomial by the construction of Y_i. So we have B–equivariant isomorphisms

$$U_i/U_{i-1} \simeq N_i \simeq M_{-\tau_i(\omega_1)} \otimes H^0(Y_i, \mathcal{L}_{\mu-\omega_1}).$$

If $\mu = \omega_1$, then $U = F$, which proves (i) in this case. Else we proceed by induction on $|\mu|$. Since $|\mu - \omega_1| = |\mu| - 1$, the flags $(F \cap U_j)/U_{j-1}, j = 1, \ldots, t$, are B–stable by the isomorphism above, so the flag F is also B–stable, which proves (i).

To prove (ii), note that the subquotients in the flag $M_{-\lambda} \otimes U$ are of the form

$$M_{-\lambda-\tau_i(\omega_1)} \otimes H^0(Y_i, \mathcal{L}_{\mu-\omega_1}).$$

Moreover, the subquotient $M_{-\lambda} \otimes U_i/U_{i-1}$ has as basis the images of the standard monomials $p(\mathcal{T})$, where $\mathcal{T}$ has τ_i as first row.

If i is such that $\lambda + \tau_i(\omega_1)$ is not a Q–dominant weight, then we do not change the flag. Note that if $\lambda + \tau_i(\omega_1)$ is not Q–dominant, then none of the standard tableaux having τ_i as first row is (Q, λ)–dominant.

If $\lambda + \tau_i(\omega_1)$ is Q–dominant and $|\mu| > 1$, then we repeat the construction of the filtration in the proof of (i) for $H^0(Y_i, \mathcal{L}_{\mu-\omega_1})$, and we refine corresponding to this filtration the flag U. So we get a flag

$$0 \subset \cdots \subset M_{-\lambda} \otimes U_{i-1} = M_{-\lambda} \otimes U_{i,-1} \subset \cdots$$
$$\cdots \subset M_{-\lambda} \otimes U_{i,p'} = M_{-\lambda} \otimes U_i \subset \cdots \subset M_{-\lambda} \otimes H^0(Y, \mathcal{L}_\mu).$$

$M_{-\lambda} \otimes U_{i,j}/U_{i,j-1}$ is isomorphic to $M_{-\lambda-\tau_i(\omega_1)-\tau'_j(\omega_a)} \otimes H^0(Y_{i,j}, \mathcal{L}_{\mu-\omega_1-\omega_a})$, where $a = 1$ if $a_1 \geq 2$ and $a = \min\{i \geq 2 \mid a_i > 0\}$ else. Further, the subquotients have as basis the standard monomials $p(\mathcal{T})$, where $\mathcal{T}$ has τ_i as first row and τ'_j as second row. Now if $\lambda + \tau_i(\omega_1) + \tau'_j(\omega_a)$ is not Q–dominant, then we do not change the flag. But if $|\mu| \geq 3$ and $\lambda + \tau_i(\omega_1) + \tau'_j(\omega_a)$ is Q–dominant, the we repeat the procedure.

So if we repeat the procedure $|\mu|$ times, then we obtain a flag

$$V : V_{-1} = 0 \subset V_1 \subset \cdots \subset V_q = M_{-\lambda} \otimes H^0(Y, \mathcal{L}_\mu)$$

having the following properties:
(a) V is a subflag of the complete flag F.
(b) There exists a number l, $1 \leq l \leq p_1$, and a standard tableau $\mathcal{S}_r$ of shape $\mu' = a_1\omega_1 + \cdots + a_{i_l-1}\omega_{i_l-1} + j_l\omega_{i_l}$ (see 2.6) such that V_r/V_{r-1} has as basis the images of the standard monomials $p(\mathcal{T})$ with $\mathcal{T}(l) = \mathcal{S}_r$.

(c) $\mathcal{S}_r(l-1)$ is (Q, λ)–dominant, and if $\mathcal{S}_r$ $(= \mathcal{S}_r(l))$ is (Q, λ)–dominant, then $l = |\mu|$, $\mathcal{S}_r = \mathcal{T}_{i_j}$ for some (Q, λ)–dominant standard tableau $\mathcal{T}_{i_j}$ of shape μ, and V_r/V_{r-1} is isomorphic to $M_{-\lambda-\nu(\mathcal{T}_{i_j})}$.

(d) If $\mathcal{S}_r$ is not (Q, λ)–dominant, then $V_r/V_{r-1} \simeq M_{-\lambda-\nu(\mathcal{S}_r)} \otimes H^0(Y_r', \mathcal{L}_{\mu-\mu'})$, where $Y_r' \subset Y$ is a union of Schubert varieties $X(\kappa_1) \cup \cdots \cup X(\kappa_t)$ such that $\pi_{i_l}(\kappa_s)$ is equal to the lth row of $\mathcal{S}_r$, $s = 1, \ldots, t$.

Denote by $\mathcal{V}_r$ the bundle on Q/B associated to the B–module V_r. Now if $\mathcal{S}_r$ is (Q, λ)–dominant, then by (b) and (c) we get

$$H^0(Q/B, \mathcal{V}_r/\mathcal{V}_{r-1}) \simeq H^0(Q/B, \mathcal{L}_{\lambda+\nu(\mathcal{T}_{i_j})}),$$

where $\mathcal{S}_r = \mathcal{T}_{i_j}$.

Now suppose that $\mathcal{S}_r$ is not (Q, λ)–dominant, so there exists a simple root α in L such that $\langle \lambda + \nu(\mathcal{S}_r), \alpha \rangle < 0$. Let $\tau^{(l)}$ be the lth row of $\mathcal{S}_r$. Since $\lambda + \nu(\mathcal{S}_r(l-1))$ is (Q, λ)–dominant and $\langle \tau^{(l)}(\omega_{i_l}), \alpha \rangle \in \{-1, 0, 1\}$, this implies $\langle \lambda + \nu(\mathcal{S}_r), \alpha \rangle = \langle \tau^{(l)}(\omega_{i_l}), \alpha \rangle = -1$.

Let $P(\alpha)$ be the minimal parabolic subgroup of Q generated by B and the unipotent subgroup $G_{-\alpha}$ associated to the root $-\alpha$. Note that $\langle \tau^{(l)}(\omega_{i_l}), \alpha \rangle = -1$ implies that $s_\alpha \tau^{(l)} < \tau^{(l)}$, and hence $s_\alpha \kappa_s < \kappa_s$ for $s = 1, \ldots, t$, and hence Y_r' is $P(\alpha)$–stable. So by the isomorphism in (d), the restriction of $\mathcal{V}_r/\mathcal{V}_{r-1}$ to $P(\alpha)/B$ is the tensor product of a line bundle of degree -1 and a trivial bundle, and all cohomology groups of this bundle on $P(\alpha)/B$ vanish. But this implies that the Leray–spectral sequence corresponding to the map $Q/B \to Q/P(\alpha)$ degenerates completely, so $H^l(Q/B, \mathcal{V}_r/\mathcal{V}_{r-1}) = 0$ for all $l \geq 0$.

Consider the flag $(V \cap M_{-\lambda} \otimes F_{i_j})/M_l \otimes F_{i_{j-1}}$. Since the only subquotient of this flag corresponding to a (Q, λ)–dominant tableau is $M_{-\lambda} \otimes F_{i_j}/F_{i_j-1} \simeq M_{-\lambda-\nu(\mathcal{T}_{i_j})}$, we get

$$H^l(Q/B, \mathcal{L}_\lambda \otimes \mathcal{F}_{i_j}/\mathcal{F}_{i_j-1}) \simeq H^l(Q/B, \mathcal{L}_{\lambda+\tau_{i_j}(\omega_1)}).$$

In particular, we see by induction on j that $H^l(Q/B, \mathcal{L}_\lambda \otimes \mathcal{F}_{i_j}) = 0$ for $l > 0$, so we get

$$H^0(Q/B, \mathcal{L}_\lambda \otimes \mathcal{F}_{i_j})/H^0(Q/B, \mathcal{L} \otimes \mathcal{F}_{i_{j-1}}) \simeq H^0(Q/B, \mathcal{L}_\lambda \otimes \mathcal{F}_{i_j}/\mathcal{F}_{i_{j-1}})$$
$$\simeq H^0(Q/B, \mathcal{L}_{\lambda+\nu(\mathcal{T}_{i_j})}),$$

which proves (ii). $\qquad\qquad\qquad\qquad\qquad\qquad\qquad\qquad\qquad\qquad\qquad\qquad\qquad\square$

3. Standard monomial theory and good filtrations

3.0 We wish to give a short introduction into the theory of standard monomials for the other simple groups. For a detailed discussion we refer to [6,7,8,9,18].

We have already seen in section 2 that one might view a standard Young tableau as a sequence of elements in W/W_i. A Young tableau for the other simple groups will be a sequence of so–called admissible quadruples of elements in

W/W_i. Note that only for $G = Sl_{n+1}(k)$ all fundamental weights are miniscule, i.e., all weights in $H^0(G/B, \mathcal{L}_{\omega_i})$ can be written as $-\tau(\omega_i)$ for some $\tau \in W/W_i$. So it is clear that in general the cosets in W/W_i do not suffice for an indexing system for a basis of $H^0(G/B, \mathcal{L}_{\omega_i})$.

The notion of a (Q, λ)–dominant tableau generalizes in a straightforward way also to these Young tableaux. We state (without proof) the generalization of the decomposition rules in 3.13 and 3.14.

Using similar identifications as in the case $Sl_{n+1}(k)$, one can associate to a Young tableau in the sense of 3.5 a Young tableau in the "classical" sense (see [10]). We discuss the case $G = Sp_4$ as an example in 3.15.

3.1 Let μ be a dominant weight. We say that μ is of type $(*)$ if the following holds:

$(*)$ Let $\omega_1, \ldots, \omega_n$ be the enumeration of the fundamental weights as in [1]. Then the coefficient a_i in $\mu = \sum_{i=1}^n a_i\omega_i$ is greater than 0 only if $i = 1, 3, 4$ for G of type F_4, $i = 1, 2, 3, 6, 7$ for G of type E_7, $i = 1, 7, 8$ for G of type E_8.

Remarks (i) If a fundamental weight ω is of type $(*)$, then $|\langle \omega, \beta \rangle| \leq 3$ for any positive root β.

(ii) SMT is also available if $a_i > 0$ for $i = 5$ for G of type E_7, $i = 2$ for G of type E_8. But for the B–stable filtration defined later one needs certain detailed information about weight multiplicities and the indexing system of the standard basis. This information is only available if μ is of type $(*)$.

3.2 We recall the indexing system for the standard basis of $H^0(G/B, \mathcal{L}_\omega)$, where ω is a fundamental weight of type $(*)$. Let P be the maximal parabolic subgoup corresponding to ω, and denote by W_P the Weyl group of P. Let $\pi : W \to W/W_P$ be the projection map. Recall that W_P is the stabilizer W_ω of ω in W.

We use the usual notation $\tau > \kappa$ and $l(\tau)$ for the Bruhat order and the length function on W and W/W_P. An m–chain for a pair (τ, κ), $\tau, \kappa \in W/W_P$, is a sequence $w_0, \ldots, w_r$ of elements in W/W_P and a sequence $\beta_1, \ldots, \beta_r$ of positive roots, such that either $r = 0$ and $\tau = w_0 = \kappa$, or $\tau = w_0 > \cdots > w_r = \kappa$, and

$$l(w_j) = l(w_{j-1}) - 1, \quad s_{\beta_j} w_j = w_{j-1} \text{ and } |\langle w_j(\omega), \beta_j \rangle| = m \text{ for } j = 1, \ldots, r.$$

Remark An equivalent way to define an m–chain for a pair (τ, κ) is the following: Let $Ch(G/P)$ be the Chow ring of G/P. For $w \in W/W_P$ let $[X(w)]$ be the element in $Ch(G/P)$ determined by the Schubert variety $X(w) \subset G/P$. Denote by H the unique Schubert variety in G/P of codimension one. Then

$$[X(w)] \cdot [H] = \sum_j d_j [X(\phi_j)], \ d_j \geq 0,$$

where the summation runs over all Schubert varieties of codimension one in $X(w)$. Now an m–chain for a pair (τ, κ) is a sequence of Schubert varieties

$$X(\tau) = X(w_0) \supset \cdots \supset X(w_r) = X(\kappa),$$

such that either $X(\tau) = X(w_0) = X(\kappa)$, or $X(w_j)$ is of codimension one in $X(w_{j-1})$ and the coefficient of $[X(w_j)]$ in $[X(w_{j-1})] \cdot [H]$ is m for $j = 1, \ldots, r$.

Definition 3.3 A quadruple $\theta = (\gamma, \delta, \sigma, \phi)$ of elements in W/W_P is called admissible if $\gamma \geq \delta \geq \sigma \geq \phi$, and there exist 3–chains for the pairs (γ, δ) and (σ, ϕ) and a 2–chain for the pair (δ, σ). The weight $\nu(\theta)$ associated to an admissible quadruple is defined as

$$\nu(\theta) := (2\gamma(\omega) + \delta(\omega) + \sigma(\omega) + 2\phi(\omega))/6.$$

Remark If G is of type A_n, then all admissible quadruples are trivial, i.e., they are of the form $(\gamma, \gamma, \gamma, \gamma)$. If G is of type B_n, C_n or D_n, then they are of the form $(\gamma, \gamma, \sigma, \sigma)$.

3.4 Denote by I the set of admissible quadruples θ in W/W_P. For a union of Schubert varieties $Y = X(w_1) \cup \cdots \cup X(w_r)$ let I_Y be the subset of I of admissible quadruples $\theta = (\gamma, \delta, \sigma, \phi)$ such that $\gamma \leq \pi(w_j)$ for some $j = 1, \ldots, r$.

First Basis Theorem ([6,8,9]) *Let ω be a fundamental weight of type* $(*)$. *There exists a basis $\{p(\theta) \mid \theta \in I\}$ of $H^0(G/B, \mathcal{L}_\omega)$, called the standard basis, such that $p(\theta)$ is a T–weight vector of weight $-\nu(\theta)$. The restriction of $p(\theta)$ to a union of Schubert varieties Y is not identically zero if and only if $\theta \in I_Y$, and the set $\{p(\theta)|_Y \mid \theta \in I_Y\}$, is a basis for $H^0(Y, \mathcal{L}_\omega)$.*

3.5 We fix an enumeration of the fundamental weights $\omega_1, \ldots, \omega_n$ (the enumeration need not coincide with the one in [1]). Let $\mu = \sum_{i=1}^n a_i \omega_i$ be a dominant weight of type $(*)$. We wish to recall the definition of standard monomials of type $(\mathbf{a}) = (a_1, \ldots, a_n)$.

Let P_i be the maximal parabolic subgroup associated to ω_i, let W_i be its Weyl group, and denote by $\pi_i : W \to W/W_i$ the projection.

A Young tableau of shape $(\mathbf{a}) = (a_1, \ldots, a_n)$ is a sequence $\mathcal{T} = (\theta_{i,j})$, $1 \leq i \leq n$, $1 \leq j \leq a_i$, where $\theta_{i,j}$ is an admissible quadruple in W/W_i. The weight $\nu(\mathcal{T})$ associated to a tableau is defined as

$$\nu(\mathcal{T}) := \sum_{\substack{1 \leq i \leq n \\ 1 \leq j \leq a_i}} \nu(\theta_{i,j}).$$

The monomial $p(\mathcal{T})$ of shape $(\mathbf{a})$ associated to $\mathcal{T}$ is the product

$$p(\mathcal{T}) := \prod_{i,j} p(\theta_{i,j}) \in H^0(G/B, \mathcal{L}_\mu),$$

where $p(\theta_{i,j}) \in H^0(G/B, \mathcal{L}_{\omega_i})$ is the section associated to the admissible quadruple $\theta_{i,j}$. The restriction of $p(\mathcal{T})$ to a union of Schubert varieties will also be
denoted by $p(\mathcal{T})$.

3.6 To describe the standard monomials we need the notion of a *defining chain*
for a Young tableau $\mathcal{T} = (\theta_{i,j})$. For $\theta_{i,j} = (\gamma_{i,j}, \delta_{i,j}, \sigma_{i,j}, \phi_{i,j})$ let $\Theta_{i,j} = (\Gamma_{i,j}, \Delta_{i,j}, \Sigma_{i,j}, \Phi_{i,j})$ be a quadruple of elements in W such that the projection
π_i maps $\Gamma_{i,j}, \Delta_{i,j}, \Sigma_{i,j}, \Phi_{i,j}$ to $\gamma_{i,j}, \delta_{i,j}, \sigma_{i,j}$, respectively $\phi_{i,j}$. Let i_0 be such
that $a_{i_0} > 0$ and $a_i = 0$ for $i < i_0$. The sequence $\Theta = (\Theta_{i,j})$ is called a *defining
chain* for $\mathcal{T}$ if

$$\Gamma_{i_0,1} \geq \Delta_{i_0,1} \geq \Sigma_{i_0,1} \geq \Phi_{i_0,1} \geq \Gamma_{i_0,2} \geq \cdots \geq \Phi_{n,a_n}.$$

Definition 3.7 The Young tableau $\mathcal{T}$ is called *standard* if there exists a defining
chain Θ for $\mathcal{T}$. If $Y = X(w_1) \cup \cdots \cup X(w_r)$ is a union of Schubert varieties,
then $\mathcal{T}$ is called *standard on Y* if there exists a defining chain Θ for $\mathcal{T}$ such that
$\Gamma_{1,1} \leq w_j$ for some $j = 1, \ldots, r$. The section $p(\mathcal{T}) \in H^0(G/B, \mathcal{L}_\mu)$ associated
to $\mathcal{T}$ is called a *standard monomial* of type (a) if the tableau $\mathcal{T}$ is standard;
and $p(\mathcal{T})$ is called *standard on Y* if $\mathcal{T}$ is standard on Y.

Second Basis Theorem [6,8,9] *Let Y be a union of Schubert varieties in
G/B and let $\mu = \sum_{i=1}^n a_i \omega_i$ be a dominant weight of type (*). The set of
standard monomials of type (a) $= (a_1, \ldots, a_n)$ on Y form a basis of $H^0(Y, \mathcal{L}_\mu)$.
Moreover, the standard monomials $p(\mathcal{T})$ are T-weight vectors of weight $-\nu(\mathcal{T})$.*

3.8 Using SMT we wish now to define a filtration of $H^0(Y, \mathcal{L}_\mu)$. To simplify
the notation we say $(i, j) < (i', j')$, $i, j \in \mathbf{N}$, if either $i < i'$ or $i = i'$ and
$j < j'$. For $i = 1, \ldots, n$ fix a total ordering "$\prec$" on W/W_i such that $\tau \prec \kappa$ if
$l(\tau) < l(\kappa)$. Denote by "$<$" the induced lexicographic ordering on the set of
admissible quadruples in W/W_i, i.e. $\theta < \theta'$ if $\gamma \prec \gamma'$, or $\gamma = \gamma'$ and $\delta \prec \delta'$, etc.
Let "$<$" also denote the induced lexicographic ordering on the set of Young
tableaux of a fixed shape; i.e., if $\mathcal{T} = (\theta_{i,j})$ and $\mathcal{T}' = (\theta'_{i,j})$ are Young tableaux
of shape (a), then $\mathcal{T} < \mathcal{T}'$ if there exists a pair (i_0, j_0), $1 \leq i_0 \leq n$, $1 \leq j_0 \leq a_{i_0}$,
such that $\theta_{i,j} = \theta'_{i,j}$ for $(i, j) < (i_0, j_0)$, and $\theta_{i_0,j_0} < \theta'_{i_0,j_0}$.

Let Y be a union of Schubert varieties and let $\mu = \sum_{i=1}^n a_i \omega_i$ be a dominant
weight of type (*). Denote by $\{\mathcal{T}_1, \ldots, \mathcal{T}_m\}$ the set of standard Young tableaux
on Y of shape (a). We suppose that the enumeration of the tableaux is such
that $\mathcal{T}_1 > \cdots > \mathcal{T}_m$. Let F_i be the subspace of $H^0(Y, \mathcal{L}_\mu)$ spanned by the
standard monomials $p(\mathcal{T}_j)$, $j \leq i$, and denote by F the complete flag $F : F_0 :=
0 \subset F_1 \subset \cdots \subset F_m = H^0(Y, \mathcal{L}_\mu)$.

Proposition 3.9 ([11]) *The complete flag F is B-stable.*

3.10 We wish to recall the definition of a (Q, λ)-dominant tableau. For an admissible quadruple $\theta = (\gamma, \delta, \sigma, \phi)$ in W/W_i let ν_l, $l = 1, \ldots, 4$ be the following

elements in $X(T) \otimes_{\mathbf{Z}} \mathbf{Q}$ (cf. Definition 3.3):

$$\nu_1 := \lambda + \frac{1}{3}\gamma(\omega_i), \;\; \nu_2 := \nu_1 + \frac{1}{6}\delta(\omega_i),$$

$$\nu_3 := \nu_2 + \frac{1}{6}\sigma(\omega_i), \;\; \nu_4 := \nu_3 + \frac{1}{3}\phi(\omega_i) = \lambda + \nu(\theta).$$

Definition 3.11 Let λ be a Q–dominant weight and let ω_i be a fundamental weight of type $(*)$. An admissible quadruple θ in W/W_i is called (Q, λ)–dominant, if $\langle \nu_i, \alpha \rangle \geq 0$ for $i = 1, \ldots, 4$ and for all simple roots α of L. A standard Young tableau $\mathcal{T} = (\theta_{i,j})$ of shape $(\mathbf{a})$ is called (Q, λ)–dominant if for all pairs (i, j), $1 \leq i \leq n$, $1 \leq j \leq a_i$, the admissible quadruple $\theta_{i,j}$ is $(\lambda + \sum_{(i',j')<(i,j)} \nu(\theta_{i',j'}))$–dominant.

Remark Denote by 1_i the base point in W/W_i. The tableau $\mathcal{T} = (\theta_{i,j})$ with $\theta_{i,j} = (1_i, 1_i, 1_i, 1_i)$ for all $1 \leq i \leq n$, $1 \leq j \leq a_i$, is the minimal standard tableau with respect to the total ordering, and $\mathcal{T}$ is (Q, λ)–dominant for any Q–dominant weight λ.

3.12 Let Y be a union of Schubert varieties in G/B, let $\mu = \sum_{i=1}^{n} a_i \omega_i$ be a dominant weight of type $(*)$, and suppose that λ is a Q–dominant weight. As in 3.8, denote by $\{\mathcal{T}_1, \ldots, \mathcal{T}_m\}$ the set of standard Young tableaux on Y of shape $(\mathbf{a})$, and let $\{\mathcal{T}_{i_1}, \ldots, \mathcal{T}_{i_s}\}$, $i_1 < \cdots < i_s$, be the subset of (Q, λ)–dominant tableaux. We suppose that the enumeration is such that $\mathcal{T}_1 > \cdots > \mathcal{T}_m$. Let

$$F' : F_0 = 0 \subset F_{i_1} \subset \cdots \subset F_{i_s} = H^0(Y, \mathcal{L}_\mu)$$

be the subflag of the complete flag F in 3.8 corresponding to the (Q, λ)–dominant tableaux. Denote by $\mathcal{F}_{i_j}$ the vector bundle on Q/B associated to the B–module F_{i_j}.

Theorem 3.13 ([11]) *Denote by* M_j *the* Q–*module* $H^0(Q/B, \mathcal{L}_\lambda \otimes \mathcal{F}_{i_j})$. *The* Q–*stable filtration* $M_0 = 0 \subset M_1 \subset \cdots \subset M_s = H^0(Q \times^B Y, \mathcal{L}_{\lambda,\mu})$ *is a good filtration such that*

$$M_j/M_{j-1} \simeq H^0(Q/B, \mathcal{L}_\lambda \otimes \mathcal{F}_{i_j}/\mathcal{F}_{i_{j-1}}) \simeq H^0(Q/B, \mathcal{L}_{\lambda+\nu(\mathcal{T}_{i_j})}).$$

Moreover, $H^l(Q/B, \mathcal{L}_\lambda \otimes \mathcal{F}_{i_j}/\mathcal{F}_{i_{j-1}}) = 0$ *for* $l > 0$.

3.14 Generalized Littlewood–Richardson rule. ([10,11]) Suppose now that k is an algebraically closed field of characteristic zero. Then every G– or L–module decomposes into the direct sum of simple modules, and the simple modules are the modules of the form $H^0(G/B, \mathcal{L}_\lambda)$ respectively $H^0(Q/B, \mathcal{L}_\lambda)$, where λ is a dominant weight in the first case, and a Q–dominant weight in the second case. So Theorem 3.13 gives us in fact a rule to compute the decomposition of the L–module $H^0(Q \times^B Y, \mathcal{L}_{\lambda,\mu})$ into simple L–modules.

In particular, if $Q = G$ and $Y = G/B$, then we obtain the tensor product decomposition rule

$$H^0(G/B, \mathcal{L}_\lambda) \otimes H^0(G/B, \mathcal{L}_\mu) = \bigoplus_{\mathcal{T}} H^0(G/B, \mathcal{L}_{\lambda+\nu(\mathcal{T})}),$$

where the sum is taken over all (G, λ)–dominant standard Young tableaux of shape (a).

Further, if we set $\lambda = 0$ and $Y = G/B$, then we obtain a restriction rule to compute the decomposition of $H^0(G/B, \mathcal{L}_\mu)$ into the direct sum of simple L–modules:

$$H^0(G/B, \mathcal{L}_\mu) = \bigoplus_{\mathcal{T}} H^0(Q/B, \mathcal{L}_{\nu(\mathcal{T})}),$$

where the sum is taken over all $(Q, 0)$–dominant standard Young tableaux of shape (a).

3.15 Example A translation of the notion of a standard Young tableau in the sense of section 3 into the "classical" notion of a Young tableau (as in section 2) can be found in [10] for the classical groups. As an example we shall discuss the case $G = Sp_4$. We use the same notation for the fundamental weights ω_1, ω_2 as in [1].

Since $|\langle \omega_i, \beta \rangle| \leq 2$, $i = 1, 2$, for all roots, the admissible quadruples are all of the form $(\tau, \tau, \delta, \delta)$, so we might rather talk about the admissible pairs (τ, δ). We identify first W/W_i with the orbit $W \cdot \omega_i$, $i = 1, 2$. We get

$$W \cdot \omega_1 = \{\epsilon_1, \epsilon_2, -\epsilon_2, -\epsilon_1\}, \quad W \cdot \omega_2 = \{\epsilon_1 + \epsilon_2, \epsilon_1 - \epsilon_2, -\epsilon_1 + \epsilon_2, -\epsilon_1 - \epsilon_2\}$$

To each weight (or coset) we associate a sequence of numbers in the following way: $\epsilon_1 : (1)$, $\epsilon_2 : (2)$, $-\epsilon_2 : (3)$, $-\epsilon_1 : (4)$, $\epsilon_1 + \epsilon_2 : (1, 2)$, $\epsilon_1 - \epsilon_2 : (1, 3)$, $-\epsilon_1 + \epsilon_2 : (2, 4)$, $-\epsilon_1 - \epsilon_2 : (3, 4)$. If $\theta = (\tau, \delta)$ is an admissible pair in W/W_i, then we identify θ with the (classical) tableau of shape (2) (for $i = 1$), respectively $(2, 2)$ (for $i = 2$), having the sequence corresponding to τ as first and the sequence corresponding to δ as second row. We have the following admissible pairs:

	1	2	3	4		12	13	13	24	34
$i = 1:$	,	,	,		$i = 2:$	,	,	,	,	.
	1	2	3	4		12	13	24	24	34

Suppose now that $\mathcal{T} = (\theta_{i,j})$ is a standard Young tableau (in the sense of section 3) of shape $\mu = a_1 \omega_1 + a_2 \omega_2$. We associate to $\mathcal{T}$ a "classical" Young tableau $\mathcal{T}'$ of shape $\mathbf{p}(\mu) := (2a_1 + 2a_2, 2a_2, 0, 0)$ in the following way: Let $\mathcal{T}'$ be the tableau having for $m = 1, \ldots, a_1$ the tableau corresponding to $\theta_{1,m}$ as $(2m-1)$st row and $2m$th row, and for $m = 1, \ldots, a_2$ the tableau corresponding to $\theta_{2,m}$ as $(2a_1 + 2m - 1)$st and $2(a_1 + m)$th row.

It is now easy to check that this correspondence gives a bijection between the standard Young tableaux $\mathcal{T}$ of shape μ in the sense of section 3 and the standard Young tableaux $\mathcal{T}'$ of shape $\mathbf{p}(\mu)$ in the sense of section 2 which have the property that for $l = 1, \ldots, a_1 + a_2$ the subtableau consisting of the $(2l - 1)$st and $2l$th row of $\mathcal{T}'$ is an admissible pair in the list above.

Let $\nu(\mathcal{T}') := (c_{\mathcal{T}'}(1) - c_{\mathcal{T}'}(4))\epsilon_1 + (c_{\mathcal{T}'}(2) - c_{\mathcal{T}'}(3))\epsilon_2$. Then $\nu(\mathcal{T}) = \nu(\mathcal{T}')$. Further, if λ is Q–dominant, then $\mathcal{T}$ is (Q, λ)–dominant if and only if $\langle \lambda + \nu(\mathcal{T}'(l)), \alpha \rangle \geq 0$ for $l = 1, \ldots, 2a_1 + 2a_2$ and all simple roots α of L.

For example, if $Q = G$ and $\lambda = \mu = \omega_1 + \omega_2$, then the (Q, λ)–dominant standard Young tableaux of shape $\mathbf{p}(\mu) = (4, 2, 0, 0)$ are

3	4
3	4
4	
4	

1	3
1	3
4	
4	

1	2
1	2
4	
4	

2	4
2	4
3	
3	

1	3
2	4
3	
3	

1	2
1	2
3	
3	

1	3
1	3
2	
2	

1	2
1	2
2	
2	

1	3
1	3
1	
1	

1	2
1	2
1	
1	

Suppose now that k is algebraically closed and char $k = 0$. Then, by 3.14, setting $V_\eta := H^0(G/B, \mathcal{L}_\eta)$ for a dominant weight η, we get the following decomposition:

$$V_{\omega_1+\omega_2} \otimes V_{\omega_1+\omega_2} \simeq V_{4\omega_1} \oplus V_{2\omega_1+2\omega_2} \oplus 2V_{2\omega_1+\omega_2}$$
$$\oplus\, 2V_{2\omega_1} \oplus V_{3\omega_2} \oplus V_{2\omega_2} \oplus V_{\omega_2} \oplus V_0.$$

4. References

[1] N. Bourbaki, "Groupes et algèbres de Lie," Chap. 4–6, Hermann, Paris, (1968).

[2] S. Donkin, "Rational Representations of Algebraic Groups," Springer Verlag, Berlin–New York, Lecture notes in Mathematics, **1140** (1985).

[3] R. Hartshorne, "Algebraic geometry," Springer Verlag, Berlin–New York, GTM, **52** (1985).

[4] J. Jantzen, "Representations of Algebraic groups," Academic Press, Orlando, Pure and Applied Mathematics, **131** (1987).

[5] S. Kumar, Proof of the Parthasarathy-Ranga-Rao-Varadarajan Conjecture, *Invent. Math.* **93** (1988), 117-130.

[6] V. Lakshmibai, Standard monomial theory for G_2, *J. Algebra* **98** (1986), 281–318.

[7] V. Lakshmibai–C. Musili–C. S. Seshadri, Geometry of G/P IV, *Proc. Indian Acad. Sci., Part A* **87** (1979), 279–362.

[8] V. Lakshmibai–K. N. Rajeswari, Towards a standard monomial theory for exceptional groups, *Contemp. Math.* **88** (1989), 449–578.

[9] V. Lakshmibai–C. S. Seshadri, Geometry of G/P V, *J. Algebra* **100** (1986), 462–557.

[10] P. Littelmann, A generalization of the Littlewood–Richardson rule, *J. Algebra* **130** (1990), 328–368.

[11] P. Littelmann, Good filtrations and decomposition rules for representations with standard monomial theory, *Preprint* (1990).

[12] O. Mathieu, Filtrations of B–modules, *Duke Math. J.* **59** (1989), 421–442.

[13] O. Mathieu, Filtrations for G–modules, *Preprint (to appear in Ann. Sc. Éc. Norm. Supér.)* (1989).

[14] V. B. Mehta–A. Ramanathan, Schubert varieties in $G/B \times G/B$, *Compos. Math.* **67** (1988), 355–358.

[15] S. Ramanan–A. Ramanathan, Projective normality of flag varieties and Schubert varieties, *Invent. Math.* **79** (1985), 217–224.

[16] A. Ramanathan, Schubert varieties are Cohen–Macaulay, *Invent. Math.* **80** (1985), 283–295.

[17] P. Polo, Modules associés aux variétés de Schubert, *C.R. Acad. Sc. Paris* **308** (1989), 37–60.

[18] C. S. Seshadri, Standard monomial theory and the work of Demazure, "Advanced Studies in pure Mathematics, Vol.I," Tokyo, (1983), 355–384.

[19] C. S. Seshadri, Geometry of G/P–I, "C. P. Ramanunjan: A Tribute," Published for the Tata Insitute of Fundamental Research, Bombay, Springer Verlag, Berlin–New York, (1978), 207–239.

[20] Wang Jian–Pian, Sheaf cohomology on G/B and tensor products of Weyl modules, *J. Algebra* **77** (1982), 162–185.

Computational Aspects of Lie Group Representations and Related Topics   107
Proceedings of the 1990 Computational Algebra Seminar
pp. 107–128 in CWI Tract 84 (1991)

Constructing Roots of Polynomials

over the Complex Numbers

Wim B.G. Ruitenburg

Department of Mathematics, Statistics and Computer Science

Marquette University

Milwaukee, WI 53233

USA

0. Introduction

Constructive proofs of the Fundamental Theorem of Algebra are known since 1924, when L. E. J. Brouwer, B. de Loor, and H. Weyl showed that nonconstant monic polynomials over the complex numbers have a complex root. Later that year Brouwer generalized this result by showing that each polynomial $f(X)$ having an invertible coefficient for some positive power of X has a root. These proofs are constructive equivalents of classical analytical proofs of the Fundamental Theorem. Modern versions of their results are in [BB, pp. 156ff] and [TvDa, pp. 434ff]. The time has come to give a constructive algebraic proof.

In [M] the authors use algebraic methods to show that the algebraic closure $\mathbf{C}^a$ of the field of rationals $\mathbf{Q}$ in the field of complex numbers $\mathbf{C}$ is algebraically closed and dense in $\mathbf{C}$. In the exercises it is indicated how one can construct roots of monic polynomials over the complexes more generally [M, p. 191]. There is, however, no indication how to accomplish this without resorting to some choice principles, or how to generalize this to polynomials of which it is only known that the coefficient of some positive power of X is invertible. We show that the more general version is indeed provable, and without resorting to choice principles.

We have two target audiences in mind: Constructivists and computer algebraists. To accommodate the former we present the algebraic results in more detail than would otherwise be necessary. For the latter, we will presently discuss some aspects of constructive mathematics, how it relates to algorithms, and why avoiding choice principles matters to us.

There exist several schools of constructive mathematics, the most well-known being Brouwer's intuitionism, Markov constructivism, and Bishop constructivism [BR]. Modern followers, however, do not always closely adhere to the philosophies of the originators, so many 'dialects' developed, some of these motivated by the existence of models for constructive logic. The mathematics we use is based on the constructive logic that holds for all topos models [G], and is also called intuitionism. This intuitionism is essentially stricter than the constructivisms mentioned above, so our results hold in all topos models, and are acceptable to most constructivists at the same time. The most important restriction is the lack of choice principles. Fortunately, only a small amount of knowledge of intuitionism is required for understanding the constructive proofs of the Fundamental Theorem.

A clear illustration of where constructivism differs from classical mathematics occurs in proving statements of the form "there exists x such that $A(x)$." Classically it suffices to show that it is impossible that there is no x for which $A(x)$ holds. A constructive proof must construct x as well as a proof of $A(x)$. In particular, a constructive proof of "A or B" must consist of a proof of A or a proof of B. If B is the statement "not A", then a constructive proof of "A or not A" means either proving A, or proving that assuming A leads to an absurdity. Such proofs cannot always be found. So the Principle of the Excluded Middle fails.

There is a difference between proving "not A" and showing that A cannot be proven. We illustrate this through examples. It is well-known that constructive proofs have computational content. So if there is a constructive proof of the existence of a function $f: \mathbf{N} \to \mathbf{N}$ such that $A(n, f(n))$ holds for all natural numbers $n \in \mathbf{N}$, then, by classical techniques outside the realm of constructivism, one can show that f is a computable function. On one hand, if by classical means we know that there is no computable function f such that $A(n, f(n))$ holds for all n, then we know that "there exists f such that $A(n, f(n))$ for all n" cannot be proven. On the other hand, a *constructive* proof of the negation of this statement implies that the negation also holds in classical mathematics: There is no solution f whatsoever. Let us identify Turing machines with natural numbers by some primitive recursive bijective encoding. By the Halting Theorem there is no computable function f such that $f(n) = 0$ exactly when Turing machine n halts, but there are noncomputable ones. So it cannot be shown constructively that such a function exists, and it cannot be shown constructively that such a function does not exist. Another example, also based on the Halting Theorem, says that there is no constructive proof to decide for all binary sequences $\alpha: \mathbf{N} \to \{0, 1\}$ whether $\alpha(n) = 1$ for some n.

The three constructive schools mentioned above accept certain choice principles that are at least as strong as the simple axiom of Countable Choice. The simple axiom of *Countable Choice* says that if $A(m, n)$ is a statement about natural numbers m, n such that for all m there exists n with the property that $A(m, n)$ holds, then there exists a function f such that $A(m, f(m))$ holds for all m. [BB] and [TvDa], in their proofs of the Fundamental Theorem of Algebra, make essential use of choice principles extending Countable Choice. Although not explicitly stated, the construction of the algebraic closure $\mathbf{C}^a$ in [M] does not make essential use of any choice principles. By avoiding choice principles, results will hold in all topos models. This implies that if we are able to construct a solution x of an equation $f(x) = 0$ over the (Dedekind) reals using topos intuitionism, then x is locally continuous in the parameters of the equation. So, for example, we cannot show the existence of a solution of $X^3 + pX + q = 0$ over the (Dedekind) reals when (p, q) is close to $(0, 0)$, because it would imply the existence of a continuous solution $X(p, q)$ in a neighborhood of $(0, 0)$ [JR]. For the same reason we cannot find a solution to the equation $X^2 + c = 0$ over the (Dedekind) complex numbers when c is near 0. With Countable Choice, however, one can find solutions. So if we allow the use of Countable Choice, then continuity of solutions in the parameters is no longer guaranteed.

The lack of choice principles does not prevent us from constructing functions. Suppose that $A(m, n)$ is a statement for which we can prove that for all $m \in \mathbf{N}$ there exists a least n for which $A(m, n)$ holds. Define f by $f(m) = $ the least n for which $A(m, n)$ holds. Then $A(m, f(m))$ holds for all m. The key distinction is that we are able to give a finite description that uniquely defines f.

Constructive mathematics without choice principles is stricter than 'computable' mathematics. Its constructive nature more than allows us to construct algorithms from the constructive proofs: It also proves the correctness of the algorithms. These implicit algorithms, however, are usually grossly inefficient since in practice constructivists concentrate on abstractness and generality rather than on the computational complexity of their results.

In §1 we prove the existence of algebraic closures of countable discrete fields (Poor Man's Algebraic Closure). In §2 these are used to construct algebraic closures of countable factorial discrete fields (Rich Man's Algebraic Closure). Within such algebraic closures we can factor nonzero polynomials into irreducible factors over many subfields. We apply these results to $\mathbf{Q}$ and, in §3, establish isomorphisms with the algebraic closure $\mathbf{C}^a$ of $\mathbf{Q}$ in $\mathbf{C}$. Then we use the algebraic closedness of $\mathbf{C}^a$ to show that many more polynomials over $\mathbf{C}$ have roots in $\mathbf{C}$, strengthening the results of [BB] and [TvDa].

1. The Poor Man's Algebraic Closure

It is not necessary to recapitulate all of algebra just because we use constructive methods. It is easily seen that many basic results from classical algebra are constructive. Therefore we concentrate on the less obvious results, or results that require an original proof, together with some glue to create one coherent presentation.

First and foremost, sets need not be discrete. A set is *discrete* if for all of its elements a, b we can determine whether $a = b$ or not. The natural numbers

N, integers **Z**, and rationals **Q** are discrete sets. Obviously, polynomial rings $R[X]$ over a discrete commutative ring R are also discrete. But the reals **R** are not: For a real to exist it suffices, for each natural number $m > 0$, to be able to give a rational interval of length at most $1/m$ 'in which the real number lies,' see §3. For each Turing machine we can construct a sequence $\{a_n\}_n$ by setting $a_n = 1/n$ if the machine does not stop in n steps, and $a_n = 1/m$ if the machine stops in $m \leq n$ steps. As a Cauchy sequence, $\{a_n\}_n$ determines a real number. By the Halting Theorem, we cannot show for each Turing machine whether the limit of its corresponding sequence $\{a_n\}_n$ equals 0 or not.

A discrete set is *finite* if there exists a bijection with an initial segment $\{0, \ldots, n-1\}$ of **N**. The empty set (if $n = 0$) is finite. Finite combinatorial theorems are essentially constructive. This is true for all finite group theory that we will need, including Sylow's Theorem. Some caution is required, though. Exceptions are statements like 'each subgroup of a finite group is finite.' For example, let $G = \{0, 1\}$ be the group of two elements, and let H be the subgroup of G generated by the image of a binary sequence $\{a_n\}_n$. Then $H = G$ if and only if $a_n = 1$ for some n, and $H = \{0\}$ if $a_n = 0$ for all n. By the Halting Theorem, such a choice cannot always be made constructively.

In classical mathematics, groups, rings, and modules are defined by simple universal equational axioms like, for rings, $x(y + z) = xy + xz$. In constructive algebra we use the same schemas to axiomatize them. A ring is nontrivial when 1 is not equal to 0.

We do not require equality on groups, rings, and modules to be discrete. This creates problems when we want to define integral domain and field. In the case of integral domains, an axiom saying that from $xy = 0$ one can conclude $x = 0$ or $y = 0$ is too restricting because of the difficulty of establishing "or": Even the real numbers cannot be shown to satisfy this axiom. Instead, one has a binary relation $x \neq y$ on the ring, classically usually equivalent to "$x = y$ is false." On **R** and **C** we define $x \neq y$ if and only if $x - y$ is a unit. Being nonzero and being a unit cannot be shown to be the same. An integral domain then satisfies: If $x \neq 0$ and $y \neq 0$, then $xy \neq 0$. Similarly, **R** and **C**—obviously—satisfy the field property: If $x \neq 0$, then x is a unit. The technical problems with inequalities grow fast, and we refer the reader to [M, pp. 41ff] and [Ru] for further details and developments. When we restrict ourselves to discrete structures, we avoid these problems because we can use the classical definitions: A discrete nontrivial commutative ring is a *discrete domain* if for all x, y such that $xy = 0$ we have $x = 0$ or $y = 0$. A discrete domain is a *discrete field* if all nonzero elements are units. One easily verifies that the standard construction of a quotient field of a discrete domain produces a discrete field.

One easily verifies that elementary finite-dimensional linear algebra over discrete fields (rank of a matrix, finite-dimensional null spaces and ranges, Gaussian elimination, determinant) is constructive. If A is a square matrix over a discrete field k, then the commutative matrix ring $k[A]$ is discrete. The *characteristic polynomial* of A is the polynomial $f(X) = \det (X - A)$ over $k \subseteq k[A]$. For all invertible S, $\det (X - A) = \det (X - S^{-1}AS)$. The *eigenvalues* of A are the roots of $f(X)$ in k or in a discrete field extension of k. The construction of roots of polynomials over discrete extension fields is a nontrivial matter. Even the existence of such roots is not guaranteed [M, p. 153], unless the base field k is countable (Theorem 1.6).

A module over a commutative ring R is *finite-rank free* if it is isomorphic to R^n, for some $n \in \mathbf{N}$.

1.0 Proposition (Cayley-Hamilton) *Let R be a commutative ring, and $f(X)$ be the characteristic polynomial of an endomorphism α of a finite-rank free R-module. Then $f(\alpha) = 0$.*

Proof For an algebraic proof, see [M, p. 72].   □

Proposition 1.0 allows for a non-algebraic proof. Let A be an $n \times n$ matrix with variables $X_{i,j}$ as entries. Then the characteristic polynomial $f(A)$ over $\mathbf{Z}$ in n^2 variables reduces to 0, as is shown by classical means. A general theorem of logic says that the same reduction must work constructively. There are several results below that can be reduced to trivialities using general theorems from logic. We refrain from using these methods so as to increase the accessibility of our results.

A polynomial over a commutative ring is *monic* if it has leading coefficient 1. A polynomial $f = a^n X^n + \cdots + a_0$ has *degree at most* n, and *degree less than* m for all $m > n$. We may not know the degree of a polynomial, because we may not know whether a 'leading' coefficient equals 0 or not. Naturally, monic polynomials and polynomials over discrete commutative rings have a degree.

An R-module M is *faithful* if $rM = 0$ implies $r = 0$, for all $r \in R$.

1.1 Proposition *Let $R \subseteq S$ be commutative rings, and $\alpha \in S$. Then the following are equivalent:*

(i) *α satisfies a monic polynomial of degree n over R.*

(ii) *$R[\alpha]$ is generated by n elements as an R-module.*

(iii) *S has a faithful R-submodule M, generated by n elements, such that $\alpha M \subseteq M$.*

Proof Obviously, (i) implies (ii), and (ii) implies (iii). Suppose (iii) holds, and let $m_1, \ldots, m_n$ generate M. There are $\beta_{i,j} \in R$ such that $\alpha m_j = \sum_i \beta_{i,j} m_i$. Let f be the characteristic polynomial of the matrix $\{\beta_{i,j}\}$. Then $f(\alpha)M = 0$, so $f(\alpha) = 0$. So (i) holds.   □

A commutative ring $S \supseteq R$ is called *integral* over the commutative ring R if all $s \in S$ are roots of monic polynomials over R. From Proposition 1.1 it now follows that if α is root of a monic polynomial over R, then so are all elements of $R[\alpha]$. We say that α is *integral* over R if $R[\alpha]$ is integral over R. If R is a discrete field, then—following tradition—we commonly use the term *algebraic* instead of *integral*.

1.2 Proposition *Let $R \subseteq S$ be commutative rings, and let $\alpha, \beta \in S$ be such that α is integral over R, and β is integral over $R[\alpha]$. Then $R[\alpha, \beta]$ is integral over R. The elements of S that are integral over R form a subring.*

Proof It suffices to prove the first claim: $R[\alpha, \beta]$ is a finitely generated module over $R[\alpha]$, and $R[\alpha]$ is a finitely generated module over R. Multiplication of the generators of the two extensions yields a finite set of generators of $R[\alpha, \beta]$ as module over R.   □

1.3 Proposition *Let R, S be commutative rings such that S is a finitely generated integral ring extension of R. Then S is a finitely generated R-module.*

Proof There exist rings $R_0 \subseteq R_1 \subseteq \cdots \subseteq R_n$ such that $R_i = R[a_1, \ldots, a_i]$, and $R_n = S$. Then R_{i+1} is a finitely generated R_i-module, for all i. Multiplication of the generators from the different extensions produces a finite set of generators for $R_n = S$ as module over $R_0 = R$.   □

1.4 Proposition *Let $R \subseteq S \subseteq T$ be commutative rings such that $T \supseteq S$ and $S \supseteq R$ are integral extensions. Then $T \supseteq R$ is integral.*

Proof For each $\alpha \in T$ there is a monic polynomial $f(X) = X^n + a_1 X^{n-1} + \cdots + a_n$ over S such that $f(\alpha) = 0$. Let $S' = R[a_1, \ldots, a_n]$. Then $S'[\alpha]$ is a finitely generated module over S', and S' is a finitely generated module over R. So $S'[\alpha]$ is finitely generated as module over R. Thus α is integral over R.   □

A set S is *countable* if there exists a function $s: \mathbf{N} \to S$ from the natural numbers onto S, that is, $S = \{s_0, s_1, s_2, \ldots\}$.

A subset $Y \subseteq X$ is called *detachable* from X if for all $x \in X$ we can decide whether $x \in Y$ or $x \notin Y$, that is, x is not an element of Y. So a commutative ring R is discrete exactly when $\{0\}$ is detachable from R. More generally, an ideal $I \subseteq R$ is detachable from R if and only if the quotient ring R/I is discrete.

Countable discrete sets may be finite or (countably) infinite, but we cannot always know which one. For example, let $p_0, p_1, \ldots$ be the ascending sequence of prime numbers, and let $\{a_n\}_n$ be a binary sequence with at most one 1. Let $P \subseteq \mathbf{Z}$ be the ideal generated by the sequence of elements $\{a_n p_n\}_n$. One easily verifies that P is a prime ideal that is detachable from $\mathbf{Z}$. The quotient ring $R = \mathbf{Z}/P$ is countable, but, by the Halting Theorem, we may not know whether it is finite or not. We may not know its characteristic either. The quotient field of R is a countable discrete field whose characteristic we cannot determine.

1.5 Proposition *Let R be a countable commutative ring whose finitely generated ideals are detachable, and let I be a proper finitely generated ideal. Then I is contained in a maximal ideal that is detachable from R.*

Proof $R = \{r_0, r_1, \ldots\}$ for some enumeration r. Construct a sequence of finitely generated ideals $I_0 \subseteq I_1 \subseteq \cdots$ as follows: Set $I_0 = I$; if $I_j + r_j R = R$, then set $I_{j+1} = I_j$, otherwise set $I_{j+1} = I_j + r_j R$. Let $M = \bigcup_j I_j$. Then $r_j \in M$ if and only if $r_j \in I_{j+1}$. So M is a detachable maximal ideal.   □

1.6 Theorem *Let f be a nonconstant polynomial over a countable discrete field k. Then there is a countable discrete field $E \supseteq k$ and $\alpha \in E$ such that $f(\alpha) = 0$.*

Proof By the Euclidean Algorithm all finitely generated ideals of the countable ring $k[X]$ are principal and detachable. So f is contained in a detachable maximal ideal M. Set $E = k[X]/M$. $\square$

Let $\{a_n\}_n$ be a binary sequence, and let k be the countable discrete field extension of $\mathbf{Q}$ generated by the sequence $\{a_n \sqrt{2}\}_n$. Then we may not know the factorization of $X^2 - 2$ over k. So in general one cannot give a minimal polynomial for α in Theorem 1.6.

A discrete field K is a *splitting field* for a monic polynomial f over a discrete field k if there exist $a_1, \ldots, a_n \in K$ such that $f = (X - a_1) \cdots (X - a_n)$ and $K = k[a_1, \ldots, a_n]$. Repeated application of Theorem 1.6 now gives:

1.7 Theorem *Let f be a monic polynomial over a countable discrete field k. Then there exists a countable discrete splitting field for f over k.* $\square$

In general one cannot show that countable discrete splitting fields are uniquely determined up to isomorphism [M, pp. 153ff].

The construction in the proof of Proposition 1.5 depends on the enumeration of the ring R. Different enumerations may give different maximal ideals. To avoid choice principles when we use Theorem 1.7 in the proof of the theorem below, we need to choose some canonical method to construct one unique splitting field K with enumeration from a given discrete field k with enumeration. Let $\{a_0, a_1, \ldots\}$ be an enumeration of a countable discrete field k. Then the *canonical enumeration* of $k[X]$ (based on $\{a_n\}_n$) is the one that lists, for $i = 1, 2, \ldots$ successively, all polynomials of degree at most i in the coefficients $a_0, a_1, \ldots, a_i$ in lexicographical order with the leading term considered most significant. If we use the canonical enumeration, then, for all $f \in k[X]$, the field extension $k[\alpha]$ of Theorem 1.6 is uniquely determined, and $k[\alpha]$ receives its (canonical) enumeration from $k[X]$. Repeating this process, using canonical enumerations at each step, the splitting field of Theorem 1.7 is uniquely determined by the enumeration of k, and by f.

1.8 Theorem (Poor Man's Algebraic Closure) *Each countable discrete field k is contained in a countable discrete field that is algebraically closed and algebraic over k.*

Proof Let $f_0, f_1, \ldots$ be an enumeration of the monic polynomials over k. Construct a chain of countable discrete fields $k_0 \subseteq k_1 \subseteq \cdots$ by setting $k_0 = k$, and by letting k_{i+1} be the canonical splitting field of f_i over k_i. Let $\Omega = \bigcup_i k_i$. Clearly, Ω is countable, discrete, and an algebraic field extension of k. Let f be a monic polynomial over Ω. By Proposition 1.6 there is a countable discrete field extension $E \supseteq \Omega$ such that $f(\alpha) = 0$ for some $\alpha \in E$. By Proposition 1.4 α is algebraic over k. So $f_i(\alpha) = 0$ for some i. But f_i splits in $k_{i+1} \subseteq \Omega$. Thus $\alpha \in \Omega$. $\square$

Note that the special construction of k_{i+1} from k_i enables us to avoid choice principles in the construction of Ω, since all k_i are uniquely determined by any enumeration of $k_0 = k$. By the uniqueness of the k_i, the union Ω is uniquely determined.

Splitting fields cannot be uniquely determined up to isomorphism, so one cannot show that countable discrete algebraic closures of a discrete field k are uniquely determined up to isomorphism.

1.9 Corollary *The field* $\mathbf{Q}$ *of rational numbers has a countable discrete algebraic closure.* $\square$

In §2 we will show that for $\mathbf{Q}$ countable discrete algebraic closures are unique up to isomorphism.

2. The Rich Man's Algebraic Closure

A discrete domain R is a GCD-*domain* if for all $a, b \in R$ there exists a greatest common divisor $c = \gcd(a, b)$. Obviously, c is unique up to a unit, and GCD-domains satisfy the familiar equations [M, pp. 108ff]

$$\gcd(\gcd(a, b), c) = \gcd(a, \gcd(b, c));$$
$$c \cdot \gcd(a, b) = \gcd(ca, cb);$$
$$\text{if } x = \gcd(a, b), \text{ then } \gcd(a, bc) = \gcd(a, xc); \quad \text{and}$$
$$\text{if } a \mid bc \text{ and } \gcd(a, b) = 1, \text{ then } a \mid c.$$

All equations are up to a unit. Equality-up-to-a-unit need not be a discrete equality relation on the equivalence classes. (Consider, for example, the subring of $\mathbf{Q}$ generated by the sequence $\{a_n/2\}_n$, for some binary sequence $\{a_n\}_n$.) Note that, by the Euclidean Algorithm, $k[X]$ is a GCD-domain for all discrete fields k.

Let f be a polynomial over a GCD-domain. Then $\operatorname{cont}(f)$, the *content* of f, is the greatest common divisor of the coefficients of f; f is *primitive* if $\operatorname{cont}(f) = 1$.

2.0 Lemma (Gauss's Lemma) *Let* f *and* g *be nonzero polynomials over a GCD-domain* R. *Then* $\operatorname{cont}(fg) = \operatorname{cont}(f)\operatorname{cont}(g)$.

Proof We may assume that f and g are primitive. Let m and n be the degrees of f and g, respectively, let $c = \operatorname{cont}(fg)$, and let $d = \gcd(c, a_m)$, where a_m is the leading coefficient of f. We complete the proof by induction on $m + n$. If $f = a_m X^m$, then we are done. Otherwise, $d \mid (f - a_m X^m)g$, so, by induction, $d \mid \operatorname{cont}(f - a_m f)\operatorname{cont}(g)$. Since g is primitive, $d \mid (f - a_m X^m)$, thus also $d \mid f$, proving $d = \gcd(c, a_m) = 1$. Similarly, $\gcd(c, b_n) = 1$, where b_n is the leading coefficient of g. So $\gcd(c, a_m b_n) = 1$. Thus fg is primitive. $\square$

Let f and g be polynomials over a commutative ring R such that g is monic. By the Remainder Theorem there are unique polynomials q and r over R, with r of a degree less than the degree of g, such that $f = qg + r$. The coefficients of q and r are polynomials in the coefficients of f and g.

2.1 Theorem (Unique Interpolation) *Let $a_0, \ldots, a_n$ and $v_0, \ldots, v_n$ be elements of a commutative ring R such that $a_i - a_j$ is a unit, for all $i \neq j$. Then there is a unique polynomial of degree at most n over R such that $f(a_i) = v_i$ for all i.*

Proof By induction on n. If $n = 0$, choose $f = v_0$. If $n > 0$, then there is a polynomial g of degree at most $n - 1$ such that $g(a_i) = (v_i - v_n)/(a_i - a_n)$ for all $i < n$. Take $f = (X - a_n)g + v_n$.

For uniqueness it suffices to show that if $f(a_i) = 0$ for all i, and f is of degree at most n, then $f = 0$. The case for $n = 0$ is trivial. Suppose $n > 0$. By the Remainder Theorem, $f = g(X - a_n)$ for some g of degree at most $n - 1$ with $g(a_i) = 0$ for all $i < n$. By induction on n, $g = 0$. So $f = 0$. □

A nonzero element p of a discrete domain R is *irreducible* if it is not a unit, and if $p = qr$ implies that q or r is a unit, for all $q, r \in R$.

A discrete domain is a *unique factorization domain* or *UFD* if each nonzero element is a unit or equals a product of irreducibles, and such that if $p_1 \cdots p_m = q_1 \cdots q_n$ are two products of irreducibles, then $m = n$ and there is a permutation π such that p_i and $q_{\pi i}$ differ by a unit, for all i. Discrete fields and $\mathbf{Z}$ are unique factorization domains. A discrete domain R is *factorial* if $R[X]$ is a discrete UFD. This definition seems unnatural at first, but is a natural generalization of the notion of factorial field: A discrete field is factorial when we can factor polynomials over it into irreducibles. See also Theorem 2.3. Algebraically closed discrete fields are factorial, since all nonconstant polynomials factor into linear terms.

A set is *infinite* if it contains arbitrarily large finite subsets. Without choice principles we cannot show that an infinite set contains a countably infinite subset.

2.2 Theorem (Kronecker 1) *If R is an infinite UFD with finitely many units, then so is $R[X]$. Thus R is factorial.*

Proof Obviously $R[X]$ has finitely many units since it has the same units as R. Let $f \in R[X]$ be of degree $n > 0$. We complete the proof by induction on n. It suffices to provide a finite collection of polynomials that includes all possible factors of f. Let $a_0, \ldots, a_n$ be distinct elements of R. If $f(a_i) = 0$ for some i, then we divide a factor $X - a_i$ out of f and apply induction. So we may assume $f(a_i) \neq 0$ for all i. Each nonzero element of R has finitely many divisors, so there are finitely many sequences $b_0, \ldots, b_n$ such that b_i divides $f(a_i)$, for all i. By the Unique Interpolation Theorem 2.1, there is for each such sequence a unique polynomial g over the quotient field of R, of degree at most n, such that $g(a_i) = b_i$. Since R is detachable from its quotient field, we can find a finite subcollection of g with coefficients in R that includes all factors of f. □

An essentially identical proof of Theorem 2.2 was given, about nine decades before Kronecker, by the astronomer Friedrich Theodor von Schubert (1758–1825) in 1793 [vS]. See also [C, pp. 136ff].

2.3 Theorem (Kronecker 2) *If R is a factorial domain, then so is $R[X]$.*

Proof For $m > 0$, let $R[X, Y]_m$ be the submodule of $R[X, Y]$ of polynomials of X-degree less than m. The submodule $R[X, Y]_m$ is closed under taking factors. Let $\varphi_m: R[X, Y]_m \to R[X]$ be the R-module map that is the restriction of the ring morphism that is the identity on $R[X]$ and maps Y to X^m, and let $\psi_m: R[X] \to R[X, Y]_m$ be the R-module map that takes X^n to $Y^q X^r$, where $n = qm + r$ with $0 \le r < m$. Then φ_m and ψ_m are each other's inverses. Each factorization of a polynomial $f \in R[X, Y]$ of X-degree less than m must be of the form $f = \psi_m(g)\psi_m(h)$. So it suffices to factor $\varphi_m(f)$ in $R[X]$. □

Note that, in the proof of Theorem 2.3, $\varphi_m(f)$ may have factorizations that do not translate into factorizations of f.

By Kronecker 1 the domain $\mathbf{Z}$ is factorial, so, by Gauss's Lemma, $\mathbf{Q}$ is factorial too. Thus, by Kronecker 2, $\mathbf{Q}(X_1, X_2, \ldots)$ is factorial, and so is $k(X_1, X_2, \ldots)$, for all algebraically closed discrete fields k. Next we will show that finite algebraic extensions of $\mathbf{Q}$ are also factorial. Since $\mathbf{Q}$ has characteristic 0, several results are proven for discrete fields of characteristic 0 only. Generalizations involving separability conditions are discussed in [M].

Elements a, b of a commutative ring R are *strongly relatively prime* if $aR + bR = R$. The derivative f' of a polynomial f is defined as usual. A polynomial f over a commutative ring is *separable* if f and f' are strongly relatively prime. This is different from tradition: One usually defines separable polynomials over discrete fields as the ones that are products of our separable polynomials [Ri]. Clearly, factors of separable polynomials are again separable, for if fg is separable, then there exist polynomials s, t such that $sfg + t(f'g + fg') = 1$; so $(sg + tg')f + tgf' = 1$. Let $R[\alpha] \supseteq R$ be commutative rings. Then α is *separable* over R if it is root of a separable polynomial over R.

Each $n \times n$ matrix over a discrete field k is also a vector of an n^2-dimensional vector space. We can find a smallest m such that the vectors $I, A, A^2, \ldots, A^m$ are linearly dependent. Then A is root of a monic polynomial p over k of degree m, the so-called *minimal polynomial* of A. Since A is root of its characteristic polynomial of degree n, we have that $m \le n$. The matrix ring $k[A]$ forms a discrete commutative ring such that $k[A] \cong k[X]/(p)$. If S is an invertible $n \times n$ matrix, then $k[A] \cong k[S^{-1}AS]$ by the isomorphism that is the identity on k and that sends A to $S^{-1}AS$. The matrix A is *separable* if its minimal polynomial p is separable.

2.4 Theorem *Let A be an $n \times n$ matrix over a discrete field k. Then the minimal polynomial of A is separable and splits into linear factors if and only if A is diagonalizable. If A is diagonalizable, then the projections of k^n onto the eigenspaces of A can be written as polynomials in A of degree at most $n - 1$.*

Proof If A is diagonalizable, with set of eigenvalues Λ, then it is root of the separable polynomial $\prod_{\lambda \in \Lambda}(X - \lambda)$. Conversely, if the minimal polynomial of A is separable and splits into linear factors, then the eigenspaces V_λ of A, being the null spaces of matrices $A - \lambda$ that are associated with the strongly relatively prime linear factors $X - \lambda$ of the minimal polynomial of A, are direct summands such that $\sum_\lambda V_\lambda = k^n$.

Suppose A is diagonalizable, and write $f = (X - \lambda)g_\lambda(X)$ for each root λ of the minimal polynomial f. As $f(A) = 0$, the matrix $g_\lambda(A)$ maps into V_λ. If $\mu \neq \lambda$ are eigenvalues, then $X - \mu$ divides $g_\lambda(X)$, so $g_\lambda(A)V_\mu = 0$. The polynomial $1 - \sum_{\lambda \in \Lambda} g_\lambda(X)/g_\lambda(\lambda)$ has a degree less than the cardinality of Λ, but has all the eigenvalues as roots; so it is identical to 0. Thus $\sum_{\lambda \in \Lambda} g_\lambda(A)/g_\lambda(\lambda)$ is the identity, and $g_\lambda(A)/g_\lambda(\lambda)$ is the projection onto V_λ. $\square$

2.5 Theorem *Let A and B be commuting diagonalizable $n \times n$ matrices over a discrete field k. Then k^n admits a basis relative to which A and B diagonalize simultaneously.*

Proof Let V_λ^A and V_λ^B be the λ-eigenspaces of A and B, respectively. Since B commutes with $A - \lambda$, for all λ, the eigenspaces of A are invariant under B, hence also under the projections onto the eigenspaces V_μ^B, which are polynomials in B. Therefore, $V_\lambda^A = \sum_\mu V_\lambda^A \cap V_\mu^B$. So $k^n = \sum_{\lambda,\mu} V_\lambda^A \cap V_\mu^B$. $\square$

The class of discrete fields admits *linear elimination*: Let k be a discrete field, and $v_1, \ldots, v_n, w$ be vectors in k^n. Then w is a linear combination of the vectors v_i with coefficients in some discrete field extension of k if and only if the rank of the matrix $(v_1, \ldots, v_n, w)$ is equal to the rank of the matrix $(v_1, \ldots, v_n)$. So if w is a linear combination of the v_i over some discrete extension field, then it is already a linear combination with coefficients in k.

2.6 Theorem *If A and B are commuting separable $n \times n$ matrices over a discrete field k of cardinality greater than $n(n-1)/2$, then there exists c such that $k[A, B] = k[A + cB]$.*

Proof Let K be a countable discrete subfield that includes the coefficients of the matrices A and B, and contains at least $1 + n(n-1)/2$ elements from k. By Theorem 1.7 we can construct a countable discrete field $L \supseteq K$ over which the minimal polynomials of A and B split into linear factors. So A and B are—simultaneously—diagonalizable over L with diagonal elements $a_1, \ldots, a_n$ and $b_1, \ldots, b_n$. Choose $c \in K$ distinct from $(a_j - a_i)/(b_i - b_j)$, for all pairs i, j with $b_i \neq b_j$. Then $a_i + cb_i \neq a_j + cb_j$ whenever $(a_i, a_j) \neq (b_i, b_j)$. By Theorem 2.4, A and B can be written as polynomials of degree at most $n - 1$ in $A + cB$. So A and B, as vectors in n^2 variables, are linear combinations of the vectors $I, A + cB, \ldots, (A + cB)^{n-1}$ with coefficients in L. By linear elimination, A and B are polynomials in $A + cB$ over K, hence over k. $\square$

The proofs of Theorems 2.4, 2.5, and 2.6 are based on [Ri]. For further improvements and strengthenings, see [M, pp. 158ff] and [Ri].

2.7 Lemma *Let R be a commutative ring containing a discrete field k, and let $\alpha, \beta \in R$ and polynomials f, g over k be such that $f(\alpha) = g(\beta) = 0$. Then there are commuting square matrices A, B of the same size over k such that*

$f(A) = g(B) = 0$, and a ring map from $k[A, B]$ onto $k[\alpha, \beta]$ that is the identity on k, sends A to α, and sends B to β.

Proof The ring $k[x, y] = k[X, Y]/(f(X), g(Y))$ is a finite-dimensional vector space over k. Multiplication by x and y are linear transformations on this vector space. With respect to some basis, these transformations are represented by commuting matrices A and B satisfying $f(A) = g(B) = 0$, and $k[A, B] \cong k[x, y]$. So we can construct the ring map from $k[A, B]$ onto $k[\alpha, \beta]$ that is the identity on k, sending A and B to α and β, respectively. $\square$

2.8 Corollary (Primitive Element) *Let R be a commutative ring containing an infinite discrete field k, and let α and β be elements of R that are separable over k. Then there exists θ such that $k[\alpha, \beta] = k[\theta]$.*

Proof There are separable polynomials $f, g \in k[X]$ such that $f(\alpha) = g(\beta) = 0$, so there is a commutative matrix ring with surjective ring map $\sigma \colon k[A, B] \to k[\alpha, \beta]$, and such that $f(A) = g(B) = 0$. By Theorem 2.6 there is $C \in k[A, B]$ such that $k[C] = k[A, B]$. Choose $\theta = \sigma(C)$. $\square$

Let $K \supseteq k$ be discrete fields such that K is finite-dimensional as a vector space over k. We shall write $[K : k]$ for the dimension. If L is a discrete field extension of K that is finite-dimensional, then so is L over k, and we have $[L : k] = [L : K][K : k]$. If two of the three dimensions are finite, then so is the third and the equation holds.

2.9 Theorem *Let $k \subseteq k[\alpha]$ be discrete fields of characteristic 0 such that k is factorial. Then $k[\alpha]$ is factorial too.*

Proof Let f be a polynomial over $k[\alpha]$ of degree $n > 0$. It suffices to give an irreducible factor. We complete the proof by induction on n. We may assume that f is separable; otherwise, the greatest common divisor of f and f' is a proper factor, and we are done by induction. Let $k[\alpha, \beta] = k[\alpha][X]/(f(X))$; $k[\alpha, \beta]$ is a finite-dimensional vector space over k. Then $k[\alpha, \beta] = k[\theta]$, with $g(\theta) = 0$ for some polynomial g over k of degree $[k[\theta] : k]$. If g is irreducible, then so is f. Otherwise, let p be a proper factor of g. Then $k[\theta]$ maps onto $k[X]/(p)$ with nonzero kernel $p(\theta) \cdot k[\theta]$. Hence $h(\beta) = p(\theta)$ is mapped to 0, for some $h(X) \in k[\alpha][X]$. Then the greatest common divisor of f and h is a proper factor of f. $\square$

Recall that there exist countable discrete fields whose characteristic we cannot determine. Theorem 2.9 can be generalized to some of such discrete fields, and to some discrete fields of finite characteristic, by replacing the characteristic 0 condition by Seidenberg's 'Condition P' [M, p. 188].

2.10 Theorem (Rich Man's Algebraic Closure) *Each countable factorial field k of characteristic 0 has a countable discrete algebraic closure Ω such that* *for each finitely generated subfield $K \supseteq k$, each element of Ω is root of an irreducible polynomial over K.*

Proof The construction of Ω is identical to that in the proof of Theorem 1.8. By Corollary 2.8, each finitely generated intermediate field is of the form $K = k[\alpha]$. Let $\beta \in \Omega$. Then $K[\beta] = k[\theta]$ for some $\theta \in \Omega$. Both θ and α are roots of irreducible polynomials over k, so $k[\theta]$ and $k[\alpha]$ are finite-dimensional vector spaces over k. Then $K[\beta]$ is a finite-dimensional vector space over K of degree

$$[K[\beta] : K] = [k[\theta] : k]/[k[\alpha] : k].$$

So θ is root of an irreducible polynomial over K of degree $[K[\beta] : K]$. $\square$

2.11 Corollary *The field of rational numbers $\mathbf{Q}$ has a countable discrete algebraic closure C such that for each finitely generated subfield $k \supseteq \mathbf{Q}$, each element of C is root of an irreducible polynomial over k.* $\square$

Without additional choice principles we cannot show that all algebraic closures of a countable factorial field of characteristic 0 are countable. But the countable algebraic closures are all isomorphic.

Let k, K be discrete fields, and $\sigma: k \to K$ a morphism. Let $k[\alpha]$ be a discrete field extension of k, and α a root of an irreducible polynomial f over k. If $\beta \in K$ is a root of $\sigma(f)$, then σ extends to a morphism from $k[\alpha]$ into K that takes α to β.

2.12 Theorem *All countable discrete algebraic closures of a countable factorial field of characteristic 0 are isomorphic.*

Proof Let $K = \{a_0, a_1, \ldots\}$ and $L = \{b_0, b_1, \ldots\}$ be countable discrete algebraic closures of the countable factorial field k. By induction we construct embeddings $\sigma_n: k_n = k[a_0, \ldots, a_{n-1}] \to L$. Naturally, $k_0 = k$ embeds into L. Suppose σ_n exists. Then a_n is root of an irreducible polynomial f over k_n, and there is a smallest, hence unique, i such that b_i is root of $\sigma_n(f)$. Extend σ_n to σ_{n+1} by setting $\sigma_{n+1}(a_n) = b_i$. The union of the σ_i is an isomorphism from K to L. $\square$

3. The Fundamental Theorem of Algebra

There are several ways to define the set of real numbers, hence at least as many ways to define the set of complex numbers. Some of these cannot be shown to be equivalent in constructive mathematics. Each choice yields another field of complex numbers for which one may try to prove some form of the Fundamental Theorem of Algebra. Below we restrict ourselves to the ones that seem most relevant to constructivists.

A (rational) Cauchy sequence is a sequence of rational numbers $\{r_n\}_n$ such that for all integers $m > 0$ there exists M such that $|r_p - r_q| < 1/m$ for all $p, q \geq M$. A Cauchy sequence is *modulated* if $M = M(m)$ is a function from $\mathbf{N}$ to $\mathbf{N}$ [TvD, pp. 253ff]. [BB, pp. 18ff] uses a 'fixed' modulus function $M(m)$. This further restriction will be inessential in what follows below. Define a binary relation $\sim$ on the collection of Cauchy sequences by $\{r_n\}_n \sim \{s_n\}_n$ if and only if for all $m > 0$ there exists M such that $|r_p - s_q| < 1/m$ for all $p, q \geq M$. One easily verifies $\sim$ to be an equivalence relation. A similar modulated equivalence relation exists where $M = M(m)$ is a function $\mathbf{N} \to \mathbf{N}$. A *Cauchy real* is an equivalence class. A *modulated Cauchy real* is a 'modulated' equivalence class of modulated Cauchy sequences. Both kinds of Cauchy reals with the canonical operations form commutative rings. A (modulated) Cauchy real is invertible exactly when it has a (modulated) Cauchy sequence $\{r_n\}_n$ for which there exist $m > 0$ and M according to the definition above, and $|r_M| > 2/m$.

A subset $Q \subseteq \mathbf{Q}$ of the rationals is a *left Dedekind cut* if it satisfies

$p < q \in Q$ implies $p \in Q$.

For all $p \in Q$ there exists q such that $p < q \in Q$.

For all integers $m > 0$ there exist $p < q$ such that $|p - q| < 1/m$, $p \in Q$, and $q \notin Q$, that is, q is not an element of Q.

Left Dedekind cuts form the set of *Dedekind reals* $\mathbf{R}$. We easily verify that $\mathbf{R}$, with the canonical operations, is a commutative ring. We write $Q > 0$, Q is positive, when $p \in Q$ for some $p > 0$, and $Q < 0$, Q is negative, when $q \notin Q$ for some $q < 0$. A Dedekind real Q is invertible, written $Q \neq 0$, exactly when $Q > 0$ or $Q < 0$. Note that this makes $\neq$ on $\mathbf{R}$ different from denial of equality. If $Q \neq 0$ is false, then $Q = 0$. Analogous to (modulated) Cauchy reals and Dedekind reals we have (modulated) Cauchy complex numbers and Dedekind complex numbers, the last ones forming the set $\mathbf{C} = \mathbf{R} + i\mathbf{R}$, with $a + ib \neq 0$ exactly when $a + ib$ is invertible. Then $a + ib \neq 0$ exactly when $a \neq 0$ or $b \neq 0$, for all $a, b \in \mathbf{R}$. The relation $\neq$ is an apartness [Ru].

We may consider $\mathbf{Q}$ a subring of the modulated Cauchy reals by identifying each rational with the equivalence class that contains the corresponding constant Cauchy sequence. The modulated Cauchy reals may be considered a subring of the Cauchy reals. The Cauchy reals may be considered a subring of $\mathbf{R}$ by identifying each Cauchy sequence $\{r_n\}_n$ with the Dedekind cut Q defined by $p \in Q$ if and only if for some $m > 0$ and M satisfying the definition of Cauchy sequence, $p + 2/m < r_M$.

If c is a (modulated) Cauchy complex number, then the absolute value $|c|$ exists and is a (modulated) Cauchy real. Similarly, if $c \in \mathbf{C}$, then $|c| \in \mathbf{R}$. A *Cauchy sequence* is a sequence $\{c_n\}_n$ of elements of $\mathbf{C}$ such that for all $m > 0$ there exists M such that $|c_p - c_q| < 1/m$ for all $p, q \geq M$. The sequence is *modulated* if $M = M(m)$ is a function. A (modulated) Cauchy sequence of modulated Cauchy sequences is a (modulated) Cauchy sequence, and a Cauchy sequence of Dedekind reals is a Dedekind real. But a Cauchy sequence of modulated Cauchy sequences is only a Cauchy sequence, and a modulated Cauchy sequence of Cauchy sequences is only a Dedekind real. With Countable Choice one can show that each Dedekind real is a modulated Cauchy real, and thus the Cauchy reals are closed under taking Cauchy sequences. Therefore, in the presence of Countable Choice, modulated Cauchy sequences are the common way by which to define reals; without choice it is the (left) Dedekind cuts [G, pp. 415ff].

A set $U \subseteq \mathbf{R}$ is open if for all $u \in U$ there exist rational numbers p, q such that $p < u < q$, and $v \in U$ whenever $p < v < q$. Open sets on $\mathbf{R}^n$ are defined by the product topology. If $\mathbf{c}, \mathbf{d} \in \mathbf{R}^n$ are such that $c_i \neq d_i$ ($c_i - d_i$ is a unit) for some i, then there exist open sets $U, V \subseteq \mathbf{R}^n$ such that $\mathbf{c} \in U$, $\mathbf{d} \in V$, and $U \cap V = \emptyset$. Functions f are *continuous* if $f^{-1}(U)$ is open for all open U. Constant functions, the identity, and the basic ring theoretic functions are continuous. Compositions of continuous functions are continuous. So all polynomial functions are continuous.

A commutative ring is *impotent* if it satisfies the axioms

$$a^2 = 0 \text{ implies } a = 0, \quad \text{and}$$
$$a^2 = a \text{ implies } a = 0 \text{ or } a = 1.$$

One easily verifies that $\mathbf{R}$ and $\mathbf{C}$ are impotent rings.

If R is impotent and $a, b \in R$ are such that $a + b = 1$ and $ab = 0$, then $a = 1$ or $a = 0$ and, therefore, $b = 0$ or $b = 1$. For if we multiply the first equation by a, and apply the second equation, we get $a^2 = a^2 + ab = a$.

3.1 Lemma *Let $R \subseteq S$ be impotent commutative rings, and $\alpha \in S$. If $f, g \in R[X]$ are strongly relatively prime, and $f(\alpha)g(\alpha) = 0$, then $f(\alpha)$ is a unit or $g(\alpha)$ is a unit. So $g(\alpha) = 0$ or $f(\alpha) = 0$.*

Proof $sf + tg = 1$ for some $s, t \in R[X]$. So $s(\alpha)f(\alpha) = 1$ or $t(\alpha)g(\alpha) = 1$. $\square$

3.2 Theorem *Let R be an impotent commutative ring with discrete subfield k. If $\alpha \in R$ is algebraic over k, then $k[\alpha]$ is a discrete field. The set of elements in R algebraic over k is a discrete subfield.*

Proof It suffices to prove the first claim. By Proposition 1.2 each $\beta \in k[\alpha]$ is algebraic over k, hence root of a monic polynomial $g \in k[X]$. We can write $g = X^m h$ with $h(0) \neq 0$. Then X^m and h are strongly relatively prime, so β^m is a unit or $h(\beta)$ is a unit. So β is a unit or $\beta = 0$. $\square$

Let $\mathbf{C}^a$ be the set of *algebraic numbers*, that is, the set of complex numbers that are algebraic over $\mathbf{Q}$, and $\mathbf{R}^a = \mathbf{C}^a \cap \mathbf{R}$ be the set of *algebraic reals*. Then $\mathbf{C}^a$ and $\mathbf{R}^a$ are discrete.

3.3 Lemma *Let $f \in \mathbf{R}^a[X]$, and $a, b \in \mathbf{R}$ such that $f(a) < 0 < f(b)$. Then there exists a modulated Cauchy real $c \in \mathbf{R}^a$ with $f(c) = 0$. If $a < b$, then $a < c < b$; otherwise, $a > c > b$.*

Proof We may assume that $a < b$. By continuity there are $a', b' \in \mathbf{Q}$ such that $a < a' < b' < b$ and $f(a') < 0 < f(b')$. For each $r \in \mathbf{R}^a$ we have $f(r) < 0$, $f(r) = 0$, or $f(r) > 0$, so we can construct sequences $\{a_n\}_n$, $\{b_n\}_n$, and $\{c_n\}_n$, where $c_n = (a_n + b_n)/2$, by:

$a_0 = a'$ and $b_0 = b'$.
$a_{n+1} = b_{n+1} = c_n$ if $f(c_n) = 0$.
$a_{n+1} = c_n$ and $b_{n+1} = b_n$ if $f(c_n) < 0$.
$a_{n+1} = a_n$ and $b_{n+1} = c_n$ if $f(c_n) > 0$.

Then $a_n \leq a_{n+1} \leq b_{n+1} \leq b_n$ and $|a_n - b_n| \leq (b' - a')(1/2)^n$, for all n. So $\{c_n\}_n$ is a modulated Cauchy sequence with limit $c \in \mathbf{R}$. By the Remainder Theorem, applied to $\mathbf{Q}[Y][X]$, there is $g \in \mathbf{Q}[X, Y]$ such that $f(X) = (X - Y)g(X, Y) + f(Y)$. There is an M such that $|g(x, y)| \leq M$ whenever $a \leq x, y \leq b$. So $|f(x) - f(y)| \leq M|x - y|$ whenever $a \leq x, y \leq b$; thus $\{f(c_n) - f(a_n)\}_n$ and $\{f(c_n) - f(b_n)\}_n$ converge to 0, with $f(a_n) \leq 0 \leq f(b_n)$. By continuity, $f(c) = 0$; and $c \in \mathbf{R}^a$ by Proposition 1.4. $\square$

3.4 Corollary *All nonzero polynomials* $f \in \mathbf{R}^a[X]$ *have a finite set of roots in* $\mathbf{R}^a$. *If* f *is of odd degree, then it has at least one root.*

Proof Suppose f is of odd degree. We may assume f to be monic. Let b be 1 plus the sum of the absolute values of the coefficients of f, and let $a = -b$. Then $f(a) < 0 < f(b)$.

Let f be nonzero and of degree $n > 1$. We complete the proof by induction on n. We may assume f to be separable. By induction, f' has a finite set of roots $r_1 < \cdots < r_m$. If f' has no roots, then f has one. Otherwise, f has one root in the interval (r_j, r_{j+1}) exactly when $f(r_j)f(r_{j+1}) < 0$, one root less than r_1 exactly when $f(r_1 - 1)f'(r_1 - 1) > 0$, and one root bigger than r_m exactly when $f(r_m + 1)f'(r_m + 1) < 0$. $\square$

Obviously, the element $i = \sqrt{-1}$ is algebraic. Let $a, b \in \mathbf{R}$ be such that $a + ib$ is an algebraic number. Then $a + ib$ is root of a polynomial with rational coefficients, so, by conjugation, $a - ib$ is root of the same polynomial. So a and b are algebraic numbers too. Thus $\mathbf{C}^a = \mathbf{R}^a + i\mathbf{R}^a$. If $c \in \mathbf{C}^a$, then the absolute value $|c| \in \mathbf{R}^a$. The order relation $<$ with restriction to $\mathbf{R}^a$ is decidable: If $a \in \mathbf{R}^a$ is nonzero, then a is invertible, so $a > 0$ or $a < 0$. Obviously we can enumerate the monic polynomials over $\mathbf{Q}$, and for each such polynomial we can enumerate its roots in $\mathbf{R}^a$ in a unique manner 'from left to right.' So $\mathbf{R}^a$ is countable, hence $\mathbf{C}^a$ is countable. Combining this with Theorem 3.2 we get:

3.5 Corollary *The set of algebraic numbers* $\mathbf{C}^a$ *is a countable discrete field.* $\square$

3.6 Corollary *All algebraic numbers are modulated Cauchy.*

Proof Let $c \in \mathbf{R}^a$. Then c is the unique root of the polynomial $f(X) = X - c$ satisfying $f(c - 1) < 0 < f(c + 1)$. $\square$

Let $\{a_n + ib_n\}_n$ be a (modulated) Cauchy sequence of algebraic numbers. Construct the (modulated) rational sequence $\{c_n/n + id_n/n\}_n$ by setting c_n equal to the largest integer less than or equal to na_n, and d_n equal to the largest integer less than or equal to nb_n. Then the rational sequence has the same limit as the sequence over $\mathbf{C}^a$. So each (modulated) Cauchy sequence of algebraic numbers has as limit a (modulated) Cauchy number.

3.7 Lemma *Let* $a, b \in \mathbf{R}^a$. *Then there exist* $c, d \in \mathbf{R}^a$ *such that* $(c + id)^2 = a + ib$.

Proof First suppose that $b = 0$. As $\mathbf{C}^a$ is discrete, either $a > 0$ or $a = 0$, or $a < 0$. If $a > 0$, then $\sqrt{a} \in \mathbf{R}^a$ is a root of $X^2 - a$, by Lemma 3.3. If

$a < 0$, then we get $i\sqrt{-a}$. In the general case we choose c and d from the roots of $X^2 - (a + \sqrt{a^2 + b^2})/2$ and $X^2 - (-a + \sqrt{a^2 + b^2})/2$, respectively. $\square$

The theory of finite groups is essentially completely constructive. One easily sees that most proofs of the class equation for finite groups are easily constructivized. So Sylow's theorem is constructive: If G is a finite group and p is a prime number such that p^n divides the order of G, then G has a finite subgroup of order p^n. A subgroup of order p^n with n maximal is called a *p-Sylow subgroup*.

Let R be a commutative ring. A polynomial $f \in R[X_1, \ldots, X_n]$ is *symmetric* in the variables $X_1, \ldots, X_n$ if $f(X_1, \ldots, X_n) = f(X_{\pi 1}, \ldots, X_{\pi n})$, for all permutations π. Clearly, the coefficients σ_i of the polynomial

$$(Y + X_1)(Y + X_2) \cdots (Y + X_n) = Y^n + \sigma_1 Y^{n-1} + \cdots + \sigma_n$$

are symmetric. They are the *elementary symmetric polynomials*. Each symmetric polynomial is element of the ring $R[\sigma_1, \ldots, \sigma_n]$ [M, pp. 73ff].

Let $K \supseteq k$ be discrete fields. An element $\alpha \in K$ *splits* over k if it is root of a polynomial over k that factors into linear factors over K. The field K is *normal* over k if each $\alpha \in K$ splits over k.

Let $K \supseteq k$ be discrete fields such that $K = k[\theta]$. Then θ splits over k if and only if K is normal over k. For if θ splits, then there is a monic polynomial f over k that splits with roots $\theta = \theta_1, \ldots, \theta_n$. The elementary symmetric polynomials in the θ_j are coefficients of f, hence elements of k. Let $\alpha \in K$. We can write $\alpha = p(\theta)$, for some $p \in k[X]$. Then α is root of the polynomial $g = \prod_j (X - p(\theta_j))$, whose coefficients are symmetric in the θ_j. So $g \in k[X]$.

Let $K = k[\theta]$ and $\theta = \theta_1, \ldots, \theta_n$ be as above, and suppose, additionally, that f is irreducible and the characteristic of k equals 0. Then all θ_j are distinct, and for each j we have a unique automorphism of K that is the identity on k and maps θ to θ_j. These automorphisms form the *Galois group* G of the extension $K \supseteq k$. If H is a finite subgroup of G, then θ is root of the polynomial $h = \prod_{\sigma \in H}(X - \sigma(\theta))$ over the field $L \supseteq k$ generated by the coefficients of h. The field L is called the *fixed field* of H, since its elements are exactly the ones that are fixed by the automorphisms of H. Obviously, h is irreducible over L. So $[K : L] = |H|$, the cardinality of H.

3.8 Lemma *Each polynomial over* $\mathbf{Q}$ *has a root in* $\mathbf{C}^a$.

Proof Let f be a monic polynomial over $\mathbf{Q}$, and let K be a splitting field of f over $\mathbf{Q}$ which, by Corollary 2.8, has a finite Galois group G. It suffices to embed K in $\mathbf{C}^a$. Let H be the 2-Sylow subgroup of G with fixed field k. Then $[k : \mathbf{Q}] = |G|/|H|$ is odd. By Corollary 2.8 there exists α such that $k = \mathbf{Q}[\alpha]$, and α is root of an irreducible polynomial of odd degree over $\mathbf{Q}$. So by Corollary 3.4 there exists an embedding of k into $\mathbf{C}^a$. The group H contains a chain of subgroups $H_0 \subseteq \cdots \subseteq H_n = H$ of order $|H_j| = 2^j$, with fixed fields $K = K_0 \supseteq \cdots \supseteq K_n = k$. So $[K_j : K_{j+1}] = 2$ for all j. By the quadratic formula, if $M \supseteq L$ are discrete fields of characteristic greater than 2 such that $[M : L] = 2$, then $M = L[\beta]$, with $\beta^2 \in L$. So by Lemma 3.7 we can extend an embedding from k_{j+1} into $\mathbf{C}^a$ to one from k_j, for all j. So K embeds into $\mathbf{C}^a$. $\square$

3.9 Theorem (Discrete Fundamental Theorem) $\mathbf{C}^a$ *is algebraically closed.*

Proof Let f be a nonconstant polynomial over $\mathbf{C}^a$. By Theorem 1.7 there exists a countable discrete splitting field of f. Let $g \in \mathbf{Q}[X]$ have all roots of f as roots, including multiplicities; so $f \mid g$. By Corollary 2.8 there is a splitting field $\mathbf{Q}[\alpha]$ of g. Let $h \in \mathbf{Q}[X]$ be the minimal polynomial of α. Then $h(\beta) = 0$ for some $\beta \in \mathbf{C}^a$. So g, and thus f, splits into linear factors over $\mathbf{Q}[\beta] \subseteq \mathbf{C}^a$. $\square$

The Discrete Fundamental Theorem enables us to study the roots of polynomials over $\mathbf{C}$ more generally through approximation by polynomials over $\mathbf{C}^a$. To make this work we must show that if two polynomials are close to each other, then their roots are close too.

Let $f = \sum_j a_{n-j} X^j$ be a polynomial over $\mathbf{C}$. Define $|f| = \sum_j |a_j|$.

Let $f = X^n + a_1 X^{n-1} + \cdots + a_n$ be a monic polynomial over $\mathbf{C}$, and let $c \in \mathbf{C}$. Then $|f(c)| \geq |c|^n - |a_1 c^{n-1} + \cdots + a_n| \geq |c|^n - \max(1, |c|^{n-1})(|f|-1)$. So if $|c| \geq |f|$, then $|f(c)| \geq |c|^{n-1}(|c| - |f| + 1) \geq |f|^{n-1}$; and if $|f(c)| < |f|^{n-1}$, then $|c| < |f|$. If g is a monic factor of f, then for all $\varepsilon > 0$ there exists a polynomial $g^* = \prod_j (X - c_j)$ over $\mathbf{C}^a$ with $|c_j| < |f|$ for all c_j, and $|g - g^*| < \varepsilon$. So $|g| \leq \varepsilon + |g^*| < \varepsilon + (1 + |f|)^n$. So $|g| \leq (1 + |f|)^n$.

If $f = (X - c_1) \cdots (X - c_n)$, $\varepsilon > 0$, and c are such that $|f(c)| < \varepsilon^n$, then $\prod_j |c - c_j| < \varepsilon^n$. Thus $|c - c_j| < \varepsilon$ for some j. Let, additionally, $R \geq |f|$, and $g = (X - d_1) \cdots (X - d_n)$. Suppose that $|f - g| < (\varepsilon/R)^n$ for some $\varepsilon > 0$. Then $|g(c_j)| < \varepsilon^n$ for all j. So for all j there exists k such that $|c_j - d_k| < \varepsilon$.

By the Remainder Theorem, there exists for all polynomials $f(X)$ a polynomial $G_f(X, Y)$ such that $f(X) - f(Y) = (X - Y)G_f(X, Y)$. The coefficients of G_f are polynomials in the coefficients of f. So given $R > 0$ and an integer $n > 0$, there exists M such that for all monic f of degree n and $z, w \in \mathbf{C}$, if $|f| < R$, $|z| < R$, and $|w| < R$, then $|G_f(z, w)| < M$.

3.10 Lemma *Let $n > 0$ be an integer, and $R, \varepsilon \in \mathbf{R}$ be such that $\varepsilon > 0$. Then there exists $\delta > 0$ such that for all $f = (X - c_1) \cdots (X - c_n)$ and $g = (X - d_1) \cdots (X - d_n)$ over $\mathbf{C}$, if $|f| < R$, $|g| < R$, and $|f - g| < \delta$, then there is a permutation π such that $|c_j - d_{\pi j}| < \varepsilon$ for all j.*

Proof We may assume that $\varepsilon < 1$. Let $S = (1 + R)^n$. Choose $M \geq 1$ such that for all monic f of degree at most n and all z, w, if $|f| < S$, $|z| < S$, and $|w| < S$, then $|f(z) - f(w)| \leq |z - w|M$. Choose $0 < \varepsilon_{2n} < \cdots < \varepsilon_1 = \varepsilon$ such that $\varepsilon_{2j} < \varepsilon_{2j-1}^j$ and $\varepsilon_{2j-1} < \varepsilon_{2j-2}^3/(100M^2 S^{n+1})$, for all j. Set $\delta = \varepsilon_{2n}/S^{n-1}$. Let $f = \prod_j (X - c_j)$ and $g = \prod_j (X - d_j)$ be monic polynomials of degree n such that $|f| < R$, $|g| < R$, and $|f - g| < \delta$. Then $|f(z) - g(z)| \leq |f - g|S^{n-1} < \varepsilon_{2n}$ for all z satisfying $|z| < S$. We complete the proof by induction on n. Suppose $n > 1$. Then there exists d_k such that $|c_n - d_k| < \varepsilon_{2n-1}$. We may assume that $k = n$. Let $f^*(z) = f(z)/(z - c_n)$ and $g^*(z) = g(z)/(z - d_n)$. For all z

satisfying $|z| < S$, $|z - c_n| > \varepsilon_{2n-2}/5M$, and $|z - d_n| > \varepsilon_{2n-2}/5M$, we have

$$|f^*(z) - g^*(z)| = |\frac{f(z)(z - c_n) + f(z)(c_n - d_n) - g(z)(z - c_n)}{(z - c_n)(z - d_n)}|$$
$$\leq |f(z) - g(z)|5M/\varepsilon_{2n-2} + |f(z)|\varepsilon_{2n-1}(5M/\varepsilon_{2n-2})^2$$
$$< \varepsilon_{2n}5M/\varepsilon_{2n-2} + RS^n\varepsilon_{2n-1}25M^2/\varepsilon_{2n-2}^2$$
$$< 50M^2S^{n+1}\varepsilon_{2n-1}/\varepsilon_{2n-2}^2 < \varepsilon_{2n-2}/2.$$

Let $|w| < S$. Then there exists z as above such that $|w - z| < \varepsilon_{2n-2}/4M$. So $|f^*(w) - g^*(w)| \leq |f^*(w) - f^*(z)| + |f^*(z) - g^*(z)| + |g^*(z) - g^*(w)| < \varepsilon_{2n-2}/4 + \varepsilon_{2n-2}/2 + \varepsilon_{2n-2}/4 = \varepsilon_{2n-2}$. By induction there exists a permutation π such that for all $j < n$ there is $\pi j < n$ such that $|c_j - d_{\pi j}| < \varepsilon$. Set $\pi n = n$. $\square$

We cannot show that all nonzero polynomials over $\mathbf{C}$ have an invertible leading coefficient, so we need to consider polynomials that are 'almost-monic.'

3.11 Lemma Let f and g be polynomials over $\mathbf{C}^a$ such that f is monic and of degree n, and g is of degree at most m. Let $0 < \varepsilon < 1/2$ be such that $|g| < (\varepsilon/(2|f|))^{m+n+1}$. If c is a root of $g(X)X^{n+1} + f(X)$, then exactly one of the following holds:
   $|c| > |f|/\varepsilon$, and $|1/c - 1/d| < \varepsilon/|f|$ for some root d of $g(X)X + 1$.
   $|c| < |f|$, and $|c - d| < \varepsilon$ for some root d of $f(X)$.

Proof Let c be a root of $g(X)X^{n+1} + f(X)$. Then $|c| \geq 2|f|$ or $|c| < 2|f|$. Suppose $|c| \geq 2|f|$. Then $|g(c)c + 1| \leq (|f| - 1)/|c| < 1/2$. So $|c|^{m+1}|g| \geq |g(c)c| > 1/2$. Thus $|c|^{m+1} > (|f|/\varepsilon)^{m+1}$, hence $|c| > |f|/\varepsilon$. Also, $|(g(c)c + 1)/c^{m+1}| < (\varepsilon/|f|)^{m+1}$. So $|1/c - e| < \varepsilon/|f|$ for some root $e = 1/d$ of the monic polynomial $(g(1/X)/X + 1)X^{m+1}$.
   Suppose $|c| < 2|f|$. Then

$$|f(c)| \leq |g(c)c^{n+1}| \leq |g||c|^{m+n+1} < |g|(2|f|)^{m+n+1} < \varepsilon^n.$$

So there is a root d of $f(X)$ such that $|c - d| < \varepsilon$. $\square$

3.12 Lemma Let $F = a_nX^n + \cdots + a_0$ be a polynomial over $\mathbf{C}$ such that a_j is a unit. Then there exists $k \geq j$ such that a_k is a unit, and a monic polynomial F^* over $\mathbf{C}$ of degree k, such that F^* divides F. If the coefficients of F are (modulated) Cauchy numbers, then so are the coefficients of F^*.

Proof By induction on $n - j$. Write $F = a_j(b_nX^n + \cdots + b_0)$, let $r = |X^j + b_{j-1}X^{j-1} + \cdots + b_0|$, and $s = |b_nX^n + \cdots + b_{j+1}X^{j+1}|$. Then $s > 1/(2(6r)^n)$ or $s < 1/(6r)^n$. If $s > 1/(2(6r)^n)$, then a_k is a unit for some $k > j$: Apply induction. Suppose $s < 1/(6r)^n$. By continuity there exists $\gamma > 0$ such that $s + (n - j)\gamma < 1/(6(r - j\gamma))^n$. Let $\delta = |a_j|\gamma/4$. If h is a polynomial over $\mathbf{C}^a$ of degree at most n such that $|h - F| < \delta$, then it has exactly j roots $c_1, \ldots, c_j$, counting multiplicities, satisfying $|c_i| < |h|$. Define $h^* = \prod_i(X - c_i)$. Then h^* is a monic polynomial of degree j that divides h. By Lemmas 3.10 and 3.11, for all $\varepsilon > 0$ and for all G over $\mathbf{C}$ of degree at most n such that

$|G - F| < \delta$ there exists $\delta_1 > 0$ such that if h_1, h_2 are polynomials over $\mathbf{C}^a$ of degree at most n satisfying $|h_i - G| < \delta_1$, then $|h_1^* - h_2^*| < \varepsilon$. So the maps $h \mapsto h^*$ and $h \mapsto h/h^*$ can be continuously extended to all G over $\mathbf{C}$ of degree at most n that satisfy $|G - F| < \delta$. In particular, F^* divides F. $\square$

The continuity of the map $h \mapsto h^*$ cannot be strengthened to a continuous map to some linear factor of h^*, since in general the permutation π in Lemma 3.10 need not be uniquely determined.

3.13 Theorem (Fundamental Theorem for (modulated) Cauchy complex numbers) *Each polynomial $f(X)$ over the (modulated) Cauchy complex numbers having an invertible coefficient for some positive power of X has a (modulated) Cauchy root.*

Proof We may assume f to be a monic polynomial $X^n + a_1 X^{n-1} + \cdots + a_n$, where each a_j is the limit of a (modulated) rational Cauchy sequence $\{a_{j,m}\}_m$. We construct a sequence $\{c_m\}_m$ of roots $c_m \in \mathbf{C}^a$ of $f_m = X^n + a_{1,m} X^{n-1} + \cdots + a_{n,m}$ as follows: Choose for c_0 one of the roots of f_0. From c_{m-1} we select for c_m from among the roots of f_m the one that is closest to c_{m-1}, that is, $|c_{m-1} - c_m| \le |c_{m-1} - d|$ for all roots d of f_m. If there is no unique choice, then select the one with largest real part. If there are still two choices left, select the one with largest imaginary part. Then $\{c_m\}_m$ is a (modulated) Cauchy sequence whose limit is a root of f. $\square$

The uniqueness of the choice of c_m in the proof of Theorem 3.13 implies that the sequence $\{c_m\}_m$ is uniquely determined by a finite description, and no choice principles are needed.

Theorem 3.13 does not extend to all of $\mathbf{C}$: We cannot find a continuous solution $X(c)$ to the equation $X^2 + c = 0$ when $c \in \mathbf{C}$ is near 0.

3.14 Theorem *Let $n > 1$, and let $F = X^n + a_1 X^{n-1} + \cdots + a_n$ be a polynomial over $\mathbf{C}$ such that there exists j satisfying $n^j a_j \ne \binom{n}{j} a_1^j$, that is, $n^j a_j - \binom{n}{j} a_1^j$ is a unit. Then F has a proper monic factor F^* such that F^* and F/F^* are strongly relatively prime.*

Proof Given F, there exists $\gamma > 0$ such that $|(X + c)^n - F(X)| > \gamma$, for all c. So there exist ε, μ such that for all monic polynomials g over $\mathbf{C}^a$ of degree n, if $|g - F| < \mu$, then $|g| < 2|F| = R$ and g has roots c, d with $|c - d| > 2n\varepsilon$. For n, ε, R, there exists $\delta < \mu$ satisfying Lemma 3.10. Choose a monic polynomial $g = \prod_j (X - c_j)$ of degree n over $\mathbf{C}^a$ such that $|g - F| < \delta/3$. The equivalence relation on the roots of g generated by the binary relation $|c_j - c_k| < 2\varepsilon$ contains at least two distinct equivalence classes, and can be extended to a decidable equivalence relation $\sim$ that divides the collection of roots into exactly two equivalence classes C and D. For all monic polynomials $h = \prod_j (X - d_j)$ of degree n over $\mathbf{C}^a$ such that $|h - g| < \delta/2$, there is a permutation π such that $|c_j - d_{\pi j}| < \varepsilon$. The equivalence relation on the roots of g induces an equivalence relation on the roots of h, dividing them into two equivalence classes as well, say C' and D'. These classes are independent of π. Define $h^* = \prod_{d \in D'} (X - d)$. The map $h \mapsto h^*$ can be continuously extended to all monic G over $\mathbf{C}$ of degree n that satisfy $|G - g| < \delta/2$. Let $h^\circ = h/h^*$. There are unique polynomials h_* and h_o with h_* of degree less than $\deg h^\circ$ and h_o of degree less than $\deg h^*$, such that $h^* h_* + h^\circ h_o = 1$. The maps $h \mapsto h^\circ$, $h \mapsto h_*$, and $h \mapsto h_o$ are continuous wherever h^* is. So F^* is a proper monic factor of F, and F^* and $F^\circ = F/F^*$ are strongly relatively prime. $\square$

A polynomial f over $\mathbf{C}$ has a *simple root* α if $f(\alpha) = 0$ and $f'(\alpha)$ is invertible. The existence of a simple root for a monic polynomial can be expressed in terms of its coefficients. The following approach is from [W]. Let R be a commutative ring, and let $f = (Y + X_1)(Y + X_2) \cdots (Y + X_n) = Y^n + a_1 Y^{n-1} + \cdots + a_n$ be the polynomial over $R[X_1, \ldots, X_n]$ with as coefficients the elementary symmetric polynomials $a_j = \sigma_j(X_1, \ldots, X_n)$. To express that $-X_j$ is a simple root of f, we need that $E_j = \prod_{k \neq j}(X_j - X_k) \neq 0$, where $x \neq y$ stands for $x - y$ is a unit. So for f to have a simple root we need at least one $E_j \neq 0$. So $(Y + E_1)(Y + E_2) \cdots (Y + E_n) \neq Y^n$, that is, $\sigma_j(E_1, \ldots, E_n) \neq 0$ for some j. These polynomials are symmetric, so there exist polynomials $d_j(Y_1, \ldots, Y_n)$ such that $d_j(a_1, \ldots, a_n) = \sigma_j(E_1, \ldots, E_n)$. Define f to be *unramifiable*, if $d_j(a_1, \ldots, a_n) \neq 0$ for some j.

3.15 Theorem *Each unramifiable monic polynomial over $\mathbf{C}$ has a simple root.*

Proof By Theorem 3.14, an unramifiable monic polynomial f of degree $n > 1$ has a proper factorization $f = gh$, for monic g, h. Then g or h is unramifiable again. By induction on n, g or h has a simple root, which is a simple root of f. $\square$

3.16 Theorem *Let $r \in \mathbf{R}$, and let $a_1(Y), \ldots, a_n(Y)$ be rational functions over $\mathbf{C}^a$ such that $a_j(r)$ exists, for all j. Then $f(X, r) = X^n + a_1(r)X^{n-1} + \cdots + a_n(r)$ splits in $\mathbf{C}$.*

Proof We may assume that $n > 1$. We proceed by induction on n. There are rational numbers p and q such that $p < r < q$, and $a_j(s)$ exists for all $p \leq s \leq q$ and all j. If the inequality $\gcd(f(X,Y), \frac{\partial f}{\partial X}(X,Y)) \neq 1$ over $\mathbf{C}^a(Y)$ has infinitely many solutions $Y = s \in \mathbf{R}^a$ with $p \leq s \leq q$, then, by Theorem 2.1, $f(X,Y)$ and $\frac{\partial f}{\partial X}(X,Y)$ share a nonconstant factor $g(X,Y)$ over $\mathbf{C}^a(Y)$ that is monic in X. So $g(X,r)$ is a proper factor of $f(X,r)$: Apply induction. Otherwise, let $p \leq d_1 < \cdots < d_m \leq q$ be the finite set of solutions of the inequality. Set $p = d_0$ and $q = d_{m+1}$. By Lemma 3.10 we can find roots $c_1(t), \ldots, c_n(t)$ of $f(X, t)$ that are continuous in $t \in \mathbf{R}$ on each interval (d_j, d_{j+1}). Continuous roots of neighboring intervals can be pairwise connected to make a continuous solution on the whole interval (p, q), because the roots of $f(X, d_j)$ are discrete sets. $\square$

The constructions of the continuous solutions $c_k(t)$ in the proof above essentially use that the intervals (d_j, d_{j+1}) are simply connected. Theorem 3.16 does not apply to the polynomial $X^2 + c$ with $c \in \mathbf{C}$, since a complex number depends on two real values rather than one: its real and its imaginary part.

4. References

[BB]   E. Bishop & D. Bridges, *Constructive Analysis*, Grundlehren der mathematischen Wissenschaften, Vol. 279, Springer Verlag, 1985.

[BR]   D. Bridges & F. Richman, *Varieties of Constructive Mathematics*, London Mathematical Society Lecture Note Series, Vol. 97, Cambridge University Press, 1987.

[C]   M. Cantor, *Vorlesungen über Geschichte der Mathematik*, Vol. 4, Teubner Verlag, Leipzig, 1908.

[G]   R. Goldblatt, *Topoi, the categorial analysis of logic*, Studies in logic and the foundations of mathematics, Vol. 98, North–Holland, 1979.

[JR]   A. Joyal & G. E. Reyes, *Separably real closed local rings*, J. Pure Appl. Algebra, **43**(1986), 271–279.

[M]   R. Mines, F. Richman, W. Ruitenburg, *A Course in Constructive Algebra*, Universitext, Springer Verlag, 1988.

[Ri]   F. Richman, *Separable extensions and diagonalizability*, Amer. Math. Monthly, **97**(1990), 395–398.

[Ru]   W. Ruitenburg, *Inequality in constructive mathematics*, Dept. of Math., Stat. & Comp. Sci., Marquette University, Technical Report No. 285, (1988).

[vS]   F. T. von Schubert, *De inventione divisorum*, ad annum 1793, Nova acta scient. imp. Petropolitanae. Petropoli, **11**(1798), 172–182.

[TvD]   A. S. Troelstra & D. van Dalen, *Constructivism in Mathematics, An Introduction*, Vol. I, Studies in logic and the foundations of mathematics, Vol. 121, North–Holland, 1988.

[TvDa] A. S. Troelstra & D. van Dalen, *Constructivism in Mathematics, An Introduction*, Vol. II, Studies in logic and the foundations of mathematics, Vol. 123, North–Holland, 1988.

[W]   G. C. Wraith, *Generic Galois theory of local rings*, pp. 739–767 in: Applications of Sheaves (eds.: M. P. Fourman, C. J. Mulvey, D. S. Scott), Lecture Notes in Mathematics, Vol. 753, Spinger Verlag, 1979.

Computational Aspects of Lie Group Representations and Related Topics   129
Proceedings of the 1990 Computational Algebra Seminar
pp. 129–142 in CWI Tract 84 (1991)

On the computation of normal forms

Jan A. Sanders

Department of Mathematics and Computer Science

Free University

De Boelelaan 1081

1081 HV Amsterdam

The Netherlands

0. Introduction

A classic problem in differential equations is to compute the normal form of a given equation

$$\dot{x} = v(x) \qquad (x \in \mathbf{R}^n),$$

at an equilibrium point, which we assume is 0. In other words, we suppose that $v(0) = 0$. We give a brief description of how to theoretically compute a normal form of v. The normalizing process is entirely algebraic; thus, we shall assume that v is a formal power series

$$v(x) = Ax + v_2(x) + \cdots + v_\ell(x) + \cdots$$

where A is a nonzero $n \times n$ real matrix and $v_\ell \in \mathcal{F}_\ell = \mathcal{F}_\ell(W)$ is an n-vector of homogeneous polynomials of degree ℓ on $W = \mathbf{R}^n$. To simplify v we use a succession of near identity coordinate changes. Let us try to bring the quadratic terms v_2 of v into normal form using the coordinate change

$$x = \varphi(y) = y + \varphi_2(y)$$

where $\varphi_2 \in \mathcal{F}_2$. In the new coordinates v becomes

$$D\varphi(y)\dot{y} = \dot{x} = v(\varphi(y)) \quad (y \in \mathbf{R}^n).$$

In other words, with the usual notation D for derivative,

$$
\begin{aligned}
\dot{y} &= \varphi_* v(y) \\
&= (I + D\varphi_2(y))^{-1} v(y + \varphi_2(y)).
\end{aligned}
$$

Up to quadratic terms, the formal power series for $w = \varphi_* v$ is

$$
\begin{aligned}
w(y) &= (I - D\varphi_2(y) + \cdots)(A(y + \varphi_2(y)) + v_2(y + \varphi_2(y)) + \cdots) \\
&= Ay + A\varphi_2(y) - D\varphi_2(y)Ay + v_2(y) + \cdots \\
&= Ay + (v_2(y) - [A, \varphi_2](y)) + \cdots \\
&= Ay + w_2(y) + \cdots
\end{aligned}
$$

where $[A, \varphi_2]$ is the Lie bracket of the vectorfields A and φ_2. Recall that for vectorfields f, g on $\mathbf{R}^n$

$$
[f, g](x) = Dg(x)f(x) - Df(x)g(x). \tag{1}
$$

Clearly $[\,,\,]$ is defined for formal power series vectorfields as well. Since A is a linear vectorfield we have the adjoint map

$$
\mathrm{ad}_A = [A, \cdot] : \mathcal{F}_\ell \to \mathcal{F}_\ell.
$$

To remove all the quadratic terms in v we need to solve the linear equation

$$
\mathrm{ad}_A \,\varphi_2 = v_2
$$

for $\varphi_2 \in \mathcal{F}_2$, which is not always possible. To see this, consider the vectorfield on $\mathbf{R}^2$ given by

$$
\begin{pmatrix} \dot{x}_1 \\ \dot{x}_2 \end{pmatrix} = \begin{pmatrix} 0 & 0 \\ 1 & 0 \end{pmatrix} \begin{pmatrix} x_1 \\ x_2 \end{pmatrix} + \begin{pmatrix} \frac{1}{2}\alpha_1 x_1^2 + \beta_1 x_1 x_2 + \frac{1}{2}\gamma_1 x_2^2 \\ \frac{1}{2}\alpha_2 x_1^2 + \beta_2 x_1 x_2 + \frac{1}{2}\gamma_2 x_2^2 \end{pmatrix}.
$$

Let the near identity coordinate change φ be defined by

$$
\begin{pmatrix} x_1 \\ x_2 \end{pmatrix} = \begin{pmatrix} y_1 + \frac{1}{2}A_1 y_1^2 + B_1 y_1 y_2 + \frac{1}{2}C_1 y_2^2 \\ y_2 + \frac{1}{2}A_2 y_1^2 + B_2 y_1 y_2 + \frac{1}{2}C_2 y_2^2 \end{pmatrix}.
$$

Then carrying out the calculation gives

$$
w_2(y) = \begin{pmatrix} \frac{1}{2}(\alpha_1 + 2B_1)y_1^2 + (\beta_1 + C_1)y_1 y_2 + \frac{1}{2}\gamma_1 y_1^2 \\ \frac{1}{2}(\alpha_2 - A_1 + 2B_2)y_1^2 + (\beta_2 - B_1 + C_2)y_1 y_2 + \frac{1}{2}(\gamma_2 - C_2)y_2^2 \end{pmatrix}.
$$

To make w_2 zero we must solve the linear equations

$$
\begin{pmatrix} 0 & -2 & 0 & 0 & 0 & 0 \\ 0 & 0 & -1 & 0 & 0 & 0 \\ 0 & 0 & 0 & 0 & 0 & 0 \\ 1 & 0 & 0 & 0 & -2 & 0 \\ 0 & 1 & 0 & 0 & 0 & -1 \\ 0 & 0 & 1 & 0 & 0 & 0 \end{pmatrix} \begin{pmatrix} A_1 \\ B_1 \\ C_1 \\ A_2 \\ B_2 \\ C_2 \end{pmatrix} = \begin{pmatrix} \alpha_1 \\ \beta_1 \\ \gamma_1 \\ \alpha_2 \\ \beta_2 \\ \gamma_2 \end{pmatrix}. \tag{2}
$$

This is not always possible, because the matrix on the left hand side of (2) is not invertible. In fact, it is nilpotent.

To remove as many terms as possible from v_2, using the coordinate change φ, we decompose $\mathcal{F}_2$ as the direct sum of the image of ad_A and a complementary subspace C_2. Then we can write

$$v_2 = v_2' + v_2''$$

where $v_2' \in \mathrm{im}\,\mathrm{ad}_A$ and $v_2'' \in C_2$. Now choose φ_2 so that $\mathrm{ad}_A\,\varphi_2 = v_2'$. Then

$$w_2 = v_2 - (\mathrm{ad}_A\,\varphi_2) = v_2'' + v_2' - (\mathrm{ad}_A\,\varphi_2) = v_2''.$$

Thus we have brought v into the normal form w

$$w(y) = Ay + v_2''(y) + \cdots \tag{3}$$

up through quadratic terms. We can bring the cubic terms in v into normal form in the same way using the near identity coordinate change $\varphi = id + \varphi_3$ where $\varphi_3 \in \mathcal{F}_3(\mathbf{R}^n)$. Because φ is the identity up through quadratic terms, it leaves unchanged the normal form (3). Repeating this process gives a normal form

$$v(x) = Ax + v_2(x) + \cdots + v_\ell(x) + \cdots$$

where v_ℓ belongs to a complement C_ℓ of $\mathrm{im}\,\mathrm{ad}_A$ in $\mathcal{F}_\ell$. Obviously, what is meant by a normal form depends on the choice of complement C_ℓ.

There is a "natural" choice of complement for $\mathrm{im}\,\mathrm{ad}_A|\mathcal{F}_\ell$ using representation theory of $s\ell_2$, which we now explain. Suppose that

$$A = S + N$$

is the unique *semisimple-nilpotent decomposition* of A into a commuting sum of a semisimple linear map S and a nilpotent linear map N. Then by the theorem of Jacobson-Morozov [Hel] (Chapter IX, Theorem 7.4), there are linear maps M and H of $\mathbf{R}^n$ into itself such that

$$\begin{aligned}
[H, M] &= 2M \\
[H, N] &= -2N \\
[M, N] &= H \qquad \text{and} \\
[S, M] &= [S, N] = [S, H] = 0.
\end{aligned} \tag{4}$$

In other words $\{M, N, H\}$ span a Lie subalgebra of $g\ell_n(\mathbf{R})$ which is isomorphic to $s\ell_2(\mathbf{R})$. Moreover, S lies in the center of this subalgebra. Therefore ad_M, ad_N, ad_H define a representation of $s\ell_2(\mathbf{R})$ on $\mathcal{F}_\ell$. Note that ad_S commutes with $\mathrm{ad}_M, \mathrm{ad}_N, \mathrm{ad}_H$. It follows from the representation theory of $s\ell_2(\mathbf{R})$ that

$$\mathcal{F}_\ell = \mathrm{im}\,\mathrm{ad}_N|\mathcal{F}_\ell \oplus \ker\mathrm{ad}_M|\mathcal{F}_\ell.$$

Since S is semisimple, ad_S is semisimple. Therefore

$$\mathcal{F}_\ell = \ker\mathrm{ad}_S|\mathcal{F}_\ell \oplus \mathrm{im}\,\mathrm{ad}_S|\mathcal{F}_\ell.$$

But ad_S commutes with both ad_M and ad_N. Hence

$$
\begin{aligned}
\mathcal{F}_\ell &= (\mathrm{im}\,\mathrm{ad}_S \oplus (\mathrm{im}\,\mathrm{ad}_N \cap \ker\,\mathrm{ad}_S))|\mathcal{F}_\ell \oplus (\ker\,\mathrm{ad}_S \cap \ker\,\mathrm{ad}_M)|\mathcal{F}_\ell \\
&= \mathrm{im}\,\mathrm{ad}_A|\mathcal{F}_\ell \oplus (\ker\,\mathrm{ad}_S \cap \ker\,\mathrm{ad}_M)|\mathcal{F}_\ell,
\end{aligned}
$$

that is, $(\ker\,\mathrm{ad}_S \cap \ker\,\mathrm{ad}_M)|\mathcal{F}_\ell$ is a natural complement to $\mathrm{im}\,\mathrm{ad}_A|\mathcal{F}_\ell$ in $\mathcal{F}_\ell$.

The main contribution of this paper is finding an algorithm suitable for a computer, to solve the equation

$$
\mathrm{ad}_A\,\widetilde{w} = v - v^0 \tag{5}
$$

for $\widetilde{w} \in \mathcal{F}_\ell$ and $v^0 \in \ker\,\mathrm{ad}_S|\mathcal{F}_\ell$ given $v \in \mathcal{F}_\ell$, and also the equation

$$
\mathrm{ad}_A\,w = v^0 - v^{00} \tag{6}
$$

for $w \in \ker\,\mathrm{ad}_S|\mathcal{F}_\ell$ and $v^{00} \in \ker\,\mathrm{ad}_S|\mathcal{F}_\ell \cap \ker\,\mathrm{ad}_M|\mathcal{F}_\ell$ given $v^0 \in \ker\,\mathrm{ad}_S|\mathcal{F}_\ell$ *without* first bringing A into real Jordan canonical form. This is not such a big advantage in the general linear case, but it has its advantages in the Hamiltonian case, where the computation of the Jordan normal form is highly nontrivial. The appropriate setting is that of graded Lie algebras. Under appropriate technical conditions on the linear problem, our approach can be easily translated to this context.

1. The Jacobson-Morozov theorem

In this section we describe a method which implements the Jacobson-Morozov theorem. In other words, given the linear mapping A, we show how to find the linear mappings M, N, H and S.

We begin with finding the linear maps S and N which give the semisimple-nilpotent decomposition of A. We use the algorithm of [BC] to compute polynomials r_i of degree less than the degree of the minimal polynomial p of A so that

$$
S = A + \sum_{i=1}^{m-1} r_i(A)p(A)^i.
$$

Here m is the maximum of the degrees of the irreducible factors of the characteristic polynomial χ of A. This algorithm does *not* need a factorization of χ and is straightforward to program in Maple.

To implement the Jacobson-Morozov theorem for $g\ell_n(\mathbf{R})$ we first solve the linear equations

$$
[S, Z] = 0
$$
$$
[[Z, N], N] = -2N
$$

for $Z \in g\ell_n(\mathbf{R})$. Put $H = [Z, N]$. To find M we solve the linear equations

$$
[S, K] = 0
$$
$$
[N, K] = 0
$$
$$
[H, K] - 2K = [H, Z] - 2Z
$$

for $K \in g\ell_n(\mathbf{R})$. Then put $M = Z - K$. It is easy to check that M, N, H and S so obtained satisfy the bracket relations (4).

2. The semisimple case

In this section, until further notice, we suppose that $A = S$ is a nonzero semisimple linear mapping. We will show how to solve

$$\operatorname{ad}_S \tilde{w} = v - v^0 \tag{7}$$

for $\tilde{w} \in \mathcal{F}_\ell$, $v^0 \in \ker \operatorname{ad}_S | \mathcal{F}_\ell$ given $v \in \mathcal{F}_\ell$.

To motivate our approach, we first treat the special case where S is a complex diagonal matrix with respect to the standard basis of $\mathbf{C}^n$, with eigenvalues $\lambda_1, \ldots, \lambda_n$. Let $(z_1, \ldots, z_n)$ be coordinates on $\mathbf{C}^n$. Then the linear vectorfield S, written as a differential operator, is

$$S = \sum_{j=1}^n \lambda_j z_j \frac{\partial}{\partial z_j}.$$

A basis for $\mathcal{F}_\ell(\mathbf{C}^n)$ is given by the vectorfields

$$z^{\alpha_j} \frac{\partial}{\partial z_j} \qquad (j = 1, \ldots, n)$$

where $z^{\alpha_j} = z_1^{\alpha_1} \cdots z_n^{\alpha_n}$, $\alpha_j = (\alpha_{j1}, \ldots, \alpha_{jn}) \in \mathbf{Z}_{\geq 0}^n$ and $|\alpha_j| = \sum_{i=1}^n \alpha_{ji} = \ell$. Then from the definition of Lie bracket (1) it follows that

$$\operatorname{ad}_S \left(z^{\alpha_j} \frac{\partial}{\partial z_j} \right) = (\langle \alpha_j, \lambda \rangle - \lambda_j) z^{\alpha_j} \frac{\partial}{\partial z_j} \tag{8}$$

where $\langle \alpha_j, \lambda \rangle = \sum_{i=1}^n \alpha_{ji} \lambda_i$. Given the vectorfield

$$v = \sum_{j=1}^n \sum_{|\alpha_j|=\ell} c_{\alpha_j} z^{\alpha_j} \frac{\partial}{\partial z_j},$$

it follows from (8) that

$$\tilde{w} = \sum_{j=1}^n \sum_{\substack{\langle \alpha_j, \lambda \rangle \neq \lambda_j \\ |\alpha_j|=\ell}} \frac{c_{\alpha_j}}{\langle \alpha_j, \lambda \rangle - \lambda_j} z^{\alpha_j} \frac{\partial}{\partial z_j}$$

and

$$v^0 = \sum_{j=1}^n \sum_{\substack{\langle \alpha_j, \lambda \rangle = \lambda_j \\ |\alpha_j|=\ell}} c_{\alpha_j} z^{\alpha_j} \frac{\partial}{\partial z_j}.$$

solve (7).

This method of solving (7) is too dependent on the choice of basis which diagonalizes S to be of much practical use. We use a different approach. Look at the one parameter group

$$t \mapsto t^S = \mathrm{diag}(t^{\lambda_1}, \ldots, t^{\lambda_n}) \qquad \text{where } t \in \mathbf{C}^*. \tag{9}$$

This $\mathbf{C}^*$-action induces a $\mathbf{C}^*$-action on $\mathcal{F}_\ell(\mathbf{C}^n)$ given by

$$t \mapsto t^{\mathrm{ad}s}\left(z_j^\alpha \frac{\partial}{\partial z_j}\right) = t^{\langle \alpha_j, \lambda \rangle - \lambda_j}\left(z^{\alpha_j} \frac{\partial}{\partial z_j}\right). \tag{10}$$

Thus $\mathbf{C}^*$ acts on homogeneous polynomial vectorfields by *rescaling* each monomial vectorfield according to (10). This does not look like too much help. But it is because we can operate on the scaling factors rather than on the monomial vectorfields. For instance, for $t \in \mathbf{C}^*$, consider the linear operator T_t on $\mathcal{F}_\ell(\mathbf{C}^n)$ defined by

$$T_t\left(z^{\alpha_j} \frac{\partial}{\partial z_j}\right) = \int^t t^{\mathrm{ad}s}\left(z^{\alpha_j} \frac{\partial}{\partial z_j}\right)\frac{dt}{t} \tag{11}$$

Then

$$T_t\left(z^{\alpha_j} \frac{\partial}{\partial z_j}\right) = \begin{cases} \dfrac{t^{\langle \alpha_j, \lambda \rangle - \lambda_j}}{\langle \alpha_j, \lambda \rangle - \lambda_j}\left(z^{\alpha_j} \frac{\partial}{\partial z_j}\right) & \text{if } \langle \alpha_j, \lambda \rangle \neq \lambda_j \\[2mm] \log t\left(z^{\alpha_j} \frac{\partial}{\partial z_j}\right) & \text{if } \langle \alpha_j, \lambda \rangle = \lambda_j. \end{cases} \tag{12}$$

If we put

$$\tilde{w} = T_1 v \quad \text{and}$$

$$v^0 = \text{coefficient of } t^{-1} \text{ in } t^{\mathrm{ad}s} v,$$

then $\tilde{w}$ and v^0 solve (7).

The only trouble with the above approach is that S was assumed to be diagonal so that we could compute t^S. This difficulty can be circumvented as follows (see also [LR]). Let

$$p(\lambda) = \prod_{j=1}^r (\lambda - \lambda_j)$$

be the minimal polynomial of S. Thus $\lambda_j \neq \lambda_k$ if $j \neq k$. For $j = 1, \ldots, r$ set $p_j(\lambda) = p(\lambda)/(\lambda - \lambda_j)$.

2.1 Lemma For $j = 1, \ldots, r$, the mapping $\pi_j = p_j(S)/p'(\lambda_j)$ is a projection of $\mathbf{C}^n$ onto $\ker(S - \lambda_j)$.

Proof Because

$$(S - \lambda_j)\pi_j(\mathbf{C}^n) = \frac{p(S)}{p'(\lambda_j)}\mathbf{C}^n = 0,$$

we have $\pi_j(\mathbf{C}^n) \subseteq \ker(S - \lambda_j)$. Since the polynomials $\{p_j(\lambda)/p'(\lambda_j)\}_{j=1}^r$ are pairwise relatively prime, $\mathbf{C}^n = \bigoplus_{j=1}^r \pi_j(\mathbf{C}^n)$. It follows that $\pi_j(\mathbf{C}^n) = \ker(S - \lambda_j)$.

It remains to be shown that π_j is a projection. Suppose that

$$1 = \sum_{k=1}^r \pi_k(\lambda) \tag{13}$$

holds. Then multiplying both sides of (13) by $p_j(\lambda)/p'(\lambda_j)$ gives, with $p_{kj}(\lambda) = p(\lambda)/((\lambda - \lambda_j)(\lambda - \lambda_k))$,

$$
\begin{aligned}
\pi_j(\lambda) &= \sum_{k \neq j} \frac{p_k(\lambda)p_j(\lambda)}{p'(\lambda_k)p'(\lambda_j)} + (\pi_j(\lambda))^2 \\
&= \sum_{k \neq j} \frac{p_{kj}(\lambda)(\lambda - \lambda_j)p_j(\lambda)}{p'(\lambda_k)p'(\lambda_j)} + (\pi_j(\lambda))^2 \\
&= p(\lambda) \sum_{k \neq j} \frac{p_{kj}(\lambda)}{p'(\lambda_k)p'(\lambda_j)} + (\pi_j(\lambda))^2.
\end{aligned}
\tag{14}
$$

Substituting S into (14) and using $p(S) = 0$ gives $(\pi_j)^2 = \pi_j$ as desired.

To prove (13) consider the partial fraction decomposition of $p(\lambda)^{-1}$

$$\frac{1}{p(\lambda)} = \sum_{k=1}^r \frac{A_k}{\lambda - \lambda_k}. \tag{15}$$

Multiplying both sides of (15) by $\lambda - \lambda_j$ and taking the limit as $\lambda \to \lambda_j$ gives $A_j = (p'(\lambda_j))^{-1}$. Note that $p'(\lambda_j) \neq 0$, since λ_j is a simple zero of p. Therefore

$$1 = p(\lambda) \sum_{k=1}^r \frac{1}{(\lambda - \lambda_k)p'(\lambda_k)} = \sum_{k=1}^r \frac{p_k(\lambda)}{p'(\lambda_k)} = \sum_{k=1}^r \pi_k(\lambda),$$

which proves (13) and the lemma. $\square$

Using the functional calculus for holomorphic functions of a matrix and the above lemma, we find that

$$t^S = \sum_{j=1}^r t^{\lambda_j} \pi_j \tag{16}$$

for an arbitrary complex semisimple linear map S with distinct eigenvalues $\{\lambda_j\}_{j=1}^r$.

2.2 Example By way of example, we now apply the above theory to compute a normal form of the vectorfield

$$
\begin{aligned}
\begin{pmatrix} \dot{x}_1 \\ \dot{x}_2 \end{pmatrix} &= S \begin{pmatrix} x_1 \\ x_2 \end{pmatrix} + \begin{pmatrix} v_{31} \\ v_{32} \end{pmatrix} \\
&= \begin{pmatrix} 0 & 1 \\ -1 & 0 \end{pmatrix} \begin{pmatrix} x_1 \\ x_2 \end{pmatrix} + \begin{pmatrix} \frac{1}{3}\alpha_1 x_1^3 + \beta_1 x_1^2 x_2 + \gamma_1 x_1 x_2^2 + \frac{1}{3}\delta_1 x_2^3 \\ \frac{1}{3}\alpha_2 x_1^3 + \beta_2 x_1^2 x_2 + \gamma_2 x_1 x_2^2 + \frac{1}{3}\delta_2 x_2^3 \end{pmatrix}
\end{aligned}
\tag{17}
$$

up through cubic terms. The linear vectorfield S is semisimple with minimal polynomial $p(\lambda) = \lambda^2 + 1 = (\lambda - i)(\lambda + i)$. Applying the lemma with $\lambda_1 = i$ and $\lambda_2 = -i$, we get for the projection onto $\ker(S - i)$

$$\pi_1 = \frac{p_1(S)}{p'(i)} = \frac{1}{2i}(S + i) = \frac{1}{2}\begin{pmatrix} 1 & -i \\ i & 1 \end{pmatrix}$$

and for the projection of onto $\ker(S + i)$

$$\pi_2 = \frac{1}{2}\begin{pmatrix} 1 & i \\ -i & 1 \end{pmatrix}.$$

Now (16) yields

$$t^S = \frac{1}{2}t^i\begin{pmatrix} 1 & -i \\ i & 1 \end{pmatrix} + \frac{1}{2}t^{-i}\begin{pmatrix} 1 & i \\ -i & 1 \end{pmatrix}$$

$$= \frac{1}{2}\begin{pmatrix} \tau + \tau^{-1} & -i(\tau - \tau^{-1}) \\ i(\tau - \tau^{-1}) & \tau + \tau^{-1} \end{pmatrix} \quad \text{where } \tau = t^i$$

$$= \tau^{-iS}.$$

Consequently, by (11),

$$T_1\begin{pmatrix} v_{31} \\ v_{32} \end{pmatrix} = \left[\int^t t\,\text{ad}_S\begin{pmatrix} v_{31} \\ v_{32} \end{pmatrix}\frac{dt}{t}\right]_{t=1}$$

$$= \left[\int^\tau \tau^{-i\,\text{ad}_S}\begin{pmatrix} v_{31} \\ v_{32} \end{pmatrix}\frac{d\tau}{i\tau}\right]_{\tau=1}.$$

$\qquad\qquad\qquad\qquad\qquad\qquad\qquad\qquad\qquad\qquad\qquad\qquad\qquad (18)$

Observe that $T_1v \in \mathcal{F}_3(\mathbf{R}^2)$, although the intermediate steps were over $\mathbf{C}$. Evaluating the right hand side of (18) is straightforward, but is better left to a computer. We obtain

$$\tilde{w} = T_1\begin{pmatrix} v_{31} \\ v_{32} \end{pmatrix} =$$

$$= \begin{pmatrix} (-\alpha_2 + \beta_1 - \gamma_2 + \delta_1)(x_1^2 + x_2^2)x_2 + \frac{1}{8}(\alpha_1 + \beta_2 + \gamma_1 + \delta_2)(x_1^2 + x_2^2)x_1 \\ (\alpha_2 - \beta_1 + \gamma_2 - \delta_1)(x_1^2 + x_2^2)x_1 + \frac{1}{8}(\alpha_1 + \beta_2 + \gamma_1 + \delta_2)(x_1^2 + x_2^2)x_2 \end{pmatrix}.$$

This agrees with the general theory [CS], which says that the normal form of (17) is

$$S\begin{pmatrix} x_1 \\ x_2 \end{pmatrix} + \begin{pmatrix} H_1x_1 - H_2x_2 \\ H_1x_2 + H_2x_1 \end{pmatrix},$$

where $H_1, H_2 \in \mathbf{R}[[x_1^2 + x_2^2]]$.

We end this section by treating (5) for general (not necessarily semisimple) $A = S + N$. Using the above method for solving

$$\text{ad}_S\,\widetilde{w_S} = v - v^0 \qquad\qquad\qquad\qquad\qquad\qquad\qquad (19)$$

for $\widetilde{w_S} \in \mathcal{F}_\ell(\mathbf{R}^n)$ and $v^0 \in \ker \mathrm{ad}_S | \mathcal{F}_\ell$ given $v \in \mathcal{F}_\ell$, we show how to solve

$$\mathrm{ad}_A \, \tilde{w} = v - v^0 \tag{20}$$

for $\tilde{w} \in \mathcal{F}_\ell(\mathbf{R}^n)$ and $v^0 \in \ker \mathrm{ad}_S | \mathcal{F}_\ell$ given $v \in \mathcal{F}_\ell$. Put

$$\tilde{w} = \sum_{k=0}^{m} (-1)^k \mathrm{ad}_N^k \, T_1^k \, \widetilde{w_S} \tag{21}$$

where $\mathrm{ad}_N^{m+1} = 0$ (such m exists since ad_N is nilpotent). It follows from (12) that T_1 equals ad_S^{-1} on $\mathrm{im}\,\mathrm{ad}_S | \mathcal{F}_\ell$ and 0 on $\ker \mathrm{ad}_S | \mathcal{F}_\ell$. Therefore

$$\mathrm{ad}_S \, T_1^k = T_1^{k-1}. \tag{22}$$

The following calculation, which uses (22), shows that $\tilde{w}$ given by (21) solves (20)

$$
\begin{aligned}
\mathrm{ad}_A \, \tilde{w} &= \sum_{k=0}^{m} (-1)^k (\mathrm{ad}_S + \mathrm{ad}_N) \mathrm{ad}_N^k \, T_1^k \, \widetilde{w_S} \\
&= \mathrm{ad}_S \widetilde{w_S} + \sum_{k=1}^{m} (-1)^k \mathrm{ad}_N^k \, T_1^{k-1} \widetilde{w_S} + \sum_{k=0}^{m} (-1)^k \mathrm{ad}_N^{k+1} \, T_1^k \, \widetilde{w_S} \\
&= \mathrm{ad}_S \widetilde{w_S} = v - v^0.
\end{aligned}
$$

3. The general case

In this section we will show how to solve the basic normal form equation

$$\mathrm{ad}_N \, w = \mathrm{ad}_A \, w = v^0 - v^{00} \tag{23}$$

for $w \in \ker \mathrm{ad}_S | \mathcal{F}_\ell$ and $v^{00} \in \ker \mathrm{ad}_S | \mathcal{F}_\ell \cap \ker \mathrm{ad}_M | \mathcal{F}_\ell$ given $v^0 \in \ker \mathrm{ad}_S | \mathcal{F}_\ell$. Using the results of §2, we may assume that v^0 has been computed starting from a given $v \in \mathcal{F}_\ell$.

The treatment of this problem will be purely representation theoretic. To be explicit, we start with the triple $\{M, N, H\}$ providing a representation ρ of $s\ell_2(\mathbf{R})$ on a real vector space U. Then [Hum]

$$U = \ker M \oplus \mathrm{im}\, N. \tag{24}$$

Our problem is: given $w \in U$, find $w' \in \ker M$ and $w'' \in \mathrm{im}\, N$ so that

$$w = w' + w''.$$

In other words, split w along the decomposition (24). Below we give a method for obtaining this splitting which is fast and suitable for a computer. For more on the splitting algorithm, see [CS2].

Let $u \in U$. We can write

$$u = \sum_h \sum_{i=0}^{\lambda(h)} \alpha_h^i v_i^h,$$

where for fixed $h \in \mathbf{N}$ the v_i^h span an irreducible subspace with highest weight $\lambda(h)$ and obey the relations

$$\begin{aligned}
H v_i^h &= (\lambda(h) - 2i) v_i^h, \\
N v_i^h &= (i+1) v_{i+1}^h, \\
M v_i^h &= (\lambda(h) - i + 1) v_{i-1}^h
\end{aligned} \tag{25}$$

(with the convention that $v_{\lambda(h)+1}^h = v_{-1}^h = 0$).

There is a natural imbedding $\iota : U \to U \otimes \mathbf{R}[X, Y]$ given by

$$\iota u = \sum_h \sum_{i=0}^{\lambda(h)} \alpha_h^i v_i^h \otimes X^i Y^{\lambda(h)-i},$$

with a corresponding projection $\rho : U \otimes \mathbf{R}[X, Y] \to U$. We remark that when $u \in \ker M$, we can give an explicit formula for ιu:

$$\iota u = \sum_h \alpha_h^0 v_0^h \otimes Y^\lambda(h) = \sum_h \alpha_h^0 (Y^H)_* v_0^h = (Y^H)_* u. \tag{26}$$

Suppose now that we have $y \in U$ and we want to compute ιy. Assume we have computed the effect of ι on My, i.e.,

$$\iota M y = \sum_h \sum_{i=0}^{\lambda(h)-1} \alpha_h^i v_i^h \otimes X^i Y^{\lambda(h)-i}.$$

We define an $\mathbf{R}$-linear map $\sigma : U \otimes \mathbf{R}[X, Y] \to U \otimes \mathbf{R}[X, Y]$ by

$$\sigma(u \otimes f(X, Y)) = N u \otimes \frac{1}{Y} \int^Y \frac{1}{\eta} \int^X f(\xi, \eta) d\xi d\eta. \tag{27}$$

Then

$$\begin{aligned}
\sigma \iota M y &= \sum_h \sum_{i=0}^{\lambda(h)-1} \alpha_h^i N v_i^h \otimes \frac{1}{Y} \int^Y \frac{1}{\eta} \int^X \xi^i \eta^{\lambda(h)-i} d\xi d\eta \\
&= \sum_h \sum_{i=0}^{\lambda(h)-1} \alpha_h^i (i+1) v_{i+1}^h \otimes \frac{1}{i+1} \frac{1}{\lambda(h)-i} X^{i+1} Y^{\lambda(h)-i-1} \\
&= \sum_h \sum_{i=0}^{\lambda(h)-1} \alpha_h^i v_{i+1}^h \otimes \frac{1}{\lambda(h)-i} X^{i+1} Y^{\lambda(h)-i-1}.
\end{aligned}$$

Projecting down onto U and applying M we obtain

$$M\rho\iota My = \sum_h \sum_{i=0}^{\lambda(h)-1} \alpha_h^i M v_{i+1}^h \frac{1}{\lambda(h)-i}$$
$$= \sum_h \sum_{i=0}^{\lambda(h)-1} \alpha_h^i v_i^h$$
$$= My.$$

In other words, $y - \rho\iota My \in \ker M$. Thus we have

$$\iota y = \sigma\iota My + Y^H(y - \rho\iota My). \tag{28}$$

This describes how we can take one step. The splitting algorithm now works as follows: Take $y \in U$. Compute $y^0 = y$ and $y^{j+1} = My^j$. Stop when $y^{m+1} = 0$. Let $y_j = \iota y^j$ for each $j \in \{0, \ldots, m+1\}$. Applying (28) repeatedly, we obtain $y_j = \sigma y_{j+1} + Y^H(y^j - \rho\sigma y_{j+1})$ for $j = m, \ldots, 0$. Then $y = (y - \rho\sigma y_1) + \rho\sigma y_1$, where the first component is the projection on $\ker M$ and the second on $\operatorname{im} N$ by construction of σ, see (27).

3.1 The splitting algorithm

Input $v^0 \in \mathcal{F}_\ell(\mathbf{R}^n) \cap \ker \operatorname{ad}_S$.

1. For $i = 0, \ldots$ compute $v^{i+1} = \operatorname{ad}_M v^i$. Stop when $v^{m+1} = 0$.
Set $v_{m+1}(X, Y) = 0$, and $j = m$.

2_j. Compute

$$w_j(X, Y) = \frac{1}{Y} \int^Y \frac{1}{\eta} \int^X v_{j+1}(\xi, \eta)\, d\xi\, d\eta,$$
$$u_j(X, Y) = \operatorname{ad}_N w_j(X, Y),$$
$$v_j(X, Y) = u_j(X, Y) + Y^{\operatorname{ad}_H}(v^j - u_j(1, 1))$$

3. Decrease j by 1 and repeat step 2_j. Stop when $j = -1$.
Output $v^{00} = v_0(0, 1)$ and $w = w_0(1, 1)$.

As a result of the reasoning above we have

3.2 Theorem For $v^0 \in \mathcal{F}_\ell(\mathbf{R}^n) \cap \ker \operatorname{ad}_S$, the $v^{00} \in \ker \operatorname{ad}_S|\mathcal{F}_\ell \cap \operatorname{im} \operatorname{ad}_N|\mathcal{F}_\ell$ and $w \in \ker \operatorname{ad}_S|\mathcal{F}_\ell$ as determined by the above condensed splitting algorithm solve

$$\operatorname{ad}_N w = v^0 - v^{00}. \tag{29}$$

3.3 Remarks In the above algorithm, $w_j(X, Y)$, $u_j(X, Y)$, $v_j(X, Y)$ are vectorfields with scaling parameters X and Y. The exponent of the parameter Y gives the ad_H-eigenvalue of the monomial vectorfield, whereas the exponent of the parameter X gives the position of the monomial vectorfield inside an irreducible. The restriction to $\ker \mathrm{ad}_S$ is not essential.

3.4 Example We illustrate the above algorithm with the vectorfield

$$v^0 = (\frac{1}{2}\alpha_1 x_1^2 + \beta_1 x_1 x_2 + \frac{1}{2}\gamma_1 x_2^2)\frac{\partial}{\partial x_1} + (\frac{1}{2}\alpha_2 x_1^2 + \beta_2 x_1 x_2 + \frac{1}{2}\gamma_2 x_2^2)\frac{\partial}{\partial x_2}$$

on $\mathbf{R}^2$ and take as a representation of $sl_2(\mathbf{R})$ the ad of:

$$M = x_2\frac{\partial}{\partial x_1}, \quad N = x_1\frac{\partial}{\partial x_2}, \quad H = -x_1\frac{\partial}{\partial x_1} + x_2\frac{\partial}{\partial x_2}.$$

First we compute

$$v^1 = \mathrm{ad}_M\, v^0$$
$$= -(\frac{1}{2}\alpha_2 x_1^2 + (\beta_2 - \alpha_1)x_1 x_2 + (\frac{1}{2}\gamma_2 - \beta_1)x_2^2)\frac{\partial}{\partial x_1}$$
$$+ (\alpha_2 x_1 x_2 + \beta_2 x_2^2)\frac{\partial}{\partial x_2}$$

$$v^2 = \mathrm{ad}_M\, v^1$$
$$= -(2\alpha_2 x_1 x_2 + (2(\beta_2 - \alpha_1)x_2^2)\frac{\partial}{\partial x_1} + \alpha_2 x_2^2\frac{\partial}{\partial x_2}$$

$$v^3 = \mathrm{ad}_M\, v^2 = -3\alpha_2 x_2^2\frac{\partial}{\partial x_1}$$

$$v^4 = 0.$$

Then from step 2_3 of the algorithm we find that

$$w_3(X, Y) = 0$$
$$u_3(X, Y) = 0$$
$$v_3(X, Y) = Y^{\mathrm{ad}_H}(v^3) = -3\alpha_2(Y x_2)^2\frac{\partial}{\partial \frac{1}{Y} x_1}$$
$$= -Y^3(3\alpha_2 x_2^2\frac{\partial}{\partial x_1})$$

since $Y^H = \begin{pmatrix} Y^{-1} & 0 \\ 0 & Y \end{pmatrix}$. Now, for $j = 2$ in step 2_j we obtain,

$$w_2(X, Y) = -\frac{1}{Y}\int^Y \frac{1}{\eta}\int^X \eta^3(3\alpha_2 x_2^2\frac{\partial}{\partial x_1})\, d\xi\, d\eta$$
$$= -XY^2(\alpha_2 x_2^2\frac{\partial}{\partial x_1})$$

$$u_2(X, Y) = \mathrm{ad}_N\, w_2(X, Y) = -XY^2\alpha_2(2x_1 x_2\frac{\partial}{\partial x_1} - x_2^2\frac{\partial}{\partial x_2})$$

$$v_2(X, Y) = u_2(X, Y) + Y^{\mathrm{ad}_H}(v^2 - u_2(1, 1))$$
$$= -XY^2\alpha_2(2x_1 x_2\frac{\partial}{\partial x_1} - x_2^2\frac{\partial}{\partial x_2}) - Y^3(2\beta_2 - \alpha_1)x_2^2\frac{\partial}{\partial x_1}.$$

We repeat this process twice more. First to compute w_1, u_1, v_1 and subsequently to compute w_0, u_0, v_0. We give the latter:

$$w_0(X,Y) = -\frac{1}{3}X^3\alpha_2(\frac{1}{2}x_1^2\frac{\partial}{\partial x_1} - x_1x_2\frac{\partial}{\partial x_2})$$

$$+ \frac{1}{12}X^2Y^2(\alpha_1 - 2\beta_2)(2x_1x_2\frac{\partial}{\partial x_1} - x_2^2\frac{\partial}{\partial x_2})$$

$$+ \frac{1}{3}X(\alpha_1 + \beta_2)(x_1x_2\frac{\partial}{\partial x_1} + x_2^2\frac{\partial}{\partial x_2}) - \frac{1}{3}XY^2(\frac{1}{2}\gamma_2 - \beta_1)x_2^2\frac{\partial}{\partial x_1}$$

$$u_0(X,Y) = X^3(\frac{1}{2}\alpha_2x_1^2\frac{\partial}{\partial x_2}) + \frac{1}{6}X^2Y(\alpha_1 - 2\beta_2)(x_1^2\frac{\partial}{\partial x_1} - 2x_1x_2\frac{\partial}{\partial x_2})$$

$$+ X\frac{1}{3}(\alpha_1 + \beta_2)(x_1^2\frac{\partial}{\partial x_1} + x_1x_2\frac{\partial}{\partial x_2})$$

$$- \frac{1}{3}XY^2(\frac{1}{2}\gamma_1 - \beta_1)(2x_1x_2\frac{\partial}{\partial x_1} - x_2^2\frac{\partial}{\partial x_2})$$

$$v_0(X,Y) = \frac{1}{2}X^3(\alpha_2x_1^2\frac{\partial}{\partial x_2}) + \frac{1}{6}X^2Y(\alpha_1 - 2\beta_2)(x_1^2\frac{\partial}{\partial x_1} - 2x_1x_2\frac{\partial}{\partial x_2})$$

$$+ \frac{1}{3}X(\alpha_1 + \beta_2)(x_1^2\frac{\partial}{\partial x_1} + x_1x_2\frac{\partial}{\partial x_2})$$

$$- \frac{1}{3}XY^2(\frac{1}{2}\gamma_1 - \beta_1)(2x_1x_2\frac{\partial}{\partial x_1} - x_2^2\frac{\partial}{\partial x_2})$$

$$+ \frac{1}{3}Y(\beta_1 + \gamma_2)(x_1x_2\frac{\partial}{\partial x_1} + x_2^2\frac{\partial}{\partial x_2}) + \frac{1}{2}Y^3\gamma_1x_2^2\frac{\partial}{\partial x_1}.$$

Hence

$$v^{00} = \frac{1}{3}(\beta_1 + \gamma_2)(x_1x_2\frac{\partial}{\partial x_1} + x_2^2\frac{\partial}{\partial x_2}) + \frac{1}{2}\gamma_1x_2^2\frac{\partial}{\partial x_1}$$

and

$$w = -\frac{1}{3}\alpha_2(\frac{1}{2}x_1^2\frac{\partial}{\partial x_1} - x_1x_2\frac{\partial}{\partial x_2}) + \frac{1}{12}(\alpha_1 - 2\beta_2)(2x_1x_2\frac{\partial}{\partial x_1}) - x_2^2\frac{\partial}{\partial x_2})$$

$$+ \frac{1}{3}(\alpha_1 + \beta_2)(x_1x_2\frac{\partial}{\partial x_1} + x_2^2\frac{\partial}{\partial x_2}) - \frac{1}{3}(\frac{1}{2}\gamma_2 - \beta_1)x_2^2\frac{\partial}{\partial x_1}$$

solve

$$\text{ad}_N w = v^0 - v^{00}.$$

The resulting normal form v^{00} agrees with the general theory [CS1] which states that the normal form of a general formal power series vectorfield on $\mathbf{R}^2$ with linear term $x_2\frac{\partial}{\partial x_1}$ is

$$x_1\frac{\partial}{\partial x_1} + H_1(x_1\frac{\partial}{\partial x_1} + x_2\frac{\partial}{\partial x_2}) + H_2x_2\frac{\partial}{\partial x_1}$$

where $H_1, H_2 \in \mathbf{R}[[x_2]]$.

To summarize what we have done: given $v \in \mathcal{F}_\ell$ we can find $\tilde{w} \in \mathcal{F}_\ell$ and $v^0 \in \ker \text{ad}_S|\mathcal{F}_\ell$ so that

$$\text{ad}_A\tilde{w} = v - v^0,$$

see (20). Moreover, given $v^0 \in \ker \mathrm{ad}_S|\mathcal{F}_\ell$ we can find $w \in \ker \mathrm{ad}_S|\mathcal{F}_\ell$ and $v^{00} \in (\ker \mathrm{ad}_M \cap \ker \mathrm{ad}_S)|\mathcal{F}_\ell$ so that

$$\mathrm{ad}_A w = \mathrm{ad}_N w = v^0 - v^{00},$$

see (29). Adding the above two equations gives the decomposition of v

$$v = \mathrm{ad}_A(\widetilde{w} + w) + v^{00}.$$

along the subspaces $\mathrm{im}\,\mathrm{ad}_A|\mathcal{F}_\ell$ and $(\ker \mathrm{ad}_M \cap \ker \mathrm{ad}_S)|\ker \mathcal{F}_\ell$, as desired.

Acknowledgement The author gratefully acknowledges the work of the referee and the editor (beyond the call of their duty) to make this paper more readable and better organized.

4. References

[BC]   Burgoyne, N. & Cushman, R., *The decomposition of a linear mapping*, J. Lin. Alg. & Appl., **8**(1974), 515–519.

[CS]   Cushman, R. & Sanders, J., *Nilpotent normal forms and representation theory of $s\ell_2(\mathbf{R})$*, pp. 31–51 in: Multiparameter bifurcation theory (eds.: M. Golubitsky and J. Guckenheimer), Contemporary Mathematics 56, American Mathematical Society, Providence 1986.

[CS1]   Cushman, R. & Sanders, J., *A survey of applications of invariant theory to normal forms*, pp. 82–108 in: Invariant theory and tableaux (ed.: D. Stanton), Springer Verlag, IMA series, 18, 1990.

[CS2]   Cushman, R. & Sanders, J., *Splitting algorithm for nilpotent normal forms*, Dynamics and Stability of Systems, **2**(1988), 235-246.

[Hel]   Helgason, H., *Differential Geometry, Lie Groups, and Symmetric Spaces*, 1978, Academic Press, New York.

[Hum]   Humphreys, J., *Introduction to Lie algebras and representation theory*, Springer Verlag, 1972.

[LR]   London, R.R. & Rogosinski, H.P., *Decomposition theory in the teaching of elementary linear algebra*, Amer. Math. Monthly, (1990), 478–485.

CWI TRACTS

1 D.H.J. Epema. *Surfaces with canonical hyperplane sections.* 1984.

2 J.J. Dijkstra. *Fake topological Hilbert spaces and characterizations of dimension in terms of negligibility.* 1984.

3 A.J. van der Schaft. *System theoretic descriptions of physical systems.* 1984.

4 J. Koene. *Minimal cost flow in processing networks, a primal approach.* 1984.

5 B. Hoogenboom. *Intertwining functions on compact Lie groups.* 1984.

6 A.P.W. Böhm. *Dataflow computation.* 1984.

7 A. Blokhuis. *Few-distance sets.* 1984.

8 M.H. van Hoorn. *Algorithms and approximations for queueing systems.* 1984.

9 C.P.J. Koymans. *Models of the lambda calculus.* 1984.

10 C.G. van der Laan, N.M. Temme. *Calculation of special functions: the gamma function, the exponential integrals and error-like functions.* 1984.

11 N.M. van Dijk. *Controlled Markov processes; time-discretization.* 1984.

12 W.H. Hundsdorfer. *The numerical solution of nonlinear stiff initial value problems: an analysis of one step methods.* 1985.

13 D. Grune. *On the design of ALEPH.* 1985.

14 J.G.F. Thiemann. *Analytic spaces and dynamic programming: a measure theoretic approach.* 1985.

15 F.J. van der Linden. *Euclidean rings with two infinite primes.* 1985.

16 R.J.P. Groothuizen. *Mixed elliptic-hyperbolic partial differential operators: a case-study in Fourier integral operators.* 1985.

17 H.M.M. ten Eikelder. *Symmetries for dynamical and Hamiltonian systems.* 1985.

18 A.D.M. Kester. *Some large deviation results in statistics.* 1985.

19 T.M.V. Janssen. *Foundations and applications of Montague grammar, part 1: Philosophy, framework, computer science.* 1986.

20 B.F. Schriever. *Order dependence.* 1986.

21 D.P. van der Vecht. *Inequalities for stopped Brownian motion.* 1986.

22 J.C.S.P. van der Woude. *Topological dynamix.* 1986.

23 A.F. Monna. *Methods, concepts and ideas in mathematics: aspects of an evolution.* 1986.

24 J.C.M. Baeten. *Filters and ultrafilters over definable subsets of admissible ordinals.* 1986.

25 A.W.J. Kolen. *Tree network and planar rectilinear location theory.* 1986.

26 A.H. Veen. *The misconstrued semicolon: Reconciling imperative languages and dataflow machines.* 1986.

27 A.J.M. van Engelen. *Homogeneous zero-dimensional absolute Borel sets.* 1986.

28 T.M.V. Janssen. *Foundations and applications of Montague grammar, part 2: Applications to natural language.* 1986.

29 H.L. Trentelman. *Almost invariant subspaces and high gain feedback.* 1986.

30 A.G. de Kok. *Production-inventory control models: approximations and algorithms.* 1987.

31 E.E.M. van Berkum. *Optimal paired comparison designs for factorial experiments.* 1987.

32 J.H.J. Einmahl. *Multivariate empirical processes.* 1987.

33 O.J. Vrieze. *Stochastic games with finite state and action spaces.* 1987.

34 P.H.M. Kersten. *Infinitesimal symmetries: a computational approach.* 1987.

35 M.L. Eaton. *Lectures on topics in probability inequalities.* 1987.

36 A.H.P. van der Burgh, R.M.M. Mattheij (eds.). *Proceedings of the first international conference on industrial and applied mathematics (ICIAM 87).* 1987.

37 L. Stougie. *Design and analysis of algorithms for stochastic integer programming.* 1987.

38 J.B.G. Frenk. *On Banach algebras, renewal measures and regenerative processes.* 1987.

39 H.J.M. Peters, O.J. Vrieze (eds.). *Surveys in game theory and related topics.* 1987.

40 J.L. Geluk, L. de Haan. *Regular variation, extensions and Tauberian theorems.* 1987.

41 Sape J. Mullender (ed.). *The Amoeba distributed operating system: Selected papers 1984-1987.* 1987.

42 P.R.J. Asveld, A. Nijholt (eds.). *Essays on concepts, formalisms, and tools.* 1987.

43 H.L. Bodlaender. *Distributed computing: structure and complexity.* 1987.

44 A.W. van der Vaart. *Statistical estimation in large parameter spaces.* 1988.

45 S.A. van de Geer. *Regression analysis and empirical processes.* 1988.

46 S.P. Spekreijse. *Multigrid solution of the steady Euler equations.* 1988.

47 J.B. Dijkstra. *Analysis of means in some non-standard situations.* 1988.

48 F.C. Drost. *Asymptotics for generalized chi-square goodness-of-fit tests.* 1988.

49 F.W. Wubs. *Numerical solution of the shallow-water equations.* 1988.

50 F. de Kerf. *Asymptotic analysis of a class of perturbed Korteweg-de Vries initial value problems.* 1988.

51 P.J.M. van Laarhoven. *Theoretical and computational aspects of simulated annealing.* 1988.

52 P.M. van Loon. *Continuous decoupling transformations for linear boundary value problems.* 1988.

53 K.C.P. Machielsen. *Numerical solution of optimal control problems with state constraints by sequential quadratic programming in function space.* 1988.

54 L.C.R.J. Willenborg. *Computational aspects of survey data processing.* 1988.

55 G.J. van der Steen. *A program generator for recognition, parsing and transduction with syntactic patterns.* 1988.

56 J.C. Ebergen. *Translating programs into delay-insensitive circuits.* 1989.

57 S.M. Verduyn Lunel. *Exponential type calculus for linear delay equations.* 1989.

58 M.C.M. de Gunst. *A random model for plant cell population growth.* 1989.

59 D. van Dulst. *Characterizations of Banach spaces not containing l^1.* 1989.

60 H.E. de Swart. *Vacillation and predictability properties of low-order atmospheric spectral models.* 1989.

61 P. de Jong. *Central limit theorems for generalized multilinear forms.* 1989.

62 V.J. de Jong. *A specification system for statistical software.* 1989.

63 B. Hanzon. *Identifiability, recursive identification and spaces of linear dynamical systems, part I.* 1989.

64 B. Hanzon. *Identifiability, recursive identification and spaces of linear dynamical systems, part II.* 1989.

65 B.M.M. de Weger. *Algorithms for diophantine equations.* 1989.

66 A. Jung. *Cartesian closed categories of domains.* 1989.

67 J.W. Polderman. *Adaptive control & identification: Conflict or conflux?.* 1989.

68 H.J. Woerdeman. *Matrix and operator extensions.* 1989.

69 B.G. Hansen. *Monotonicity properties of infinitely divisible distributions.* 1989.

70 J.K. Lenstra, H.C. Tijms, A. Volgenant (eds.). *Twenty-five years of operations research in the Netherlands: Papers dedicated to Gijs de Leve.* 1990.

71 P.J.C. Spreij. *Counting process systems. Identification and stochastic realization.* 1990.

72 J.F. Kaashoek. *Modeling one dimensional pattern formation by anti-diffusion.* 1990.

73 A.M.H. Gerards. *Graphs and polyhedra. Binary spaces and cutting planes.* 1990.

74 B. Koren. *Multigrid and defect correction for the steady Navier-Stokes equations. Application to aerodynamics.* 1991.

75 M.W.P. Savelsbergh. *Computer aided routing.* 1991.

76 O.E. Flippo. *Stability, duality and decomposition in general mathematical programming.* 1991.

77 A.J. van Es. *Aspects of nonparametric density estimation.* 1991.

78 G.A.P. Kindervater. *Exercises in parallel combinatorial computing.* 1991.

79 J.J. Lodder. *Towards a symmetrical theory of generalized functions.* 1991.

80 S.A. Smulders. *Control of freeway traffic flow.* 1991.

81 P.H.M. America, J.J.M.M. Rutten. *A parallel object-oriented language: design and semantic foundations.* 1991.

82 F. Thuijsman. *Optimality and equilibria in stochastic games.* 1991.

83 R.J. Kooman. *Convergence properties of recurrence sequences.* 1991.

84 A.M. Cohen (ed.). *Computational aspects of Lie group representations and related topics. Proceedings of the 1990 Computational Algebra Seminar at CWI, Amsterdam.* 1991.

85 V. de Valk. *One-dependent processes.* 1991.

MATHEMATICAL CENTRE TRACTS

1 T. van der Walt. *Fixed and almost fixed points.* 1963.

2 A.R. Bloemena. *Sampling from a graph.* 1964.

3 G. de Leve. *Generalized Markovian decision processes, part I: model and method.* 1964.

4 G. de Leve. *Generalized Markovian decision processes, part II: probabilistic background.* 1964.

5 G. de Leve, H.C. Tijms, P.J. Weeda. *Generalized Markovian decision processes, applications.* 1970.

6 M.A. Maurice. *Compact ordered spaces.* 1964.

7 W.R. van Zwet. *Convex transformations of random variables.* 1964.

8 J.A. Zonneveld. *Automatic numerical integration.* 1964.

9 P.C. Baayen. *Universal morphisms.* 1964.

10 E.M. de Jager. *Applications of distributions in mathematical physics.* 1964.

11 A.B. Paalman-de Miranda. *Topological semigroups.* 1964.

12 J.A.Th.M. van Berckel, H. Brandt Corstius, R.J. Mokken, A. van Wijngaarden. *Formal properties of newspaper Dutch.* 1965.

13 H.A. Lauwerier. *Asymptotic expansions.* 1966, out of print; replaced by MCT 54.

14 H.A. Lauwerier. *Calculus of variations in mathematical physics.* 1966.

15 R. Doornbos. *Slippage tests.* 1966.

16 J.W. de Bakker. *Formal definition of programming languages with an application to the definition of ALGOL 60.* 1967.

17 R.P. van de Riet. *Formula manipulation in ALGOL 60, part 1.* 1968.

18 R.P. van de Riet. *Formula manipulation in ALGOL 60, part 2.* 1968.

19 J. van der Slot. *Some properties related to compactness.* 1968.

20 P.J. van der Houwen. *Finite difference methods for solving partial differential equations.* 1968.

21 E. Wattel. *The compactness operator in set theory and topology.* 1968.

22 T.J. Dekker. *ALGOL 60 procedures in numerical algebra, part 1.* 1968.

23 T.J. Dekker, W. Hoffmann. *ALGOL 60 procedures in numerical algebra, part 2.* 1968.

24 J.W. de Bakker. *Recursive procedures.* 1971.

25 E.R. Paërl. *Representations of the Lorentz group and projective geometry.* 1969.

26 European Meeting 1968. *Selected statistical papers, part I.* 1968.

27 European Meeting 1968. *Selected statistical papers, part II.* 1968.

28 J. Oosterhoff. *Combination of one-sided statistical tests.* 1969.

29 J. Verhoeff. *Error detecting decimal codes.* 1969.

30 H. Brandt Corstius. *Exercises in computational linguistics.* 1970.

31 W. Molenaar. *Approximations to the Poisson, binomial and hypergeometric distribution functions.* 1970.

32 L. de Haan. *On regular variation and its application to the weak convergence of sample extremes.* 1970.

33 F.W. Steutel. *Preservation of infinite divisibility under mixing and related topics.* 1970.

34 I. Juhász, A. Verbeek, N.S. Kroonenberg. *Cardinal functions in topology.* 1971.

35 M.H. van Emden. *An analysis of complexity.* 1971.

36 J. Grasman. *On the birth of boundary layers.* 1971.

37 J.W. de Bakker, G.A. Blaauw, A.J.W. Duijvestijn, E.W. Dijkstra, P.J. van der Houwen, G.A.M. Kamsteeg-Kemper, F.E.J. Kruseman Aretz, W.L. van der Poel, J.P. Schaap-Kruseman, M.V. Wilkes, G. Zoutendijk. *MC-25 Informatica Symposium.* 1971.

38 W.A. Verloren van Themaat. *Automatic analysis of Dutch compound words.* 1972.

39 H. Bavinck. *Jacobi series and approximation.* 1972.

40 H.C. Tijms. *Analysis of (s,S) inventory models.* 1972.

41 A. Verbeek. *Superextensions of topological spaces.* 1972.

42 W. Vervaat. *Success epochs in Bernoulli trials (with applications in number theory).* 1972.

43 F.H. Ruymgaart. *Asymptotic theory of rank tests for independence.* 1973.

44 H. Bart. *Meromorphic operator valued functions.* 1973.

45 A.A. Balkema. *Monotone transformations and limit laws.* 1973.

46 R.P. van de Riet. *ABC ALGOL, a portable language for formula manipulation systems, part 1: the language.* 1973.

47 R.P. van de Riet. *ABC ALGOL, a portable language for formula manipulation systems, part 2: the compiler.* 1973.

48 F.E.J. Kruseman Aretz, P.J.W. ten Hagen, H.L. Oudshoorn. *An ALGOL 60 compiler in ALGOL 60, text of the MC-compiler for the EL-X8.* 1973.

49 H. Kok. *Connected orderable spaces.* 1974.

50 A. van Wijngaarden, B.J. Mailloux, J.E.L. Peck, C.H.A. Koster, M. Sintzoff, C.H. Lindsey, L.G.L.T. Meertens, R.G. Fisker (eds.). *Revised report on the algorithmic language ALGOL 68.* 1976.

51 A. Hordijk. *Dynamic programming and Markov potential theory.* 1974.

52 P.C. Baayen (ed.). *Topological structures.* 1974.

53 M.J. Faber. *Metrizability in generalized ordered spaces.* 1974.

54 H.A. Lauwerier. *Asymptotic analysis, part 1.* 1974.

55 M. Hall, Jr., J.H. van Lint (eds.). *Combinatorics, part 1: theory of designs, finite geometry and coding theory.* 1974.

56 M. Hall, Jr., J.H. van Lint (eds.). *Combinatorics, part 2: graph theory, foundations, partitions and combinatorial geometry.* 1974.

57 M. Hall, Jr., J.H. van Lint (eds.). *Combinatorics, part 3: combinatorial group theory.* 1974.

58 W. Albers. *Asymptotic expansions and the deficiency concept in statistics.* 1975.

59 J.L. Mijnheer. *Sample path properties of stable processes.* 1975.

60 F. Göbel. *Queueing models involving buffers.* 1975.

63 J.W. de Bakker (ed.). *Foundations of computer science.* 1975.

64 W.J. de Schipper. *Symmetric closed categories.* 1975.

65 J. de Vries. *Topological transformation groups, 1: a categorical approach.* 1975.

66 H.G.J. Pijls. *Logically convex algebras in spectral theory and eigenfunction expansions.* 1976.

68 P.P.N. de Groen. *Singularly perturbed differential operators of second order.* 1976.

69 J.K. Lenstra. *Sequencing by enumerative methods.* 1977.

70 W.P. de Roever, Jr. *Recursive program schemes: semantics and proof theory.* 1976.

71 J.A.E.E. van Nunen. *Contracting Markov decision processes.* 1976.

72 J.K.M. Jansen. *Simple periodic and non-periodic Lamé functions and their applications in the theory of conical waveguides.* 1977.

73 D.M.R. Leivant. *Absoluteness of intuitionistic logic.* 1979.

74 H.J.J. te Riele. *A theoretical and computational study of generalized aliquot sequences.* 1976.

75 A.E. Brouwer. *Treelike spaces and related connected topological spaces.* 1977.

76 M. Rem. *Associons and the closure statement.* 1976.

77 W.C.M. Kallenberg. *Asymptotic optimality of likelihood ratio tests in exponential families.* 1978.

78 E. de Jonge, A.C.M. van Rooij. *Introduction to Riesz spaces.* 1977.

79 M.C.A. van Zuijlen. *Empirical distributions and rank statistics.* 1977.

80 P.W. Hemker. *A numerical study of stiff two-point boundary problems.* 1977.

81 K.R. Apt, J.W. de Bakker (eds.). *Foundations of computer science II, part 1.* 1976.

82 K.R. Apt, J.W. de Bakker (eds.). *Foundations of computer science II, part 2.* 1976.

83 L.S. van Benthem Jutting. *Checking Landau's "Grundlagen" in the AUTOMATH system.* 1979.

84 H.L.L. Busard. *The translation of the elements of Euclid from the Arabic into Latin by Hermann of Carinthia (?), books vii-xii.* 1977.

85 J. van Mill. *Supercompactness and Wallman spaces.* 1977.

86 S.G. van der Meulen, M. Veldhorst. *Torrix I, a programming system for operations on vectors and matrices over arbitrary fields and of variable size.* 1978.

88 A. Schrijver. *Matroids and linking systems.* 1977.

89 J.W. de Roever. *Complex Fourier transformation and analytic functionals with unbounded carriers.* 1978.

90 L.P.J. Groenewegen. *Characterization of optimal strategies in dynamic games.* 1981.

91 J.M. Geysel. *Transcendence in fields of positive characteristic.* 1979.

92 P.J. Weeda. *Finite generalized Markov programming.* 1979.

93 H.C. Tijms, J. Wessels (eds.). *Markov decision theory.* 1977.

94 A. Bijlsma. *Simultaneous approximations in transcendental number theory.* 1978.

95 K.M. van Hee. *Bayesian control of Markov chains.* 1978.

96 P.M.B. Vitányi. *Lindenmayer systems: structure, languages, and growth functions.* 1980.

97 A. Federgruen. *Markovian control problems; functional equations and algorithms.* 1984.

98 R. Geel. *Singular perturbations of hyperbolic type.* 1978.

99 J.K. Lenstra, A.H.G. Rinnooy Kan, P. van Emde Boas (eds.). *Interfaces between computer science and operations research.* 1978.

100 P.C. Baayen, D. van Dulst, J. Oosterhoff (eds.). *Proceedings bicentennial congress of the Wiskundig Genootschap, part 1.* 1979.

101 P.C. Baayen, D. van Dulst, J. Oosterhoff (eds.). *Proceedings bicentennial congress of the Wiskundig Genootschap, part 2.* 1979.

102 D. van Dulst. *Reflexive and superreflexive Banach spaces.* 1978.

103 K. van Harn. *Classifying infinitely divisible distributions by functional equations.* 1978.

104 J.M. van Wouwe. *Go-spaces and generalizations of metrizability.* 1979.

105 R. Helmers. *Edgeworth expansions for linear combinations of order statistics.* 1982.

106 A. Schrijver (ed.). *Packing and covering in combinatorics.* 1979.

107 C. den Heijer. *The numerical solution of nonlinear operator equations by imbedding methods.* 1979.

108 J.W. de Bakker, J. van Leeuwen (eds.). *Foundations of computer science III, part 1.* 1979.

109 J.W. de Bakker, J. van Leeuwen (eds.). *Foundations of computer science III, part 2.* 1979.

110 J.C. van Vliet. *ALGOL 68 transput, part I: historical review and discussion of the implementation model.* 1979.

111 J.C. van Vliet. *ALGOL 68 transput, part II: an implementation model.* 1979.

112 H.C.P. Berbee. *Random walks with stationary increments and renewal theory.* 1979.

113 T.A.B. Snijders. *Asymptotic optimality theory for testing problems with restricted alternatives.* 1979.

114 A.J.E.M. Janssen. *Application of the Wigner distribution to harmonic analysis of generalized stochastic processes.* 1979.

115 P.C. Baayen, J. van Mill (eds.). *Topological structures II, part 1.* 1979.

116 P.C. Baayen, J. van Mill (eds.). *Topological structures II, part 2.* 1979.

117 P.J.M. Kallenberg. *Branching processes with continuous state space.* 1979.

118 P. Groeneboom. *Large deviations and asymptotic efficiencies.* 1980.

119 F.J. Peters. *Sparse matrices and substructures, with a novel implementation of finite element algorithms.* 1980.

120 W.P.M. de Ruyter. *On the asymptotic analysis of large-scale ocean circulation.* 1980.

121 W.H. Haemers. *Eigenvalue techniques in design and graph theory.* 1980.

122 J.C.P. Bus. *Numerical solution of systems of nonlinear equations.* 1980.

123 I. Yuhász. *Cardinal functions in topology - ten years later.* 1980.

124 R.D. Gill. *Censoring and stochastic integrals.* 1980.

125 R. Eising. *2-D systems, an algebraic approach.* 1980.

126 G. van der Hoek. *Reduction methods in nonlinear programming.* 1980.

127 J.W. Klop. *Combinatory reduction systems.* 1980.

128 A.J.J. Talman. *Variable dimension fixed point algorithms and triangulations.* 1980.

129 G. van der Laan. *Simplicial fixed point algorithms.* 1980.

130 P.J.W. ten Hagen, T. Hagen, P. Klint, H. Noot, H.J. Sint, A.H. Veen. *ILP: intermediate language for pictures.* 1980.

131 R.J.R. Back. *Correctness preserving program refinements: proof theory and applications.* 1980.

132 H.M. Mulder. *The interval function of a graph.* 1980.

133 C.A.J. Klaassen. *Statistical performance of location estimators.* 1981.

134 J.C. van Vliet, H. Wupper (eds.). *Proceedings international conference on ALGOL 68.* 1981.

135 J.A.G. Groenendijk, T.M.V. Janssen, M.J.B. Stokhof (eds.). *Formal methods in the study of language, part I.* 1981.

136 J.A.G. Groenendijk, T.M.V. Janssen, M.J.B. Stokhof (eds.). *Formal methods in the study of language, part II.* 1981.

137 J. Telgen. *Redundancy and linear programs.* 1981.

138 H.A. Lauwerier. *Mathematical models of epidemics.* 1981.

139 J. van der Wal. *Stochastic dynamic programming, successive approximations and nearly optimal strategies for Markov decision processes and Markov games.* 1981.

140 J.H. van Geldrop. *A mathematical theory of pure exchange economies without the no-critical-point hypothesis.* 1981.

141 G.E. Welters. *Abel-Jacobi isogenies for certain types of Fano threefolds.* 1981.

142 H.R. Bennett, D.J. Lutzer (eds.). *Topology and order structures, part 1.* 1981.

143 J.M. Schumacher. *Dynamic feedback in finite- and infinite-dimensional linear systems.* 1981.

144 P. Eijgenraam. *The solution of initial value problems using interval arithmetic; formulation and analysis of an algorithm.* 1981.

145 A.J. Brentjes. *Multi-dimensional continued fraction algorithms.* 1981.

146 C.V.M. van der Mee. *Semigroup and factorization methods in transport theory.* 1981.

147 H.H. Tigelaar. *Identification and informative sample size.* 1982.

148 L.C.M. Kallenberg. *Linear programming and finite Markovian control problems.* 1983.

149 C.B. Huijsmans, M.A. Kaashoek, W.A.J. Luxemburg, W.K. Vietsch (eds.). *From A to Z, proceedings of a symposium in honour of A.C. Zaanen.* 1982.

150 M. Veldhorst. *An analysis of sparse matrix storage schemes.* 1982.

151 R.J.M.M. Does. *Higher order asymptotics for simple linear rank statistics.* 1982.

152 G.F. van der Hoeven. *Projections of lawless sequences.* 1982.

153 J.P.C. Blanc. *Application of the theory of boundary value problems in the analysis of a queueing model with paired services.* 1982.

154 H.W. Lenstra, Jr., R. Tijdeman (eds.). *Computational methods in number theory, part I.* 1982.

155 H.W. Lenstra, Jr., R. Tijdeman (eds.). *Computational methods in number theory, part II.* 1982.

156 P.M.G. Apers. *Query processing and data allocation in distributed database systems.* 1983.

157 H.A.W.M. Kneppers. *The covariant classification of two-dimensional smooth commutative formal groups over an algebraically closed field of positive characteristic.* 1983.

158 J.W. de Bakker, J. van Leeuwen (eds.). *Foundations of computer science IV, distributed systems, part 1.* 1983.

159 J.W. de Bakker, J. van Leeuwen (eds.). *Foundations of computer science IV, distributed systems, part 2.* 1983.

160 A. Rezus. *Abstract AUTOMATH.* 1983.

161 G.F. Helminck. *Eisenstein series on the metaplectic group, an algebraic approach.* 1983.

162 J.J. Dik. *Tests for preference.* 1983.

163 H. Schippers. *Multiple grid methods for equations of the second kind with applications in fluid mechanics.* 1983.

164 F.A. van der Duyn Schouten. *Markov decision processes with continuous time parameter.* 1983.

165 P.C.T. van der Hoeven. *On point processes.* 1983.

166 H.B.M. Jonkers. *Abstraction, specification and implementation techniques, with an application to garbage collection.* 1983.

167 W.H.M. Zijm. *Nonnegative matrices in dynamic programming.* 1983.

168 J.H. Evertse. *Upper bounds for the numbers of solutions of diophantine equations.* 1983.

169 H.R. Bennett, D.J. Lutzer (eds.). *Topology and order structures, part 2.* 1983.